# BECOMING
# TRADER
# JOE

# BECOMING TRADER JOE

## How I Did Business **My Way**
and Still Beat the Big Guys

## JOE COULOMBE,
Founder of Trader Joe's,
with **PATTY CIVALLERI**

HarperCollins
LEADERSHIP

Published by HarperCollins Leadership, an imprint of HarperCollins Focus LLC.

Excerpt from *The Name of the Rose* by Umberto Eco, translated by William Weaver. Copyright © 1980 by Gruppo Editoriale Fabbri-Bompiani, Sonzogno, Etas S.p.A.

English translation copyright © 1983 by Houghton Mifflin Harcourt Publishing Company. Reprinted by permission of Houghton Mifflin Harcourt Publishing Company. All rights reserved.

ISBN 978-1-4002-2541-5 (eBook)
ISBN 978-1-4002-2543-9 (PBK)

Library of Congress Control Number: 2021935943

Printed in the United States of America

23 24 25 26 27 LBC 11 10 9 8 7

# Table of Contents

Foreword by Leroy D. Watson     ix

Preface: What's in a Name?     xi

Coauthor's Note     xv

A Trader Joe's Sampler
*Before we get into the details, here are some Trader Joe's products
that have especially interesting stories*     xvii

## SECTION 1

## HOW WE GOT THERE

**1. The Milk Train Doesn't Stop Here Anymore**
*In 1965, I was forced by competitive pressures to convert a
convenience store chain, Pronto Markets, into Trader Joe's*     3

**2. The God of Fair Beginnings**
*How I got started with Pronto Markets as a subsidiary of the giant
Rexall Drug Co. in the 1950s*     7

**3. The Guns of August, the Wages of Success**
*I bought Pronto Markets in September 1962 and made the most*
*important decision of my career: pay high wages*                        14

**4. On the Road to Trader Joe's**
*Those high wages force me into merchandising moves, which led to*
*Trader Joe's*                                                           24

**5. How *I Love Lucy* Homogenized America**
*I smelled a chance to be different*                                     28

**6. Good Time Charley**
*Aloha! The first version of Trader Joe's, 1967, was the*
*fun-leisure-party store*                                                35

**7. Uncorked!**
*How we managed to break price on wine despite the Fair Trade Laws*      45

**8. Whole Earth Harry**
*A serious recession forces me to marry the health food store to the*
*party store, and I got Whole Earth religion in the process*             60

**9. Promise, Large Promise**
*Fearlessly advertising Trader Joe's*                                    67

**10. Hairballs**                                                        80

### SECTION 2

## MAC THE KNIFE

**11. Mac the Knife**
*End of Fair Trade on milk and alcohol in 1977 leads to the third*
*and final version, which I called "Mac the Knife"*                      93

**12.** Intensive Buying
*Honest, we love middlemen*                                    100

**13.** Virtual Distribution
*Outsourcing? So that's what you call it!*                    113

**14.** Private Label Products
*Academic jokes for the overeducated and underpaid*           125

**15.** From Discrete to Indiscretions
*Standards are okay, up to a point*                           132

**16.** Too, Too Solid Stores
*"Nymph, in thy orisons be all my sins remember'd!"*          140

**17.** Skunks in the Office
*Tom Peters runs amok in the organization chart*              153

**18.** Double Entry Retailing
*3-D tennis in the check stand*                               159

**19.** Demand Side Retailing
*Geometry. Advantageous, but not necessarily true*            163

**20.** Supply Side Retailing
*Government Intrusion, a supply-side opportunity?*            182

**21.** The Last Five Year Plans
*Russia and Coulombe give up Five Year Plans in the same year, 1988*   203

## SECTION 3

## FIRST I SELL, THEN I LEAVE

**22.** Employee Ownership
*Founders yah, too bad. And that it led to . . .*             211

**23.** The Sale of Trader Joe's
*Money talks*      217

**24.** Goodbye to All That
*Auf Wiedersehen*      228

# ADDENDUM

Post De-Partum
*Or my ten years as a consultant*      235

List of Companies      253
Index      254

# Foreword

In 1957, I was hired to join Joe Coulombe (1930–2020) in opening the first Pronto Market, a project that would expand to become Trader Joe's. I did not know what an incredible adventure I was getting myself into. As the first employee, Vice President of Trader Joe's, and later Senior Vice President of Operations, I had the privilege of working side by side with Joe as he applied his unique marketing concepts and creative imagination to the grocery industry.

His first rule for new ideas was to always think outside the box, but always consider our customers and employees.

During this time, we found ourselves working against a backdrop of the incredible economic, political, and cultural changes that tsunamied us into the future.

In this book, Joe details the invaluable lessons we learned along the way.

His marketing genius, photographic memory, and impeccable integrity will inspire and educate not only entrepreneurs and students of business, but also the loyal customers who have come to appreciate the unique Trader Joe's experience. In an entertaining and informative read, Joe describes the creative marketing strategies that still apply today.

Hope you enjoy the book as much as I enjoyed my forty-three years at Trader Joe's—and still enjoy being a customer.

—Leroy D. Watson
Senior Vice President of Operations,
Trader Joe's, retired

# Preface

---

## What's in A Name?

Books are not made to be believed, but to be subjected to
inquiry. When we consider a book we mustn't ask ourselves
what it says but what it means, a precept that the
commentators of the holy books had very clearly in mind.
Perhaps the mission of those who love mankind is to
make people laugh at the truth, to make the truth laugh,
because the only truth lies in learning to free ourselves
from insane passion for the truth.

–Umberto Eco, *The Name of the Rose*

## Joe Coulombe or Joe Colomba or Joe Colombe

Nobody had last names until the fifteenth century, except the top nobility like the Hapsburgs, Hohenzollerns, Plantagenets, Valois, Bourbons, and so on. Then, rather quickly, non-nobility got last names. Some took the name of the city where they lived, and so we get *Tony Roma*'s for ribs, and Leonardo da Vinci.

Many others took the name of their work, like the Coopers, Smiths, Fletchers, Shepherds, and *Coulombes*. Coulombes?

Another privilege of nobility, besides having a last name, was the sole right to raise pigeons for food. The nobles built big, tall, round stone towers called *columbaria* after the Latin for dove, *columba*, which housed thousands of the birds. And they must have employed mobs of peasants to tend these towers, because when the Time of Last Names arrived, suddenly we get people all over Europe with names derived from *columba*.

Regrettably, no one could spell, not even the nobles. Furthermore, there was no general agreement on how words should be spelled until the nineteenth century. Columba was very susceptible to creative spelling. Nowhere was this more true than in Quebec, where in the 1660s Louis XIV's new finance minister, Colbert, initiated a policy of deliberately populating New France with stolid peasants from Normandy— among them a Louis Colombe—to make sure the place would always be French. In some ways he succeeded all too well.

These hardworking but illiterate people had a genius for adding or subtracting letters to the base name without regard to pronunciation. Colombe became, among other spellings, *Coulombe*. And that is why you will not find *Coulombe* in the Paris phone book, whereas there are pages of 'em in Montreal.

The point is that *Coulombe* is pronounced coo-LOAM. I thought this book would be an easier read if you knew that. Whether the mild paranoia generated by a name that few people can pronounce was a factor in my shaping Trader Joe's, I leave to your judgment. Whether the substantial paranoia generated by being a left-hander in a right-handed world was a factor in putting a left-handed spin on Trader Joe's, however, is beyond dispute. For some competitors, Trader Joe's has been sinister in at least two meanings of the word.

For the meaning of that cryptic remark, please read on . . .

I tried to explain about marketing,
but they wanted to hear about miracles.

–Roger Fitzgerald, senior editor of *Seafood Leader* magazine,
discussing a disappointing meeting with some
Asian seafood exporters in 1990

I wrote this book to help entrepreneurs and would-be entrepreneurs. That's why there's a lack of miracles and a surplus of marketing details including buying, advertising, distributing, and running stores; and lots of discussion of "the wages of success"—how we built a successful business on high wages.

But how well did Trader Joe's work? It clearly is a *succes d'estime* but was it a *succes de l'argent*? Too often we see books and movies that the critics rave about but which don't bring in bucks. Too often we see rave reviews of companies that crash and burn only a few years after they have been held up as paragons of management.

Voila! In a 1958 partnership with *Rexall Drug Co.*, we started *Pronto Markets*. After growing it to six stores, I bought out Rexall's shares in 1962. Then, in 1967, when I had reached eighteen Pronto locations, I began the transition of Pronto into Trader Joe's. I resigned at the end of 1988. During those twenty-six years, our sales grew at a compound rate of 19 percent per year.

During the same twenty-six years, our net worth grew at a compound rate of 26 percent per year. Furthermore, during the last thirteen years of that period, we had no fixed, interest-bearing debt, only current liabilities. We went from leveraged to the gills in the early days to zero leverage by 1975. Furthermore, we never lost money in a year, and each year was more profitable than the preceding year despite wild swings in income tax rates.

Since I left Trader Joe's at the end of 1988, its sales as reported in the press have continued to grow at about 20 percent per year. I submit there are few companies that have maintained such a rate of growth for the last thirty-five years. Since I have no access to Trader Joe's internal figures, I don't know how well net worth has done, but I'm sure it's done very well, too.

Still, judgment can be rendered that I failed, that I fell short of what I should have achieved. We will examine this late in the book. But I hope you'll consider the following, my favorite quote from my favorite book on management, *The Winning Performance* by Clifford and Cavanaugh:

The fourth [general theme in winning corporations] is a view of profit and wealth-creation as inevitable by-products of doing other things well. Money is a useful yardstick for measuring quantitative performance and profit and an obligation to investors. But . . . making money as an end in itself ranks low.

In 1994 *Stanford* Business School published a study of winning companies (companies that have endured for a hundred years) called "Built to Last," which came to pretty much the same conclusion.

Along the way in this book, you'll find the angst of a struggling entrepreneur and his wife who didn't get a clothes dryer until she was thirty-nine and all the kids were toilet trained (in that pre-*Pampers* era); the slings and arrows of outrageous good fortune and bad fortune; and a lot of the detail of everyday life in the twentieth century that may interest the Fernand Braudel–type historians of the twenty-fifth century.

# Coauthor's Note

**J**oe's professional life dealt heavily in brands. That is the nature of the retail grocery business, the nature of his life. In this book, we have acknowledged all brands that carry or maintain a "TM" (Trademark) or an "®" (Registered Trademark), or a "©" (Copyright) with *italics* the first time they are mentioned. All brands mentioned in this book are acknowledged from a position of admiration and respect.

Joe's life includes an inordinate number of people, many of whom have contributed in one way or another to the success of Trader Joe's. All people mentioned in this book have been captured in the positive light that they have earned, are remembered fondly, and are mentioned with the utmost respect and esteem.

We wish we could have mentioned all of our true followers, our customers. You are not forgotten.

—Patty Civalleri

# A Trader Joe's Sampler

## Some of the Best Deals
## We Ever Made

In March 1998, I gave a lecture for the *Culinary Historians Society*, a lecture that led to this book. One of the questions from the floor was, "What are some of the best deals you ever made?"

## Canned Pilchard

In 1981, *Newsweek* ran a story about a fish called pilchard, which was a lot like tuna but much cheaper, which was being promoted in New England. I don't know how the story got planted, because we soon learned that the pilchard had failed to sell: the importer offered it to us. We cut the cans and were impressed by the high quality of fish, which was seemingly as good as white meat or Albacore tuna.

By this time we were beginning to realize that Trader Joe's was becoming a powerful brand. We took the pilchard, relabeled it, and blew it out at a price two-thirds that of green-labeled tuna and half the price of albacore.

I became intrigued by this and located the source of the pilchard: a packer in Peru. In June 1982, my wife, Alice, and I went to Lima to visit the canning plant. We witnessed something very interesting: the United States had a quota for imported tuna. Once Peru's quota had been filled, a biological miracle occurred right there on the canning line. What had been tuna was now pilchard, a member of the herring family, on which there was no quota. The like hasn't been seen since the Sea of Galilee! To this day, Trader Joe's is virtually the only retailer of pilchard.

Again with big eye tuna, government regulations created a bargain. Big eye, *Parathunnus mebachi*, are huge tuna with excellent flesh.

In Canada they can be called "albacore" or "white meat" because they meet Canada's spectroscopic test of whiteness. Our government, however, says that only *Thunus alalongus* can be labeled albacore. One more bargain for the table, thanks to the product knowledge we built up at Trader Joe's.


# Whey Butter

One of the first products of the *Mac the Knife* program was whey butter from the famous *Tillamook* cheese company in Oregon. When you make cheese from milk, most of the butterfat goes into the cheese. A small amount, however, is left in the whey (mixed in with lactose; whey is about 60 percent lactose). Tillamook found they could separate this "whey cream" from the whey and sell it as butter. Chemically it's the same as butter, only it has no casein.

There are some special advantages to whey butter: it has more of a "buttery" flavor; and it tends to be more malleable when you take it out of the refrigerator.

By 1977, we had become a big customer of Tillamook, and they approached us about shipping down whey butter along with cheese. We liked the idea, because it gave us a chance to break the price of butter in Los Angeles. There were two drawbacks to their butter:

1. It was packaged only in one-pound sizes. No quarter-pound inner wraps, and the packaging was only a heavy parchment, not a cardboard carton. For 20 percent less than regular butter, we figured our brainy customers could accept this.

2. California, ever protectionist in its dairy laws, made us label it "second quality." Oregon has no such regulation, but California so defined first quality that whey butter had to be labeled second quality.

So, we put it on sale and it was a great success. Unfortunately, one year and five hundred thousand pounds later, Tillamook had improved its cheesemaking process so there was almost no butterfat left in the whey. Obviously they made more money from cheese than from butter, but they relented and agreed to supply us, but only during the holidays, for the big baking season.

Then the Feds intervened. Shipping butter from Oregon to California was interstate commerce. Federal regulations do not recognize such a thing as whey butter. So Tillamook had to take the "whey" designation off the label. This confused our customers to no end: all they saw was "second quality."

So we found a California producer who would make whey butter for us. By exiting interstate commerce we were again able to label it whey butter. But, of course, still second quality. Without the prestigious Tillamook name, we changed the label to "Trader Joe's La Cuisine de Beurre." It was still 15 percent cheaper than regular butter, and better.

# Maple Syrup

During the pit of the Depression, my mother taught grades four through six *and* served as principal of the two-room Solana Beach elementary school *and* as principal of the nearby Eden Gardens school for about $150 per month. That was until the biggest real estate developer in San Diego County went broke and there were no property taxes to pay the teachers, so for a while she taught for nothing.

Most of my childhood days, therefore, were spent with my grandmother, neè Blanche Greenwood (anglicized from Boisvert) Dumas. She was a third-generation Vermonter, her people having left Quebec long before my grandfather. In darkest Southern California, she re-created her Vermont village, Northfield Falls. Monday was wash day; on Wednesday she baked all the bread and rolls for the next seven days; on Saturday you ate Red Flannel hash, the week's leftovers put through the food grinder and deeply colored by beets. Now, very late in my life, I realize that the beets not only imposed uniform color on the leftovers, but they added sweetness, a trick of Chinese chefs. (My mother, neè Carmelita Hardin, despite her Spanish first name, was born and bred in Bristol, Tennessee, and thought Red Flannel hash was fit only for animals.) Always on the shelf was maple syrup, especially for Wednesday's bread: oven-hot and oven-moist. And if you were very good, maple candies in the shape of maple leaves might appear on the shelves.

When I got into the grocery business, I couldn't understand the scant attention paid to this greatest of all syrups. All the major brands like *Aunt Jemima* were mostly cane syrup with a little maple thrown in. Cary's was the only brand of pure maple syrup that was sold in tiny jugs at very high prices by supermarkets who thought it had no volume potential.

Putting our Intensive Buying (please read that chapter) and Virtual Distribution (please read that chapter) to work, we made a deal with the leading cooperative in Quebec to buy syrup in fifty-gallon drums.

We brought it to Los Angeles, had it bottled (*Pilgrim Joe's* label), and we didn't just break the price—we destroyed the price!

Maple syrup appealed to our wine-retailing instincts: each vintage is different in quantity and quality. So 1981 was to maple syrup what 1982 was to Bordeaux. It all depends on the right combination of freezing nights and sunny days in March.

We not only broke the price of maple syrup, but we were the only retailers selling the rare, first-run maple syrup. For many years, there was none available at all. It was water-white, and most Californians neither recognized it nor liked it. They were accustomed to Grade B, dark syrup with a kicker of a taste. But we persevered and became outstanding not only for prices but for our assortment of maple syrup. From time to time we also brought in syrup from Wisconsin, another first here.

As far as I know, Trader Joe's is the largest retailer of maple syrup in the United States. If only Grandma Blanche had lived to see it!

## Wild Rice

This is pretty much the same story as maple syrup. No strong brand demand, nobody interested in helping the public buy it right. Putting Intensive Buying and Virtual Distribution to work, we became the largest retailer of wild rice in the United States.

## Brie Cheaper Than Velveeta!

This was my favorite headline of all the headlines in all the years of our magazine, the celebrated *Fearless Flyer*. Leroy Watson, a man whose name will appear so often that he'll just be known as Leroy throughout the book, broke the code on how to get cheap brie and we did sell it for less than *Velveeta* on occasion. This was especially satisfying since

Velveeta, in our eyes, represented the nadir of the American food supply. Later, Bob Johnson perfected our cheese logistics in Europe, leading to a string of bargains.

## Bran the Blessed

As we will see in the "Whole Earth Harry" chapter, my friend Dr. Jim
Caillouette introduced me to medical research on the high fiber diet as
a preventative of colon cancer. That got us interested in wheat bran
(which, in turn, for freight reasons, got us into nuts and dried fruits).
We promoted *"Bran the Blessed"* (named for Bran, the Celtic fertility
god). Because my grandfather had died of colon cancer at age six-
ty-three, this product had a special meaning for me. I was very proud
of what we did to popularize wheat bran, and ten years later, to be the
first to promote oat bran, which may help control cholesterol.

## Almond Butter

The processing of almonds leaves a lot of bits and pieces of almonds
behind. Doug Rauch came up with the idea of grinding almonds into
an analog for peanut butter. Easier said than done. The technology for
grinding almonds is completely different than the technology for grinding peanuts. Finally, Doug, whom you will meet often in these pages,
found a religious colony in Oregon who had mastered the trick and
taught it to Doug. For years we were almost the only retailer with almond butter. In some years, we could sell it cheaper than peanut butter,
depending on the relative supplies of almonds and peanuts in any given
year.

Using those broken almonds was profoundly satisfying to the
"Whole Earth Harry" side of our nature. And one of our doctor customers prescribed it to cure acne!

On the other hand, Doug also came up with cottonseed "butter." Again profoundly ecological, it was really cheap and good. Unfortunately, several customers went into anaphylactic shock after eating it and we hastily withdrew it from the market. (About 5 percent of the population goes anaphylactic from peanut butter, too.)

## Kibble

We were approached by a dog food manufacturer who said he had a new formula for kibble that was devised by the University of California at Davis, the university's agricultural campus. It seems that dogs don't digest corn well. So we brought out this no-corn kibble at half the price of premium dog food, and advertised it as the Davis formula. The university raised hell and we hastily withdrew the claim. But not the dog food.

Maybe I should start eating the stuff. My eleven-year-old Lab survives our daily three-mile hikes a lot better than I do. All she gets is Trader Joe's Kibble and, as a special treat, Trader Joe's Peanut Butter Dog Bones. Alice points out that our three-year-old granddaughter, Odette, will also eat the kibble if we don't get the bowl off the floor before she arrives. For that matter blue jays will hop inside the kitchen to eat it, if we don't keep the door closed.

## Ketchy

The Feds have "standards of identity" for certain products like mayonnaise and catsup. If your product doesn't have all the ingredients specified you can't use the name. Unfortunately, the standard for catsup requires 30 percent sugar. Tomatoes are naturally sweet, but not *that* sweet!

So a vendor offered us a no-sugar-added catsup. But when we submitted the Trader Joe's Catsup label for approval, it was bounced: not enough sugar! My son, young Joe, raised his head from his *Macintosh* long enough to suggest a different name, *ketchy*. Even with our health food clientele, however, ketchy never caught on. We tried it several times and gave up. But it was a worthy effort. You'll meet Young Joe again in the Virtual Distribution chapter. And you'll encounter still more thrilling episodes of our repeated conflicts with government regulations. I suggest that you take the Supply Side Retailing chapter to heart.

## Non-Value-Added Frozen Fish

We virtually created this product category, as you will read in the chapter on Intensive Buying. It was thrilling to offer such bargains in good food. We were gratified when both *Sunset* magazine and *Seafood Leader* supported our position that frozen fish, if it's frozen at the time it's caught, is often superior to fresh fish.

So here we go to an autumn afternoon in 1965, in a bar where Trader Joe's was not so much born as extruded.

# SECTION 1

---

# HOW WE
# GOT THERE

# 1

## The Milk Train
## Doesn't Stop Here Anymore

Trader Joe's got its start in a bar on La Cienega Boulevard, where a crisis broke over my head on a Friday afternoon in October 1965. The *Tail O' the Cock* was a prominent watering hole on La Cienega's "restaurant row," where Los Angeles and Beverly Hills expensively and alcoholically come together. One drives La Cienega just after the "lunch" hour at the risk of one's life.

My host, Merritt Adamson Jr., had just finished drinking his normal ration of three Gibsons. When he ordered a fourth, I knew something was up.

I was thirty-five years old, President and controlling stockholder of Pronto Markets, a sixteen-store chain of "convenience" markets in Los Angeles. Just three years earlier, we had hovered on the edge of bankruptcy with the six stores I had bought from the giant Rexall Drug Co., under whose aegis I had founded Pronto in 1958. After I bought Pronto using extreme leverage (I had no money), Merritt had provided much of the capital, which had helped fuel our expansion to sixteen stores and a recovery to lots of black ink.

Merritt wasn't much older than I, but he had been thrust into the presidency of *Adohr Milk Farms* ten years earlier when his father had suddenly died. The Tail O' the Cock was just a few blocks north of Adohr's offices and creamery. We were having our monthly business luncheon, and Pronto, as small as it was, had become his largest customer for milk and ice cream. Our business wasn't enough, however: Adohr was slowly sinking because Merritt was a rare ethical player in the now wholly corrupt California milk business.

In 1935, in the pit of the Depression, when milk was being sold below cost, Merritt's father had helped write the "milk control" laws, which partly govern California's milk business (they have since been updated several times), especially the relations between the milk companies and grocery stores. After World War II, these laws increasingly were honored in the breach, as the big creameries and the big supermarket chains cut deals for illegal rebates or illegal financing or both.

This is the normal result of quasi-fascist laws that try to regulate the marketplace. But in 1935, Benito Mussolini's concept of binding state and industry together (the *fasces* is a Roman symbol, an ax with a bundle of sticks tied around its handle; the sticks represent the industries and the church, the ax represents the state, a one-for-all-and-all-for-one construct) was so popular around the world that Franklin D. Roosevelt tried to copy it with the Blue Eagle National Recovery Administration, until the Supreme Court threw it out in 1937. Relics of Mussolini, however, linger in all the states of the union, sometimes in milk control laws (and always in alcoholic beverage laws).

When Merritt Adamson Sr. wrote the laws, most milk was sold by home delivery; there were hardly any supermarkets. After the war, Adohr was stuck with home delivery while the new suburbs shifted their milk purchases massively to the newly dominant supermarkets. But to get supermarket business, Merritt Jr. would have had to go against his own father's legislation. He refused to play ball, and Adohr was sinking. His thousand-head herd of Golden Guernsey cattle out in

Ventura County, the nation's largest and another legacy from his father, was producing more milk than he could sell.

Despite my desperate need for money as Pronto emerged from Rexall in 1962, I'd had a bellyful of under-the-table offers from creameries. "We'll pay you in cash, if you'll just meet us anywhere outside the United States—our foreign subsidiaries will fund it, and the IRS will never know." That was a typical pitch. I was prudent enough to guess, however, that it would expose me to blackmail should I ever try to switch brands.

My ethics were not, shall we say, entirely ethical in their genesis nor had my hands been entirely clean while I was running Pronto for Rexall. To quote the late, great senator Sam Ervin in the Watergate hearings, when he was asked if he had ever broken the law, "the statute of limitations has expired on all my sins."

The institution of blackmail was not unknown in the grocery industry. At the big conventions, innocent (I'm positive!) grocers found themselves trapped—yes, trapped!—in hotel rooms with awfully friendly ladies, and hidden cameras. Some bread companies were notorious for this.

In 1962, Merritt and I got together on common ground. He'd get our milk business; we'd get capital; but whatever we did would be squeaky clean with the state. His attorney, Julian Burke, created such a financing plan. (Burke later became a noted turnaround specialist. Then, at age seventy, he was in charge of the Metropolitan Transit Agency of Los Angeles.) This plan worked well, but it wasn't enough to move all that Golden Guernsey milk (noted for its high butterfat content in a society that was moving to skim).

Merritt had another problem: he and his sisters had inherited Malibu.

His mother, Rhoda (*Adohr* is *Rhoda* spelled backward) Rindge, was heiress to the Spanish land grant that we peasants call Malibu. But it was a big problem. The Adamsons were land-rich but cash-poor; they lacked the funds to develop the magnificent property. They were having to sell off pieces for far less than they potentially were worth.

So the fourth Gibson came to slake our waning thirst. Merritt, a huge bear of a man whose face looked perpetually sunburned, was very shy: hence the Gibsons. After drinking the fourth one, he finally got the story out. Painfully, he confessed, "Joe, I've sold Adohr. And I've sold it to *Southland Corporation*."

Southland, for the uninitiated, is the owner of *7-Eleven Markets*. As a partner of Rexall, I had started Pronto in 1958 as a copy of 7-Eleven, because there were no 7-Elevens in California, partly because of the labor issues discussed in "The Guns of August" chapter. What Merritt was telling me was (a) my source of financing was cut off and (b) a competitor a thousand times greater in wealth was coming to town, and (c) they had found some way to avoid California's high labor costs.

I knew we would be crushed, if only inadvertently, by this monster. The convenience store business is 90 percent real estate, 10 percent all other (merchandising, personnel, etc.). In real estate, it's the tenant's balance sheet that counts. Between Southland and Pronto, it would be no contest.

Suddenly stone sober, I drove home, got Alice and the kids, and holed up for two days in a cabin at Lake Arrowhead, in California, while I tried to figure out what the hell to do. And that's how Trader Joe's got started.

# 2

# The God of
# Fair Beginnings

The God of Fair Beginnings
Hath prospered here my hand—
The cargoes of my lading,
And the keels of my command.

—Rudyard Kipling, "The Song of Diego Valdez"

Late in my career at Trader Joe's, about 1986, I decided that we needed to juice up management with a freshly minted MBA who could bring the latest management theories to us. We had built Trader Joe's with only one four-year college graduate, Dave Yoda, our Controller. The people who are responsible for what Trader Joe's is today all came from the School of Hard Knocks.

The first candidate to bring Management Enlightenment to us was a young lady just out of my alma mater, Stanford University. Over coffee I explained how I ran the company while she listened, obviously with growing impatience. "Oh, Joe," she finally burst out, "you do all the right things for all the wrong reasons!" She didn't get the job.

Condescension is typical of wet-eared MBAs, and few have been so condescending as I on my first job, even though it was the only job I could get in June 1954, during the first of the three Eisenhower recessions. Few people knew or cared what an MBA was in those days. I was lucky to get hired for $325 a month, especially since I had never taken a course in retailing at Stanford and had no interest in retailing whatsoever. I was even luckier in the man who hired me, who put up with me, who encouraged me, and who taught me everything I know about being a chief executive officer: Wayne H. "Bud" Fisher Jr., to whom this chapter is dedicated: my god of fair beginnings.

Once, I had the chance to thank him in public. Thirty years after the events in this chapter, the Stanford Business School's Los Angeles Alumni group honored me as Entrepreneur of the Year. Even though that night was their fortieth wedding anniversary, Bud and his wife attended the banquet, and to his embarrassment I paid him full tribute.

For a while I wondered how that association, which lasted almost forty years until his death in 1993, was forged, until I realized it was simple: we were both left-handed. I think that handedness is the most important thing one can know about a person. The question was never on the employment application forms, and it's probably verboten to ask these days. But dyslexia lurks in the brain of every left-hander, which means, we see the world differently, sometimes profitably. That's why, when I interview people, I try to get them to write something. At one point I was accused of running a cabal of left-handers at Trader Joe's. One of them, Doug Rauch, is President of Trader Joe's on the East Coast as of this writing.

Bud Fisher, the handsome scion of one of the founding families of Southern California; an alumnus of *Pomona*, *Harvard*, and Stanford; a first lieutenant in the Normandy landings; married to a beautiful blonde, was then Executive Vice President of the *Owl Rexall Drug Co.*, a moribund chain of three hundred stores on the West Coast. *Sav-on* drugstores, a brilliant new concept in self-service retailing created by two Latter Day Saints, Messrs. Call and Clark, had hit Los Angeles like napalm. Every time one Sav-on opened, three Owl Drug stores closed.

Bud hired me to find out why. Shall we count the ways? For once, an MBA's condescension, not to say scorn, was justified. The Owl Drug

Co. was the pits with only one asset, Fisher, who had just recently come on board. What was not justified was my impolitic way of expressing my disgust. Bud defended me against my own brashness, even though he quietly viewed the Byzantine management of his superiors at Rexall no more forgivingly than I did. But he was ten years older than I chronologically, and far older than that because of his experience at Normandy. All of those men who had experienced both the Great Depression and World War II are dead and gone from management now, but they were powerful forces in shaping postwar America.

In the course of our research on alternatives for Owl, we discovered 7-Eleven stores in Texas. There were none in California. Grocery stores intrigued me.

I then quit. I told Bud that I had learned all I could at Owl, and that I was afraid I would begin to lose my Stanford standards for management if I stayed. I went to *Hughes Aircraft* and became the financial planner for their Semiconductor Division, which sextupled during the short time I was there.

Neither Bud nor I, however, had forgotten the business opportunity we saw in 7-Eleven. According to *Dun & Bradstreet*, the typical grocer's return on investment was 54 percent in the early 1950s.

Eighteen months after I quit, he called me: he had persuaded Rexall to hire me back to clone 7-Eleven. And that's how at age twenty-seven I became President of Pronto Markets.

## We Build Pronto Markets;
## But Dart Buys *Tupperware*

There were no 7-Elevens in California at the time, so the first, experimental chain of six Prontos that we built was successful. Two years into the project, however, lightning hit: Justin Dart, the famous President of Rexall (twenty-two years later he was a member of President Reagan's kitchen cabinet) bought Tupperware, against, I am told, the unanimous

vote of his board of directors ("nothing but a goddamned party formula!"). Within a year, Tupperware was generating a third of Rexall's
profits.

Dart gave orders to liquidate all 1,100 drugstores he owned (*Lane
Drug* in the South, *Liggett Drug* in the East, and Owl) to raise cash so he
could go into partnership with *El Paso Natural Gas* and produce all the
plastic that he needed for Tupperware. What was vertical integration
for Tupperware was going to be horizontal disintegration for The Owl
Drug Co., and Pronto.

But Dart had a problem: nobody wanted to buy the molting Owl
Drug. Today it would be fought over by the vulture capitalists, but
neither ventures nor vultures were common in those days. Thirty-two
years later, when I was in charge of liquidating *Thrifty Drug Stores* in
1992, we had eight eager vultures bidding for it. But the U.S. in 1960
was like Europe or Japan today. The advent of ventures and vultures is
one of the major reasons why the U.S. has outstripped the Europeans
and the Japanese.

With no buyers in sight, I talked to Bud. By then, Dart had made
him President of Owl. I suggested that to pull it out of its nosedive, we
would do a public offering of just the best Owls, about one out of five
stores. The stock market was hot in 1961, selling at twenty times earnings. The profit of the best stores, at even a thirteen multiple, would
generate enough cash to cover the costs of closing the dogs. During the
banking crisis of 1990, this same strategy was employed by the authorities under the name *Good-Bank Bad-Bank*. Bud and I would wind up
running the public company, in which Pronto would be a minor but
profitable part. The two dyslexics agreed.

Dart, no dyslexic (he'd been a star quarterback at *Northwestern* and
tended to hire ex-football players like I later hired left-handers—only
my left-handers were smarter than his football players), liked the idea,
and we went to work. None of the top underwriters, however, would
touch it ("Not with a ten foot pole," a prominent San Franciscan declared to us in the *Pacific Union Club*). But Bud and I flew up and down

California, gluing together a stable of "pink sheet" stockbrokers, the kind who deal in the diciest public offerings.

Things dragged on, however, because it is difficult for the MBAs of today to understand how slow, how hard it was to assemble financial data in the days before computers or even electronic calculators, never mind fax machines or even decent photocopying machines. (I ran Pronto with an adding machine and a *Keuffel & Esser* slide rule. I'm not sure they have even heard of slide rules at Stanford today.) This was brought home to me in the 1992 liquidation of Thrifty Drug Stores: *Morgan Stanley*, our investment banker, was able to assemble a complete "book" to present to the vultures in five days!

It took six months to assemble figures that Pricewaterhouse would certify, partly because Owl had never been audited separately from Rexall. By the time we had everything assembled for the Securities & Exchange Commission, John Kennedy had got into an argument with Big Steel in Spring 1962. The stock market got queasy. Our deal, which at best required a strong stomach, was dead. Bud and I suddenly were personae non-grata at Rexall, whose corporate politics were always quicksand. Bud quit, and was hired instantly by *Lucky Supermarkets*. Brilliant, he became CEO of Lucky just a few years later, a post he held until he retired in 1980, one of the most acclaimed executives in retailing.

I either had to buy Pronto or find a new job.

The decline of the stock market accelerated. I walked into the office of the treasurer of Rexall one day in May 1962. He was on the phone with the *Wall Street Journal*, trying to explain why Rexall's stock had just gone from 60 to 21. I put a note on his desk: "I will buy Pronto Markets for book value." He cupped his hand over the phone and muttered, "Ten thousand dollars over book and you've got it." I shook his hand. I needed to raise the money within ninety days.

# The Problem Was I Didn't Have Any Money

Just in case you wondered, Alice and I were charter members of the *U-Haul* Club: when we left Stanford, where we had married as graduate students, all of our belongings fit in the smallest U-Haul trailer you could rent. By the time I bought Pronto Markets, it might have taken only a slightly bigger trailer, mostly to accommodate the cribs for the two kids we now had.

We did find the money, somehow. Rexall was willing to take back paper. (Dart was in a hurry to wind up his retailing affairs. This was a big advantage for me, because if I walked away, he'd be left with a crumb of a bastard business.) We had $4,000 from Alice's savings from her teaching school before she had the kids (we lived on my $325) and we sold our little house in which we had an equity of $7,000. I borrowed $2,000 from my grandmother and $5,000 from my father. (Pop, an engineer, spent most of his career being alternately employed and dis-employed by *General Dynamics* depending on the vagaries of the aerospace business; in between he owned a series of small businesses. I think he even had a *Mac Tool* route in 1962.) Seventeen years later, when I finally sold the company, the cost basis of my total investment was only $25,000.

And I sold half the stock to my employees (at book value, no blue sky). God bless those people who had such faith in me!

But we were still way short when I went to see Tom Deane at *Bank of America*. I presented my case; and—on the spot (!)—he loaned me the money on our (Alice's and mine) personal signatures. Years later, I asked him how he had been so ballsy. "It's simple," he replied. "Rexall was on Pronto's leases, and I figured they wouldn't let you go bankrupt."

So there I was, the controlling stockholder of seven Pronto Markets, living with Alice (who did the accounts payable at home) and two kids, now in a house we rented for $150 a month. We were leveraged to the gills. Furthermore, the county had opened a massive flood control project outside our new, seventh Culver City store. For six months, no one could enter the store except by walking a plank over a twenty-foot ditch. Culver City, along with the servicing costs of the leveraged balance sheet, was consuming all the profits of the other stores. Chapter 11 was a possibility.

When I dragged home at night, we'd play the *Threepenny Opera** ("Victoria's messenger does not come riding often . . . And a reply to a kick-in-the-pants is always one more kick-in-the-pants!") while I, the future guru of the wine trade, sipped, partly from poverty (we were overstocked in the stuff) but mostly from ignorance, *Paul Masson* Cream Sherry.

But I was reading *The Guns of August,* by Barbara W. Tuchman, with its implicit concept of multiple solutions to non-convex problems.

And I did have seven keels at my command . . .

---

* All quotes from the *Threepenny Opera* are based on the Loew's-MGM original (American) cast recording issued about 1960, starring the great Lotte Lenya.

# 3

## The Guns of August, the Wages of Success

It is better to be vaguely right than exactly wrong.

—Carveth Read

If all the facts could be known,
idiots could make the decisions.

—Tex Thornton, cofounder of *Litton Industries*,
quoted in the *Los Angeles Times* in the mid-1960s.
This is my favorite of all managerial quotes.

Basically I didn't like Pronto Markets as it existed in the summer of 1962. After four years of operating the 7-Eleven formula, and after observing several other attempts to clone 7-Eleven in California, I was aware of the formula's extreme exposure to the supermarkets lengthening their hours. This was happening in the wake of the same 1962 recession that had aborted our public offering the previous spring. But I didn't know how to modify the formula.

In 1962, Barbara Tuchman published *The Guns of August*, an account of the first ninety days of World War I. It's the best book on management—and, especially, mismanagement—I've ever read.

The most basic conclusion I drew from her book was that, if you adopt a reasonable strategy, as opposed to waiting for an optimum strategy, and stick with it, you'll probably succeed. Tenacity is as important as brilliance. The Germans and French both had brilliant general staffs, but neither side had the tenacity to stick with their prewar plans. As a result, the first ninety days of war ended in four years of bloody stalemate.

Twenty-eight years later, the *Economist* of November 10, 1990, put it this way:

> . . . non-convex problems . . . are puzzles in which there may
> be several good but not ideal answers which classical search
> techniques may wrongly identify as the best one.

I concluded that I didn't have to find an optimum solution to Pronto's difficulties, just a reasonable one. Trying to find an optimum solution in business is a waste of time: the factors in the equation are changing all the time.

But you've got to have something to hang your hat on. The one core value that I chose was our high compensation policies, which I had put in place from the very start in 1958. This may sound like a strange way for polarizing a business, but I did not want to destroy the faith that Pronto Markets' then-handful of employees had in me and in our common future. After all, they had just ponied up half the equity money needed to buy out Rexall.

This is the most important single business decision I ever made: to pay people well. First Pronto Markets and then Trader Joe's had the highest-paid, highest-benefited people in retailing. Now how was I going to afford it?

## The Wages Of Success

I hope that readers looking for romance in the history of Trader Joe's aren't disappointed by the following rather technical discussion of employee policies. But the real romance I had for thirty years was the one with those people who made the company work, and who came up with so many good ideas for which I am given credit.

**This is the most important single business decision I ever made: to pay people well.**

Time and again I am asked why no one has successfully replicated Trader Joe's. The answer is that no one has been willing to pay the wages and benefits, and thereby attract—and keep—the quality of people who work at Trader Joe's. My standard was simple: the average full-time employee in the stores would make the median family income for California. Back in those days it was about $7,000; as I write this, it is around $40,000. What I didn't count on back there in the 1960s was that so many spouses would go to work in the national economy. When I started, average family income was about the same as average employee income. The great social change of the 1970s and 1980s moved millions of women into the workplace. Average family income soared ahead. But we stuck with our standard, and it paid off.

## Selfish Altruism Works!

Much as I would like to pose as an altruistic visionary, my policy was grounded partly by the desire to stay un-organized by the *Retail Clerks Union*, which under the direction of the legendary Joe DeSilva terrorized the market industry of those days. We really didn't pay more per hour than union scale, but we gave people hours. Because union scale is so high, the supermarkets are very stingy with hours and will do anything to avoid paying overtime. I simply built overtime into the system: everyone was to work a five day, forty-eight-hour week. Actually, because of fluctuations in the business, employees often alternate between four-day and six-day weeks (38.5 hours to 57.5 hours). This generates a lot of three-day weekends, which is quite popular with the troops.

[The problem with unions is not their pay scales; it's their work rules and seniority rules. Union membership in the U.S. had collapsed since I left Stanford in 1954, largely because employers struggle to dump the work rules. Europe, where work rules were imposed more by law than by union contracts, faces the same problem today; it is not dealing well with it. In fairness, however, those work rules did not spring from the ground like dung beetles working it over. They came from inexcusable employer practices. Why is it that, when an opera singer leaves the stage at the end of a performance, a minion of management is waiting with a certified check for his or her services that night? It is because so many singers got screwed by impresarios since the Monteverde.]

In 1963, we became big enough to be covered by the Fair Labor Standards Act for the first time. I had to find a way to preserve our high pay scales within the context of that Act. Thanks to a trade association, I discovered an obscure 1937 Supreme Court decision on the Fair Labor Standards Act that made the administration of my forty-eight-hour payroll system much easier. I won't even try to describe the ruling. Suffice it to say it works and has certainly been audited, as you will see in the "Hairballs" chapter.

Our employees were never really approached by the Retail Clerks Union. Yes, the high compensation program (which later was augmented with benefits like health and retirement) was important, but . . .

## Letting Off Steam

Equally important was our practice of giving every full-time employee an interview every six months. At Stanford I'd been taught that employees never organize because of money: they organize because of un-listened-to grievances. We set up a program under which each employee (including some part-timers) was interviewed, not by the immediate superior, the store manager, but by the manager's superior. The principal purpose of this program was to vent grievances and address them where possible. And I think this program was as important as pay in keeping employees with us.

Productivity in part is the product of tenure. That's why I believe that turnover is the most expensive form of labor expense. I am proud that, during my thirty years at Pronto and Trader Joe's, we had virtually no turnover of full-time employees, except for the ordinary human problems of too, too solid flesh. Almost all the full-timers came out of part-time ranks. And, oh yes, nepotism is rife. Between part-timers and relatives, we never had to run an ad for full-time help.

In a lecture at the *University of Southern California* Business School, I talked about this. A young woman raised her hand: "But how could you afford to pay so much more than your competition?" The answer, of course, is that good people pay by their extra productivity. You can't afford to have cheap employees.

---

I don't use the euphemism "associates."
It joins "vertically challenged," "significant other,"
and other obfuscations in the contemporary lexicon.

–Sam Walton

---

# Investing for Productivity

In tackling the "non-convex" problem, I was limited, of course, by the fact that we were tied into long-term leases for convenience markets, about sixteen of them, by the time Merritt Adamson sold to 7-Eleven in 1966.

The problem with a convenience store (a small store with a small inventory and few fixtures) is that it is hard to invest enough money to let the people be productive enough to justify high wages and benefits. I had put the cart—the high wages—before the horse—the convenience market. Perhaps, as the young lady from Stanford commented in 1986, I had done the right thing for the wrong reason. Much of my career was spent trying to find ways to pay the high wages to which I was totally committed.

First we upped the investment ante by taking only prime locations, which could generate the most sales, even though the rents were higher.

A lease is an investment, perhaps the most serious and certainly the least changeable a retailer can make. Financially, a lease is simply a long-term loan. When I bought Pronto Markets, not only was the overt balance sheet leveraged, but the subliminal balance sheet was even worse, because of the de facto debt created by the leases. This kind of hidden debt is recognized only in the footnotes the auditors prepare. *And* they recognize only the rent amount itself. They don't include the "common area" charges, which can equal one-third of the base rent and are just as payable. Most retail bankruptcies come from bad real estate leasing decisions. That's how Rexall itself went bankrupt in 1930: bad leases from the glory days of the Roaring Twenties.

Early in my career I learned there are two kinds of decisions: the ones that are easily reversible and the ones that aren't. Fifteen-year leases are the least-reversible decisions you can make. That's why, throughout my career, I kept absolute control of real estate decisions as I will discuss in the "Too, Too Solid Stores" chapter. The need in the early 1960s to take only prime locations because of my wage policy is one reason why the arrival of 7-Eleven in 1966 was such a challenge. With their balance sheet and low labor costs, they could take the best locations.

## The Road to Serfdom

What had kept 7-Eleven out of California was Joe De Silva's aggressive organizing tactics. 7-Eleven didn't have that problem in Texas and the other Southern states where they operated. We thought it would keep them out of, if not California, at least Los Angeles. But they were astute. They adopted a franchise system, even though it meant that they could not buy or warehouse alcohol as a chain. By law, you have to have common ownership of all the stores to do that.

Their "franchise" system amounted to serfdom, in my jaundiced opinion, but it staved off the union and gave 7-Eleven wage costs about one-third those of Pronto. With their strong balance sheet and low wage costs, they could go in across the street from Pronto, absorb the losses, and drive us out of business.

I was never a fan of franchising. We saw terrible abuses in the field, which have led to elaborate, protective franchising laws in California and other states. I used to get several calls a month from people who wanted to franchise a Trader Joe's. I didn't just tell them "no," but "Hell no."

## On the Sauce

As a second way to pump investment into the Pronto stores, to support our high wage costs, we began to add hard liquor, instead of just beer and wine, to the stores. (We did this well before 7-Eleven's arrival.) The cost of a liquor license in those days was so great that the addition of a liquor license, and its added high-value-per-cubic-inch inventory, doubled our investment in a store without expanding beyond the 2,400 square foot conventional convenience store module.

In those days, California had Fair Trade on all alcoholic beverages: the manufacturer set a minimum retail price, and the state enforced it with criminal—not just civil—penalties. This was another of the quasi-fascist laws that was born of the Great Depression. So there was no discounting alcohol to the consumer, just as there was no discounting milk as I discussed in "The Milk Train" chapter. Owning a liquor license meant owning a guaranteed income stream. That's why the licenses cost so much. (Today, since Fair Trade ended, they're almost free.) By the time 7-Eleven showed up, we had liquor licenses in about a third of the stores.

## Extra Large Eggs: Trader Joe's Gets Laid

For the first time, we had begun to get a little product knowledge after buying out Rexall. That thirty-two-year-old almost-bankrupt president of Pronto, sipping his *Paul Masson* Cream Sherry, knew nothing about wine, or anything else he sold. In this, he was like all grocers of that day, and today. The buyers at the supermarket chains knew nothing about what they sold, and they don't want to know. What they did know all about was extorting slotting allowances, cooperative ad revenue, failure allowances, and back-haul concessions from the manufacturers.

Our first product knowledge breakthrough was Extra Large Eggs, a story that graduate students love to hear. A desperate egg supplier came to the tiny office I opened after the Rexall buyout.

In that office were myself and Bernice Cliff, an Owl Drug Accounting Department refugee and True Believer in me. Bernice did payroll and general ledger accounting. I wish to make it clear that she was not my secretary; in fact, I never had a secretary in my thirty years at Pronto and Trader Joe's. I don't believe in 'em. (And that's why I think that typing was the most valuable course I ever took at San Diego High School. Today, the internet just potentiates the value of this skill.)

We couldn't afford Dave Yoda, another Owl Drug accounting émigré and True Believer, full-time. He kept the books half-time; Bud Fisher helpfully put him to work at *Lucky Stores* the other half. I did all the leasing, construction, buying, pricing, merchandising, hiring, and store supervision, with lots of help from my right arm for thirty years, Leroy, the first and best employee I ever hired. Whenever I couldn't answer "the bell" (like when I went into a coma for three weeks after unloading a truck in a rainstorm), Leroy did, in addition to managing one of the seven stores. When we crossed the ten store level, I got both Leroy and Dave into the office full-time.

That's why, in 1962, I needed the capital from Adohr so desperately: I couldn't afford central management on seven stores.

So into my tiny office came the egg man. He had a problem: too many Extra Large AA eggs. He offered them to me at the same cost as Large AA, the size that all the supermarkets advertised. I would be able to sell Extra Large, which by state regulation weighed about 12 percent more than Large, for the same price as Large!

*And*, even more importantly, the supermarkets couldn't follow. The supply of Extra Large simply wasn't great enough to cover a *Safeway* ad. A moment's reflection makes one grasp that Extra Large are laid only by the eldest hens, the ones approaching, uh, retirement. There just aren't that many of those old girls.

The ads that we began running revolutionized Pronto Markets and they helped to generate the profits I needed first to stay afloat, and later to build Trader Joe's. To this day, the promotion of Extra Large AA eggs is one of the foundations of Trader Joe's merchandising, not just because of the program per se, but because it set me to wondering whether there weren't other discontinuities out there in the supplies of merchandise. Eight years later, we built Trader Joe's on the principle of discontinuity.

The Pronto Market chain, at the time of 7-Eleven's arrival, had the highest sales per store of any convenience store chain in America by a factor of three, thanks to the high wage policy, the strong locations, a few liquor licenses, and the beginnings of differentiation through product knowledge exemplified by the egg program. Now where were we going to go with it? We didn't know it yet, but we were well on the road to Trader Joe's.

# 4

## On the Road to Trader Joe's

Uncertainty ... has become so great as to render futile, if not
counterproductive, the kind of planning most companies
still practice: forecasting based on probabilities ...
Planning for Uncertainty asks: What has already happened
that will create the future? The first place to look
is in demographics.

–Peter Drucker, "Planning for Uncertainty,"
the *Wall Street Journal*, July 22, 1992

I guessed that I had maybe two or three years before the 7-Eleven guillotine would drop on Pronto. For the near term, Southland needed our milk business. We reached an accommodation with them that included my being able to exercise my right to buy out Adohr's interest in Pronto.

We had been making a lot of money in Pronto, following the success of the egg program (which is shorthand for a series of merchandising moves no longer of import). I was able to pay off Adohr quickly, with some more help from Bank of America. Merritt Adamson acted like a prince in facilitating this. (He died in 1986 after having brought his family's fortune to a new height through a series of astute real estate moves; moves that the sale of Adohr made possible. One of his key moves was getting *Pepperdine University* relocated to Malibu.)

Throughout my career I've been very lucky in the help I've received from others, like Bud Fisher, Tom Deane, Merritt Adamson, and Nate Bershon. Mr. Bershon, a wealthy real estate developer, gambled on Pronto's crummy net worth and built five Prontos for us. One of them, at National and Westwood in West Los Angeles, is still there under the Trader Joe's banner and has one of the highest sales-per-square-foot of any store in America, around $3,000. Nate Bershon died at ninety-three in 1985, still able to make out his own tax returns for his real estate empire. More than anything, he taught me that there are people out there whose handshake is better than any contract. When I finally sold Trader Joe's, it was basically on a handshake.

I would say that Southland treated us honorably up to the point in 1971 when I dropped their milk because they could not supply us with certified raw milk for our new health food program in Whole Earth Harry. Southland later went bankrupt, because of unwise expansion and tough competition from the gas station companies, like *ARCO's AM-PM* chain.

The milk business is quite different today: as the supermarket chains grew bigger and went public, they simply built their own creameries, gave up the deals with the branded dairies, and made more money from milk than ever. Most of the milk companies that were cutting those deals in the 1950s have disappeared or been radically transformed. Adohr is now owned by its own management, after having been rescued by (former Los Angeles mayor) Dick Riordan's venture capital company about 1990 after the collapse of Southland.

## The Keystone of Trader Joe's

I realized that convenience store retailing was an opportunity far too "good" for my financial resources. There was no way I could exploit it. Many other guys who tried the convenience store business in the United States didn't wise up soon enough, and were wiped out in the collapse of the industry in the late 1980s: Southland wasn't the only one that failed, just the biggest. The basic problem is that convenience store retailing is a commodity business that is hard to differentiate.

What I needed was a good but small opportunity for my good but small company: a non-commodity, differentiated kind of retailing. Yes, I could have sold out to 7-Eleven and gone to work for them, or somebody else. But the Byzantine management atmosphere at first Rexall and then Hughes Aircraft had convinced me that the only real security lies in having your own business, and this left-hander was well ahead of the curve on that one.

*Also*, I was convinced that I was on a holy mission in preserving a company owned significantly by its employees. My hope was that someday it would be 100 percent owned by them. On that one I proved to be wrong. But this conviction, along with the desire to stay the hell out of Byzantium, gave me the hubris to think we could pull it off.

The clue, the *keystone* of the arch of Trader Joe's, was a small news item in *Scientific American* in 1965. When we left Stanford, my father-in-law, Bill Steere, a professor of botany, gave me a subscription to *Scientific American.* In terms of creating my fortune, it's the most important magazine I've ever read.

The news item said that, of all the people in the United States who were qualified to go to college in 1932, in the pit of the Depression, only 2 percent actually did. By contrast, in 1964, of all the people qualified to go to college, 60 percent in fact actually did. The big change, of course, was the GI Bill of Rights that went into effect in 1945. It was the greatest experiment in mass higher education ever attempted by any society in any era. By 1965, we were into the second generation of veterans going to college (and the pace stepped up later, because of Vietnam).

A second news item, one from the *Wall Street Journal,* told me that the *Boeing 747* would go into service in 1970, and that it would slash the cost of international travel. (It did: the real cost of going to Europe today is about one-fifteenth of what it was in 1950.) In Pronto Markets

we had noticed that people who traveled—even to San Francisco—
were far more adventurous in what they were willing to put in their
stomachs. Travel is, after all, a form of education.

Anticipating Peter Drucker's advice by almost thirty years, Trader
Joe's was conceived from those two demographic news stories. What I
saw here was a small but growing demographic opportunity in people
who were well educated. 7-Eleven, and the whole convenience store
genre, served the most basic needs of the most mindless demographics
with cigarettes, *Coca-Cola*, milk, *Budweiser*, candy, bread, eggs. Dimly, I
saw an opportunity to differentiate ourselves radically from mainstream
retailing to mainstream people.

Just how homogenized America had become by 1966 deserves its
own chapter, which follows. What I saw in those news stories were the
first cracks in the homogenization.

# 5

# How *I Love Lucy*
# Homogenized America

## The Rise of Brands

The early nineteenth century saw the displacement of barter societies with cash economies, which in turn permitted retailers to appear. Retailers sold most products in bulk, however, because food technology had not progressed much past the art of filling barrels. Brands, essentially, did not exist. The retailer's name, in effect, became the de facto brand name for the flour, salt, sugar, and coffee sold from barrels.

In response to Napoleon's problems with feeding his huge army, Nicolas Appert invented canning in 1809. This was the first step away from bulk retailing. About thirty years after Waterloo, America had its first branded canned food, which was probably *Underwood's* deviled ham. During the Civil War, which also stimulated food technology, Gail Borden invented canned milk, and after that an avalanche of branded food products appeared: *Royal Baking Powder*, *Baker's Chocolate*, et al. The avalanche also included non-foods, such as *Pear's Soap*, patent medicines like *Lydia Pinkham*, and *Usher's Green Stripe*, the first branded Scotch. This phenomenon was worldwide; the great brands of champagne, for example, rose at this time, starting with *Veuve Clicquot*; the brands of Swiss chocolate, like *Lindt*, etc.

The pace quickened after the first automatic glass bottle machine was built in the 1890s, making possible the soft drink brands like Coca-Cola (as opposed to being dispensed in bulk from soda fountains). World War I established branded cigarettes, which heretofore had been regarded as effeminate, compared with cigars.

In the meantime, the *Kraft* brown paper bag was invented about 1870, making it possible to put all your store-bought purchases in a paper bag, a phenomenon that even today is unusual in Europe.

## Brands and Advertising

The brands had to advertise. Print media was all that was available, and the great mass-circulation magazines like the *Saturday Evening Post* and *Collier's* rose on the strength of brand advertising, such as George Washington Hill's immortal "Reach for a Lucky instead of a sweet." Newspapers also thrived on brand advertising.

In the late 1920s, however, network radio began to spark. The first great success was *Amos 'n Andy*. They were sponsored by an obscure brand of toothpaste from Chicago called *Pepsodent*. Overnight, it became No. 1. (See Charles Luckman's autobiography, *Twice in a Lifetime*.) Ever after, electronic media have been dominant.

The Great Depression began in 1930. The drug chains, which had coalesced before World War I, began to "price bomb" Pepsodent to draw foot traffic, thereby establishing a symbiosis between retailers and powerful brands that has lasted ever since. (This pattern was compromised for a while by the passage of federal and state Fair Trade laws about 1935. These laws were vitiated about 1960. Even during the heyday of Fair Trade, however, most food manufacturers chose not to "fair trade" their brands.)

The new radio networks signed up great theatrical performers, and these great personalities became incredibly identified with the brands that sponsored them: *Jack Benny/Jello; Fibber McGee & Molly/ Johnson's Wax; Edgar Bergen and Charlie McCarthy/Chase & Sanborn coffee; Bing Crosby/Kraft Cheese; Bob Hope/Lever Bros.*; and *Ed Wynn* the *Texaco* Fire Chief. These half-hour, nighttime big star shows were just the top of a pyramid that included:

1. Half-hour nighttime shows completely identified with a brand, such as *Lucky Strike Hit Parade, Camel Caravan, Lux Radio Theater,* etc.

2. Fifteen-minute daytime soap operas, each named for a fictitious heroine and sponsored by a specific brand of soap: *Ma Perkins, Mary Noble, Mary Marlin, Stella Dallas,* etc.

3. Fifteen-minute late afternoon "kid" shows like the *Lone Ranger/ Weber's Bread* (where is my magic decoder ring?), *Jack Armstrong/ Wheaties, Little Orphan Annie/Ovaltine,* etc.

4. Special events like *Gillette/World Series, Texaco/Metropolitan Opera,* and newscasts like the *Richfield* (gasoline, in case you've forgotten the brand) *Reporter.*

All this detail is presented, because it's easy to forget that network radio came from nowhere, and almost overnight inextricably combined entertainment and advertising in the public mind. This is why brands became so powerful, and why retailers became eunuchs—albeit wealthy eunuchs—distributing the brands.

## Radio & Parking Lots Shape the Supermarket

The supermarket, like network radio, also began about 1930. What distinguished the supermarket was its parking lot, not what was inside the store. ("Self-service" had started fifteen years earlier.) The supermarket rose to prominence because it recognized the automobile, something that department stores did not recognize until after World War II. Because of this, early supermarkets were free-standing or carved into existing business districts next to stores that themselves had no parking. "Shopping centers" are mostly a post–World War II phenomenon. The supermarket was then perfected by yet another set of wheels, when the shopping cart was invented in 1937.

The supermarket came into existence coincidentally with the rise of network radio, which was so effective that advertised brands inevitably came to dominate supermarket merchandising. So supermarkets were shaped by network radio from their beginning. As a result, supermarket merchandising has always been brand-oriented. One result of this has been that supermarkets have rarely been known for their product knowledge, about what they sold. Indeed, the supermarkets of the 1930s usually operated only the dry grocery department, which was mostly branded goods; bakery, produce, meat, and liquor were usually concessions.

**Television was the most powerful advertising medium ever invented, and it began to homogenize American culture to a startling degree.**

As we evolved Trader Joe's, its greatest departure from the norm wasn't its size or its decor. It was our commitment to product knowledge, something which was totally foreign to the mass-merchant culture, and our turning our backs to branded merchandise.

World War II completed the triumph of network radio/advertised brands. This system represented security to Americans in a time of trouble, like Mom, apple pie, and "God Bless America" (introduced by Kate Smith on her network radio show, which was sponsored by A&P).

The market chains that predated radio, like A&P, *National Tea*, and others had grown on their private labels. Even though they began to build supermarkets to replace their old, three-thousand-square-foot stores, their refusal to acknowledge the new dominance of branded goods led to their long, painful decline throughout the post–World War II period.

The triumph of brands, of course, affected many retailers besides markets. The drug chains like Rexall, which had been built on private label merchandise before 1930, were compromised by the new dominance of branded health and beauty aids: *Anacin* (Mr. Keene, Tracer of Lost Persons), *Jergens* (Walter Winchell), et al., were heavy radio advertisers. When the brilliant Sav-on drugstores opened just after World War II, it carried almost no private labels. (Most supermarkets carried no health and beauty aids until after 1950, so the brunt of this advertising fell on drugstores and on variety stores, which were then major marketers of health and beauty aids.)

## Television Finishes the Homogenization

Network radio had reshaped the living patterns of Americans like nothing else in history. But, after twenty years of dominance, it disappeared in only three short years, after the coaxial cable was driven across the U.S. in 1950, making network TV possible. TV wiped out not only network radio, but the mass circulation magazines, and most evening newspapers. Television was the most powerful advertising medium ever invented, and it began to homogenize American culture to a startling degree.

The great brands, already powerful because of network radio, reached new heights of dominance, as TV audience penetration reached almost 100 percent through the 1960s. For one thing, network TV became so expensive that only the biggest companies could afford to buy time. This led to the disappearance of many smaller brands, including almost all small breweries and the weaker soft drink brands. The supermarket, shaped first by network radio, was shaped now by network TV. Many other retailers were also impacted, such as appliance dealers (Betty White/*Westinghouse*; Ronald Reagan/*General Electric*).

This is where we were in 1966, a nation whose regional accents, modes of dress, and menus were being reduced to a common (low) denominator of *Swanson TV Dinners, Minute Maid Orange Juice, Best Foods Mayonnaise*, and *Folgers* coffee. Grocers didn't need to know anything except what was going to be advertised next on *I Love Lucy* and *Gunsmoke*.

## Network TV Peaks

In 1966, I made a correct prediction, as usual, for the wrong reasons. I guessed that network TV, with its 95 percent audience share, just couldn't go any further. The networks' audiences of the 1960s were the people who hadn't been able to afford to go to college in the 1930s and 1940s. I felt that the newly educated group that was slowly emerging would be dissatisfied with this mass culture: that they would be more demanding; that they would want something different.

In fact, network TV did peak in 1970. When John Wayne got the Oscar for *True Grit*, that was it. It was with considerable satisfaction that I saw network TV's market share drop steadily ever since. By 1997, the *NBC-CBS-ABC* share was below 50 percent. And that remaining share generally represented the lowest purchasing power in society.

In 1966, I thought that Public Television would be a big factor in this shift. I was wrong. Its market share has remained constant at about 3 percent. What happened was:

1. **Technology.** Cable and satellite TV displaced the networks; and the VCR displaced all of them. (*Sony*, when it developed the

VCR, never dreamed it would be used mostly to watch movies, rather than to tape TV shows.)

2. **Immigration.** Cable is full of Spanish, Korean, Japanese, and Chinese channels. (The top radio stations in Los Angeles are now all Hispanic.)

3. **Public Television** has gone nowhere; however, similar cable channels like *The History Channel*, *Bravo*, and all-news stations like *CNN* have eroded the networks' place.

Nothing in America has become more de-homogenized, more fragmented than electronic media! For example, in Los Angeles, we have more than seventy radio stations. And now, the internet has fragmented electronic media almost to an infinite extent.

Trader Joe's was part of this fragmentation. It created an opportunity for independent-minded people to split off the main track. You might think of Trader Joe's as one of the more esoteric cable channels; the supermarkets as NBC-CBS-ABC.

# 6

## Good Time Charley

Give me a fruitful error any time, full of seeds, bursting
with its own corrections. You can keep
your sterile truth for yourself.

–Pareto's comment on Kepler, quoted by
Stephen Jay Gould in *The Panda's Thumb*

I'm going to disillusion those dear souls—there seem to be a lot of them out there—who think that Trader Joe's sprang, fully developed, from my brain, like Athena from the head of Zeus. To continue the metaphor, it was more like an elbow here, a toenail there over a period of eleven years, with an occasional painful delivery of a major hunk of torso. Non-metaphorically, there were three major versions of Trader Joe's between 1966 and 1977: Good Time Charley of 1967, Whole Earth Harry of 1971, and Mac the Knife of 1977, which retained few vestiges of Good Time Charley.

## The Basic Ground Rules for Good Time Charley

Good Time Charley represented the coming together of these ideas:

1. We were going to track the small but emerging group of well-educated, well-traveled people.

2. The correlation between alcohol consumption and levels of education is about as perfect as one can find in marketing.

3. As reported earlier, in order to support the high wages we paid, I kept trying to invest more per job: the easiest way was to add distilled spirits. As we retrofitted more Pronto Markets with spirits, however, it became increasingly apparent that a convenience store was not the ideal platform for selling booze. For one thing, we were about to be inundated with dozens of 7-Elevens, none of which would carry hard liquor. The public image of a convenience store did not lead it to expect to find hard liquor there.

4. The advantage of hard liquor merchandise was that it met three tests:
   a. A high value per cubic inch, essential to a small store format.
   b. A high rate of consumption.
   c. It had to be easily handled.

If we could have added a fourth test, it would be that we had to be outstanding in the field. That would be an ideal category. Accordingly, this new store, as yet unnamed, would carry The World's Largest Assortment of Alcoholic Beverages, which in practice in Good Time Charley turned out to be a hundred brands of Scotch, seventy brands of bourbon, fifty brands of rum, fourteen brands of tequila, and so on. And wine. About wine, more on that later. Remember: Fair Trade on alcohol ruled in California back then. We could not become outstanding in terms of price; therefore, we would become outstanding in terms of assortment.

Still trying to maximize the use of a small store, I looked for other categories that met the Four Tests: high value per cubic inch, high rate of consumption; easily handled; and something in which we could be outstanding in terms of price or assortment. For example, diamonds met the first test but flunked the second. Fruits and vegetables met the first and second tests but flunked the third because produce requires constant reworking (nowadays, however, new plastic wraps are changing that). Fresh meat flunked the third test even more.

At that point, in February 1966, I wrote what I call a white paper, something that I have tried to do at every important turn of events. I started with the founding of Pronto Markets. In a white paper you try to write down everything you plan to do, and the reason why you think you should do it. That way, when things don't work out, you can't play the role of a Soviet historian and airbrush history.

The other important use of a white paper is to circulate it to the troops, to engage their support and solicit their ideas.

Most of my ideas about how to act as an entrepreneur are derived from *The Revolt of the Masses* by Jose Ortega y Gasset, the greatest Spanish philosopher of the twentieth century. Although it was published in 1929, the year before I was born, I believe this book still offers the clearest explanation of the times in which we live. And I believe it offers a master "plan of action" for the would-be entrepreneur, who usually has no reputation and few resources.

That was me, reading the book while I was selling *Kirby* vacuum cleaners door-to-door during my last year at Stanford.

Ortega offers an explanation of how such a person can get an enterprise started. In the context of the career of Julius Caesar, an entrepreneur who started without power, Ortega says of the state:

> Human life, by its very nature, has to be dedicated to something, an enterprise glorious or humble, a destiny illustrious or trivial. . . .
>
> The State begins when groups, naturally divided, find themselves obliged to live in common. This obligation is not of brute force, but implies an impelling purpose, a common task which is set before the dispersed groups. Before all, the State is a plan of action and a Programme of Collaboration. The men are called upon so that together they may do something. . . . It is pure dynamism, the will to do something in

common, and thanks to this the idea of the State, is bounded by no physical limits. . . .

Never has anyone ruled on this earth by basing his rule essentially on any other thing than public opinion. . . . Even the man who attempts to rule with janissaries depends on their opinion and the opinion which the rest of the inhabitants have of them. The truth is that there is no ruling with janissaries. As Talleyrand said to Napoleon, "You can do everything with bayonets, sire, except sit on them!" (*The Revolt of the Masses*, chapter 14, "Who Rules in the World?")

Most of my career has been spent selling "plans of action and programmes of collaboration," whether to Rexall to start up Pronto Markets; or Bank of America to buy out Pronto; or landlords; or vendors, many of whom have been very skeptical of, if not outright hostile to, my plans; and above all to my employees. If you want to know what differentiates me from most managers, that's it. From the beginning, thanks to Ortega y Gasset, I've been aware of the need to sell everybody.

That's why, throughout my career, my policy has been full disclosure to employees about the true state of our affairs, almost to the point of imprudence. I took a cue from General Patton, who thought that the greatest danger was not that the enemy would learn his plans, but that his own troops would not.

I also was taught (perhaps warped is a better term) by Bud Fisher, who could be shockingly frank—even if it was against his own interests. That frankness was one of Bud's secrets in gaining and keeping the loyalty of everyone from the janitors to the executive vice presidents of any company he ran.

It's a hard policy to sell to most managements. Even to my own management! For years I used to take all new employees to lunch. Among other admonitions, I told them that if they ever got a better offer, they should take it. As soon as they could, my field supervisors ended those lunches. Another frank idea was vetoed by my top people:

I wanted to publish their salaries and bonuses, and mine, every year when we issued our annual compensation bulletins.

## No Place for Secrets

People like secrets, because secrets bring power. Consider the priests of ancient Greece who kept the secret of pi. This is one reason I never had a secretary. When I found "executive secretaries" in the various companies I took over after leaving Trader Joe's, I got rid of them. They hold too many secrets and are actively interested in augmenting their inventory. There's a place for secrets, and it's usually in the office of the head of Human Resources. But it should not be in the chain of command, where the CEO's secretary too often gets inserted by force of circumstance if not by force of personality.

After circulating the white paper to the troops, several interesting ideas came from the field, which we experimented with in Pronto Markets during 1966. One of our managers, Jim Francis, was an ardent hunter. He suggested ammunition. That's right, bullets: high value per cubic inch, high rate of consumption, easily handled, and we could be outstanding in terms of price. It was easy to cream *Sears Roebuck* on price. Within a short time we were doing 2 percent of sales in bullets. Robert Kennedy was assassinated, which prompted a flood of regulations, so we dropped bullets. With all those forms to be filled out, they now flunked Test Three, "easily handled." But Jim's idea absolutely met the tests.

## Naming Trader Joe's

In 1966, the United States was at a peak of prosperity. Of Lyndon Johnson's policy of guns and butter, only the butter was yet on view. Vietnam had not yet gone on TV. There was virtually no inflation or unemployment. The op-ed pieces in the *LA Times* fretted about how we would spend all that leisure time, since the thirty-five-hour workweek was now a sure thing. The inflation-adjusted *Dow Jones Industrial Average* was at an all-time peak not equaled again until the 1990s.

So Trader Joe's was conceived in an atmosphere of fun-leisure-party-prosperity. A couple of years earlier, we had done the *Jungle Cruise* at *Disneyland,* which stuck in my head. "Yellow Bird" and "Beyond the Reef" were being played in the hotel lobbies. *Trader Vic's* was at its peak. The thirty-somethings (including us) of that day were drinking not Chardonnay but Mai Tais and Fog Cutters (you know, those drinks that come with little umbrellas) to protect the booze from the "Rain on the Roof" feature of those Polynesian bars. And somewhere in the dim recesses of childhood I must have seen *Red Dust* with Jean Harlow and Clark Gable, and read *White Shadows in the South Seas* and something about Trader Horn.

Since we were going to appeal to the well traveled, Trader Joe's simply coalesced out of all those stimuli. We did a trademark search and found that Trader Joe's Market was okay. We also did a phone book search and found a Trader Joe's, which was a used hubcap dealer in the somewhat seedy suburb of Sunland, California.

One marketing expert thought it was a terrible name: "Trader" to him was not a romantic term of the South Seas but something associated with selling defective horse flesh. Others, correctly, thought we would be confused with Trader Vic's, which happened for years, until we became better known than Trader Vic's. Other people are still convinced that it's owned by the Italian family that operates Little Joe's, an Italian restaurant in LA's Chinatown (and a great institution).

The logo for Trader Joe's was mostly designed by Fred Schroeder, a small maker of signs who had gotten the *Marie Callender* restaurant account. I had admired Marie's signs, because they always had a roof over them, making them look cherished. That's how I met Fred, who came up with the vaguely east-of-Suez lettering.

The first Trader Joe's, which opened in August 1967 on Arroyo Parkway in Pasadena, had a quasi-tori gate sign, the sheltered sign motif, and a Polynesian roof. At first, most drivers on Arroyo Parkway thought it was a restaurant, a negative that I had not anticipated. Inside was a riot of marine artifacts including a ship's bell, oars, netting, and half a rowboat. The check stand was an island with its own sort of pagoda roof, the counters made of old hatch covers in which seashells had been fiberglassed, the whole thing sitting on smashed-up barrels. This was before marine artifacts became trendy: I could go down to the marine salvage joints on the waterfront of LA's harbor and pick up stuff for pennies per pound.

All the employees wore Polynesian shirts and Bermuda shorts; the manager was called Captain; the assistant, First Mate; the box boys Native Bearers. Hawaiian music played on the loudspeakers until the employees threw the records away: one can listen to that somewhat limited repertoire for only so many days without going mad. (I had read in the *New Yorker* that Hawaiian music, played in stores, slowed the customers down.)

That was the name and visual image we developed by late 1966. Working with Leroy and Frank Kono, we developed a prototype store of 4,500 square feet.

Here's a good question: Given my need to get away from convenience stores, why did I stick with small stores? If in 1967 it was justified because I had eighteen of them already, surely it was no longer justified in the 1980s when Trader Joe's had become a powerful, successful operation. The answer was verbalized for us in *In Search of Excellence*, Tom Peter's best-selling book on management that appeared in 1983. He called it "The Power of Chunking":

> The essential building block of a company is the section [which] within its sphere does not await executive orders but takes initiatives. The key factor for success is getting one's arms around almost any practical problem and knocking it off. . . . The small group is the most visible of the chunking devices.

The fundamental "chunk" of Trader Joe's is the individual store with its highly paid Captain and staff: people who are capable of exercising discretion. I admire *Nordstrom*'s fundamental instruction to its employees: use your best judgment.

Trader Joe's finally settled down at an average of about eight thousand square feet in the 1980s, but the concept of a relatively small store with a relatively small staff remains in force. When we first opened Good Time Charley, it was open 7:00 a.m. to midnight, like Pronto. As time went on, we progressively shortened the hours down to 9:00 a.m. to 9:00 p.m. Each time we shortened hours, we made more money: there were fewer "shifts" and more interaction among the staff.

## Backing into Wine

The ideal location I found for the first Trader Joe's was a 1911 bottled water plant on Arroyo Parkway in Pasadena. My real estate broker—and a de facto member of Trader Joe's top management—had one hell of a time negotiating the lease with an obdurate lawyer, Patrick James Kirby. Kirby was so tough that later Alice said if she ever got a divorce, she was going to hire Kirby. He liked that.

Furthermore, the trade thought I was nuts paying top dollar for a site on Arroyo Parkway, which at that time was little more than an industrial slum. What only my realtor understood was that the site was ideal for my new plan: Pasadena was an extended campus, with *Cal Tech, Pasadena City College, Fuller Theological Seminary, Ambassador College* (which proved to be a major customer), an Armenian college, and *Occidental College* and *Cal State LA* not too far away. The *Huntington Hospital* is a major employer of people with advanced degrees, as are some big engineering firms like *Parsons*. In short, Pasadena probably had more well-educated, well-traveled people than any city of its size in California.

Another problem with the Arroyo Parkway building was its size, almost twice as big as the 4,500 square feet we had in mind for Trader Joe's. We coped with this in two ways:

1. We sublet a portion for a service meat market. I was uneasy about tackling the well-educated, well-traveled market without service meat. We got real lucky in Ron Dessin, our butcher, because he was a rarity: a meat cutter, a truly great artist of a meat cutter, who was also an entrepreneur. Ronnie was such a factor in the success of the first Trader Joe's that we installed service meat shops in the next four Trader Joe's. Unfortunately, Ronnie proved to be the only butcher who was also an entrepreneur. As time and ethics permitted, we eased the other guys out. From then on, we expanded without meat markets.

2. We recognized the really important use of the extra space was to expand the planned wine department. Please remember, we knew little about wine. We had conducted some experiments in Pronto during the pre-opening of Trader Joe's. They were inconclusive or outright disappointing. Thanks to one of our managers, Frank Kono, and George McCoul, a huge Armenian who had owned a meat market next to a Pronto and was now in the Napa Valley, we were introduced to several small California winemakers. As a result we decided to install "the world's greatest variety of California wine." That was seventeen brands. By contrast, *Jurgensen's*, the leading gourmet market of the era, carried only seven brands.

## But Who Was Going to Drink the Wine?

The primary market for wine in 1967 was zilch; the secondary market for California wine was even worse. By great good fortune we became the first retailer to offer plenty of shelf space to tiny wineries that later became famous, like *Heitz, Schramsberg, Mayacamas, Souverain, Freemark Abbey,* and the controversial *Martin Ray,* probably the greatest wine-maker I have ever known, and the most devious. To our astonishment, it was the wine program that was the big hit, helped by strong-sell methods of the first Captain, Jack Button. And of course it was all fair traded so we had a guaranteed profit. We began publishing a wine newsletter called, sardonically, the *Insider's Report,* and wine sales kept booming. We hired George McCoul for the next four years and began conducting wine tastings, learning seriously about wines.

Otherwise, the Pasadena Trader Joe's had a convenience store's assortment of groceries (we didn't know anything about food) augmented with the giant liquor department, and some of the programs that met my four tests and that had been tested in Pronto. Among these were: discounting magazines including *Playboy;* discounting paperback books; discounting hosiery; discounting phonograph records (a terrible idea we soon dropped); and discounting photo finishing. The latter was right on: it was a big success and zeroed in exactly on our target clientele.

Trader Joe's was off to a good start. We began converting the demo-graphically suitable Prontos in West LA, Culver City, Fullerton, etc., and selling off the less suitable Prontos, ones that we had leased in our rush to sell more Adohr milk. At the beginning of 1970, it looked like we were on a roll, leasing more locations.

Then the economy went to hell. The era of fun-vacation-leisure party was no longer operative. Trends were shifting toward a more wholesome, health-conscious consumption. This was when we saw Trader Joe's shift from the fun-providing Good Time Charley into the more health-savvy Whole Earth Harry by 1971.

# 7

# Uncorked!

I have a remedy against thirst, quite contrary to that which
is good against the biting of a mad dog. Keep running after a
dog, and he will never bite you; drink always before the
thirst, and it will never come upon you.

–Rabelais, *Gargantua*

## The Lousy Economy of the Early Seventies

To date, 1970 was the most important single year in the history
of Trader Joe's.

Let's start, like a good MBA, with the economic background. It was
terrible. After a booming 1969 in both the economy and the stock
market, Richard Nixon, although three years away from giving up in
Vietnam, started to cut back the defense establishment. Almost overnight one hundred thousand aerospace jobs were lost in Southern
California. In some towns, one out of every ten houses was for sale.
The *Los Angeles Times*'s op-ed articles, the ones that had been fretting
about how we were going to spend all the leisure time created by thirty-
five-hour workweeks, now were obsessed with the emigration from Los
Angeles.

What happened in 1970 in Los Angeles was the worst economic episode I've ever had to fight through. Unlike the post–Cold War Recession, we did not have the waves of in-migration from Mexico, nor were drug sales as great. I believe the underground economy was a silent savior of Los Angeles during 1990–94. The Kent State Massacre and the *Pentagon Papers* scandal didn't help the 1970 scene.

Furthermore, things didn't get better in the early 1970s. The sharp recession of 1970 was followed by a sudden inflation caused by Vietnam spending. Nixon "slammed the gold window shut." From 1945 to 1971, the U.S., under the Bretton Woods Agreement, had agreed to back its currency to a limited extent with gold at $35 per ounce. Other nations' central banks were withdrawing our gold so fast that Nixon had to renege on the promise. This was followed in 1973 by the end of fixed currency exchange rates. The dollar plummeted. Traveling to the wine country of France in the summer of 1973, I was unable to cash *American Express* dollar-denominated traveler's checks. Inflation jumped with the 1973 Energy Crisis. Nixon imposed wage and price controls. Then Watergate, accompanied by the Dow Jones hitting bottom in 1974.

## Three Initiatives to Turn the Tide

Against all this, Trader Joe's mounted three initiatives. In chronological order:

1. We launched the *Fearless Flyer* early in 1970.

2. We broke the price of imported wines in late 1970 thanks to a loophole in the Fair Trade law.

3. Most importantly, in 1971, we married the health food store to the Good Time Charley party store, which had been the 1967–70 version of Trader Joe's.

Together these three elements comprised the second version of Trader Joe's, Whole Earth Harry. This chapter, "Uncorked!," talks about the loophole in Fair Trade and what ensued; the following chapter brings in the health foods; finally, in the chapter "Promise, Large Promise" I discuss the *Fearless Flyer* and the overall advertising of Trader Joe's.

## The Loophole in Fair Trade

Prohibition was never "repealed." It was amended in 1933 to give each state the absolute right to regulate alcohol. Some states, like Kansas, went totally dry. Some, like Pennsylvania, made all forms of alcohol a state monopoly. Some, like, Washington, made hard liquor a state monopoly, but left beer and wine in private hands. California chose a relatively free-market solution. The state did not go into the liquor business, but it passed two basic laws:

1. The "tied house" laws: A retailer could not be owned by a manufacturer or a wholesaler of beer, wine, or liquor. Retailers could do business directly with California wineries, but they could not import wine-beer-liquor except through a licensed importer. "Import" was defined literally: a retailer could not "import" wine from Oregon or Washington.

2. Each "brand" of alcohol had to have a minimum consumer price "posted" with the state monthly. If a retailer broke any of the thousands of prices, the state could go after him with criminal penalties, take away his off-sale license, and even put him in jail.

I am going into these matters in great detail for the benefit of anyone who is in this business. As I learned time and again, success in business often rests on a minute reading of the regulations that impact your business. This point will be emphasized later in this book in the "Hairballs" chapter.

In June 1970, we were promoting a gallon jug of Spanish wine, *Marqués de Olivar*. It was imported by Monsieur Henri, the wine wholesaling arm of *Pepsi Cola*. M. Henri existed mostly to distribute *Stolichnaya*. Pepsi had a deal with the Soviet government: the Soviets would export vodka through M. Henri, and the Soviets would give Pepsi a lock on the USSR soft drink market. But M. Henri carried a lot of non–Iron Curtain stuff, too.

**We had found a loophole in the law, and by God we drove a truck through it!**

Most wine wholesalers "posted" minimum consumer prices, which gave the retailer a minimum of a 33 percent gross profit (a 50 percent markup on cost). I noticed that Marqués de Olivar, however, had a posted gross profit of only 6 percent. I called Eddie Randolph, manager of M. Henri. He explained, "We can post any price we like as long as it's at least 6 percent above cost. I posted it that way so guys like you could have a hot price."

This led us to comb through the price postings of the wholesalers. What intrigued us was that many famous French wines had different posted prices by different wholesalers.

For example, the 1966 vintage of *Chateau Lafite Rothschild* might be posted for $10 by *Young's Market Co.*; $11 by *Bohemian Distributors*; and $9.89 by *Southern Wines & Spirits*. The reason? No one was the exclusive distributor for Lafite in the U.S. or California. All three prices showed a 33 percent gross profit to the retailer. The variance may have been explained by different acquisition costs for the three wholesalers, or by each wholesaler making a different profit on the wine.

The "brand" posting with the state was not for 1966 *Lafite*, but for Young's Market '66 *Lafite*, Bohemian '66 *Lafite*, or Southern Wines & Spirits '66 *Lafite*. Each was a separate "brand" in the eyes of the state!

We then met with a great gentleman and veteran importer, Ezra Webb. Ezra had a tiny wholesale and importing company that supplied us with private label bourbon. Yes, indeed, he said, our analysis was correct. Furthermore, he could buy Lafite, indeed any of the famous Bordeaux vineyards, for much less than the big wholesalers were paying, and he would post the retails as low as we wanted! Wow! Trader Joe's was Uncorked! The first gleam of Mac the Knife's steel now glinted in the wineglass seven years before we loosed the monster on the trade.

We had found a loophole in the law, and by God we drove a truck through it! Within three years, we were the leading retailer of imported wines in California! This was the real beginning of the Legend of Trader Joe's.

We were to wine connoisseurs what that great airline, *PSA*, was to travelers before the airlines were deregulated in 1981. Like us, PSA's pricing was based on a close reading of FAA regulations, which in those days set the fare for every air route in the U.S. As long as PSA flew only within California, however, they were free of FAA price regulation. PSA had been one of my heroes, and now I was glad to join it in offering great value to our customers.

Almost thirty years later, people come up to me to talk about how they bought *Latour* for $5.99; or *Pichon Longueville Lalande* for $3.69, and so on. These prices seem impossible today when the same wines from the same vineyards sell for ten to twenty times as much. Some of the increase is due to inflation, sure, but the big change is that the great wines that are hot now, are infinitely more popular now than they were in 1970, and a lot more buyers are chasing wines of very limited production.

We were aided in our bargain buying of great wines by the recession of 1970 and the troubled economic times all around the world that followed the end of the Bretton Woods fixed exchange rates. The wine business tanked. Several wholesalers in California liquidated, including M. Henri. We got fabulous bargains from those liquidations.

---

I went in and ate dinner. It was a big meal for France but seemed very carefully apportioned after Spain. I drank a bottle of wine for company. It was a Chateau Margaux. It was pleasant to be drinking slowly and to be tasting the wine and to be drinking alone. A bottle of wine was good company.

–Ernest Hemingway, *The Sun Also Rises*

---

## Our Brief Reign as #1 in Premier Cru Wines

In 1924, Hemingway's bottle of *Chateaux Margaux* would cost maybe $3 in current purchasing power. Today it costs more like $150. But during the 1970s, Margaux, at Trader Joe's, was closer to $3 than $150, and the wine collectors . . . they were in very good company.

Over in Bordeaux, the giant Swiss food company, *Nestlé*, had made a huge, mistaken commitment to Bordeaux wines. I went there in 1974 and bought large quantities at bargain prices. (Nestlé later owned Beringer in California and recouped its fortunes.)

Then the pinnacle of our great wine buying came in 1976, and it damn near bankrupted us. One of the biggest "shippers" of Bordeaux wine, *Delors*, was liquidated by its British owners. They turned their immense inventory over to *Christie's*. In March 1976, I flew to London to attend the biggest auction of wines from Bordeaux ever held.

I went to the auction room, a hick from California amidst four hundred veteran buyers from all over the world. The prices seemed very cheap to me, so I kept buying. After the two-day auction ended, the hick was the biggest buyer at the auction!

I was staying at the Connaught, an appropriate venue for such a (suddenly) big deal, when Bob Berning, our wine buyer, called me. Trouble!

Our competitors were scheming with the state to impose a new regulation: the name of the licensed importer had to be on the main, front label on the bottle. Any wine already in California would be grandfathered, but any new imports would have to comply with the new regulation.

This was easy for the big distributors: they could arrange to have labels specially printed with additional height to accommodate their names. But all of the Delors wine at Christie's was already labeled!

If I couldn't import the Delors wines, I would have had to dump them in the European market. It might not have bankrupted us, but it sure as hell would have put a dent in our balance sheet.

Then that genius Ezra Webb came up with the solution. He simply had transparent decals printed that said, "Ezra Webb Imports." He airmailed these to Christie's. We then paid Christie's a little extra to open each case, put the decal on the main label of each bottle, and ship the now perfectly legal wine.

The wines that I bought still grace some of the most important wine cellars of California and Mexico. The following year, Bob Berning went to London and cleaned up on the big auction of Ginestet wines, including *Gruaud LaRose*, *Meyney*, *Clos des Jacobins*, et al. And they all bore Ezra's decal. That was the last year that Fair Trade was in force.

## Wines for the Overeducated and Underpaid

I don't want you to think, however, that all we were interested in were great wines. What's described above was an anomaly, an opportunity we seized, but the wines were not what I had in mind for the core competency of Trader Joe's: I wanted to make sure that every family could afford a bottle of decent wine on the table every night. One of my obsessions is the association of wine with food, as opposed to those great wines that are judged straight up and argued over endlessly. I think that blind tastings of wine are useless, because I think that a given wine has no meaning except in the presence of a given dish.

Bob Berning, therefore, began importing large quantities of cheap but good wines, $1.49 in those days. One of the first was *Serradayres*, a red wine I found in Portugal in 1971, and *Jean Gleizes*, which I found in France in 1972. These wines had no other importers in the U.S. so Ezra had no problems with the postings. Twenty-seven years later, I noticed yet another shipment of *Serradayres* at Trader Joe's.

## The Wine Bank

The real power in the enterprise remained in imported wines and, increasingly, our private label California wines, which Bob Berning was developing in great quantities. Still, many of the wines we sold were subject to Fair Trade. Besides carrying our great assortment of California "boutique" wines, there wasn't much we could do to promote them, and then I thought of the *Wine Bank*.

In the heart of the 1970–71 recession the *LA Times* interviewed a *Cadillac* dealer in Hollywood who was doing just fine, thank you, because, as he explained, "the rich are always with us." One thing the rich, or at least those not wiped out by the aerospace recession, were starting to do was to collect wine. Their problem: Where to store it?

The Wine Bank was my answer: lockers where customers could store their wine, and at the lowest prices in Los Angeles. This was a form of price competition that the Fair Trade laws did not regulate.

We created two Wine Banks at stores twenty miles apart, and wound up storing thousands of cases for customers. Our low rates helped build the popularity of Trader Joe's with the real wine freaks.

The day that Fair Trade on alcohol ended in 1978, however, I would have happily blown up both Wine Banks. They were a pain in the ass. For example, when a man and wife are just thinking about divorce, one of them comes in and cleans out the wine locker as a preemptive strike, and there the Wine Banker is, in the middle of a lawsuit.

With Fair Trade gone, we no longer needed this marginal form of competition. Still, we honored our commitment to our customers and hung on for the rest of my tenure at Trader Joe's. About five years after I left, my successors closed the Wine Banks. This was a very good business decision, but one that distressed people who had been our good customers for a very long time.

# Credit Cards:
# Another Way to Beat Fair Trade

Another form of unregulated competition was credit. Many wine retailers and the leading gourmet grocery chain, Jurgensen's, had charge accounts. These were black holes as far as I could see; they sucked up your cash, and then the customers stonewalled you on payment.

We did, however, install *Visa* and *Master Charge,* becoming one of the first grocers in the U.S. to do so. (Jurgensen's didn't do it until just before it folded.) This was regarded as a radical step by the trade because of the fees charged to retailers by the credit card companies. And Visa, neé *BankAmericard*, and Master Charge themselves were quite new in a field that had been dominated by *American Express.*

It's hard to remember how difficult it was to administer credit cards back in those days when you didn't just swipe the card through an electronic slot, which is online with a computer that approves or disapproves the credit right then and there. In the troubled times of the 1970s, however, bad checks were so common that the risks of fraudulent credit cards were minimal by comparison, even though online approval was so far out we never even imagined the day when it would arrive.

## Trader Joe's Winery (License)

Why not have a winery? A close reading of the regulations showed that a retailer could own a Master Wine Grower's License, the same kind that, say, *Gallo* or *Robert Mondavi* owned. So Bob and I went hunting for a California Master Wine Grower's license. We could have gotten a new one from the state for about $300. But we wanted an old one. We found one in the now-abandoned vineyard country east of Los Angeles, in Cucamonga. In the late 1800s, the largest vineyard in the world was in that area. In 1973, a half dozen dormant and near-dormant wineries lingered there. Dr. Aggazotti (a master vinegar maker who had a winery license as a sideline) decided to sell his license, which had been issued in 1933, and we bought it for $10,000.

## Why an Old License?

New Master Wine Grower licenses didn't have the same grandfathered privileges of that 1933 license. With that license, we could legally hold wine tastings of any wine, even if it didn't have our label on it. We could also legally act as a wholesaler of any wine, and this led to the sales of thousands of cases to some of the best private clubs and restaurants of Los Angeles.

That wholesaling privilege was internally valuable to us, too. As you will learn much later in the chapter "Employee Ownership," for tax reasons we operated the stores under eight separate corporations. Technically, these stores could not buy wine as a group. But with Pronto Market No. 1, Inc. holding the Master Wine Grower license, it could in effect wholesale Trader Joe label wines, and all those imports, to the other seven corporations.

The license also gave us special rights in dealing with California wine growers. For example, when *Oakville Winery* went bankrupt, one of its vendors, the cooper who had built its barrels, was paid off in bulk wine. He didn't know what to do with it. Moreover, he was a Latter Day Saint who did not drink! So we bought the whole inventory and had it labeled under our name. Without the license, we could not have bought the inventory directly from him.

There was a little catch, however: we had to operate a winery! I had bought a bankrupt electronics factory in South Pasadena (it had started life in 1932 as a five-thousand-square-foot supermarket) to use as an office building. The factory had added assorted toolsheds. We took about four hundred square feet of a toolshed and declared it Trader Joe's Winery! We bought a crusher, a stainless-steel fermentation tank, and used whiskey barrels. (Bourbon, by law, can be aged only in new oak barrels that have been charred. After that single use, they are sold to coopers who take them apart, scrape the charring off the oak, reassemble them, and sell them to wineries.) We bought a truckload of grapes from Riverside County, and the whole office staff pitched in, including their kids, to crush grapes. Fortunately, Berning had five kids.

## How to Crush Grapes

A little-noted aspect of winemaking is the presence of bees. Bees are crazy about the free run juice, which is about 28 percent sugar. I never will forget my first visit to *Ridge Winery*, high in the Santa Cruz Mountains, in 1968. Its founder, the late, great Dave Bennion, was there, stripped to the waist, heaving lugs of grapes into the de-stemmer/crusher. A swarm of bees flew around him like a shroud, just inches from his naked, sweating torso, but never stinging him.

This was during the Whole Earth Harry era when, as part of my Damascene conversion, I was keeping bees on the roof of the office. All that I will say here is that our grape stompers did not share Dave Bennion's luck.

And there's another joy of winemaking that I have never seen portrayed on the silver screen. Let's take your typical medieval Italian peasant girl, let's say, Kate Winslet, who is standing in the fermentation vat, tromping grapes. Suddenly espying Prince di Caprio, she flashes a smile that reveals hitherto unsuspected triumphs of fifteenth-century orthodonture, daintily steps out of the vat, casually wipes off her gorgeous gams, like she's been crushing nothing more than the bubbles in *San Pellegrino,* and minces off to get her bodice ripped.

Now, imagine Kate stepping out of a tub of first-run maple syrup that she's been standing in right up to her drip-bucket. First-run syrup has about the same degree of stickiness as grape must. Furthermore, imagine maple syrup that is full of millions of tiny barbs, the stems and stemlets of the grapes that leave your legs feeling like they have just been shaved by a medieval razor blade.

That's why I think the medieval winemakers of Beaujolais were the only guys who thought things through: they fermented whole bunches of grapes. That's the way they still make Beaujolais. It's called maceration carbonique, and I award them the Edwards Deming prize for cutting out the unnecessary.

The wine we made was awful. One principal reason was that we did not slug the grapes with sulfur to kill the wild yeasts. All grapes come covered with yeast, that powdery stuff you see on the skin, and is proof positive that God intended for grapes to be fermented into wine. Different yeasts give different fermentation results. The yeasts that have set our aesthetic standards for what wine should taste and smell like are Mediterranean yeasts, principally French. The wild yeasts of California give quite different aesthetic results; my wife, Alice, says the aesthetics are those of *STP.* Professional winemakers, therefore, hit the grapes when they arrive at the winery with a sulfur solution that kills the wild

Californian yeasts. Then they crush the grapes and inoculate the must with French yeast, especially a strain called Montrachet. We didn't do that.

Still, the wine kept us legal. Each year the Bureau of Alcohol, Tobacco & Firearms came out and recertified our winery. We didn't offer the inspector any samples. I forget what kind of story Berning fed him. Today, of course, it would have been impossible to build that winery in South Pasadena without getting an environmental pollution permit.

There was one privilege that came with the license, however, which the Department of Alcoholic Beverage Control refused to let us have: the right to import wine. They told us that we could have the license, if we stopped selling distilled spirits in the stores. This was illogical; furthermore, there were four other companies in California that were doing everything we wanted to do. I fought the issue to the Appeals level of the Department of Alcoholic Beverage Control, lost again, and dropped the matter. The arrangement with Ezra Webb was working out so well, we didn't need to import wine ourselves.

By 1976, Trader Joe's had become a powerhouse retailer of wines, especially low-priced values both from Europe and, under our label, from California. Yes, we were briefly "number one" in great wines, thanks to the Christie's auctions of 1976–77, but far more importantly we became the best place in the world to buy a good bottle of wine for less than $2.00. That's a position we held for the rest of my days at Trader Joe's. It absolutely addressed our prime market, the overeducated and underpaid people of California.

# The Great Gray Market of 1984–85

In the mid-1980s, the dollar soared against all other currencies because of high interest rates here. Against the French franc it went from four francs per dollar in 1973 to six francs in 1981 to ten francs in 1985.

The big importers of branded French wines, especially champagnes, however, didn't lower their wholesale prices to reflect the new reality. As a result, several different entrepreneurs took to buying huge quantities of premium champagnes and flying them to the United States in chartered 747s. It was economic for them to use air freight because the interest cost on the champagnes would have been so great had they shipped the wines by boat.

Bob Berning began buying with both arms. At times 10 percent or even 20 percent of our total sales were in the world's greatest champagnes: *Dom Ruinart, Roderer Cristal, Tattinger Comtes de Champagne, Dom Perignon, Perrier Jouet Flower Bottle,* and on and on.

We had competitors but they were mostly one-store operations. Also, we had cash. We were willing to pay as soon as the champagnes were rolled off the 747s and into our distribution centers. So I guess we were the biggest retailer of gray market Grand Marque Champagnes in the mid-1980s. Again, like the Christie's auction eight years earlier, these magnificent wines did not match our specific mission, providing wines to the overeducated and underpaid. But it was an exhilarating experience while it lasted.

Unfortunately, it led the wholesalers to try to buy a law in Sacramento that would have prevented it from ever happening again. And they actually got it through the legislature, which I suppose should be no surprise. While they were lobbying it through, many wine merchants tried to stop it. I went on television, and my friend Tony Day at the *LA Times* editorialized against it. But it took Safeway, which was starting up a discount liquor store chain called *Liquor Barn,* to get to Governor Deukmejian's ear: he vetoed it.

In late 1985, the Group of Seven met and talked the dollar down. It was back to six francs when I left Trader Joe's. But we all live for those ten-franc days to reappear, even if the exchange rate is expressed in Euros.

# Back to the Core Wine Business

So we went back to offering wines for the overeducated and underpaid. In 1986, we switched a lot of our private red wines from California to the Midi, in southern France, because we felt the greatest value was there even with a weaker dollar. Today the Midi produces 10 percent of all the wines sold in the world, and many Californians including Robert Mondavi have invested there.

Another inexpensive category of wine that we promoted successfully because nobody else was interested was white wine from Bordeaux. It was a measure of the growing sophistication of our customers that this hard-edged, often graceless wine sold so well. But like all wines, there are foods that go well with it. It gave us a useful alternate to the Chardonnay craze that became the prelude to the later popularity of Californian Sauvignon Blanc.

Trader Joe's has been limited in most states from selling wine as it can in California, or from selling wines at all, like in New York or Pennsylvania. I'm glad I didn't have to deal with those problems. Being king of the low-price, high-value wine trade in California was one of the greatest satisfactions of my career.

# 8

# Whole Earth Harry

> Many people, however, are concluding on the basis of
> mounting and reasonably objective evidence that the length
> of life of the biosphere as an inhabitable region for
> organisms is to be measured in decades rather than in
> hundreds of millions of years. This is entirely the fault of
> our own species. It would seem not unlikely that we are
> approaching a crisis that is comparable to the one that
> occurred when free oxygen began to accumulate
> in the atmosphere.
>
> —G. Evelyn Hutchinson, Sterling Professor of Zoology at Yale,
> writing the introductory article to *Scientific American*,
> September 1970

As I described in the "Uncorked!" chapter, the economic background in 1970 was turning grim, and sales were weakening. I was concerned. And then, once again, *Scientific American* came to the rescue.

Each September that wonderful magazine devotes its entire issue to a single subject. In September 1970, it was the *biosphere*, a term I'd never seen before. It was the first time that a major scientific journal had addressed the problem of the environment. Rachel Carson's *Silent Spring*, of course, had been serialized in the *New Yorker* in the late sixties, so the danger to the biosphere wasn't exactly news, but it could be considered alarmist news. The prestige of *Scientific American*, however, carried weight. In fact, it knocked me out.

# I Suffered a Conversion
# on the Road to Damascus

Within weeks, I subscribed to *The Whole Earth Catalog*, all the *Rodale* publications like *Organic Gardening and Farming, Mother Earth*, and a bunch I no longer remember. I was especially impressed by Francis Moore Lappé's book *Diet for a Small Planet*. I joined the board of *Pasadena Planned Parenthood*, where I served for six years.

Paul Ehrlich surfaced with his dismal, and proved utterly wrong, predictions. But hey! This guy was from Stanford! You *had* to believe him! And in 1972 all this was given statistical veracity by Jay Forrester of *MIT,* in the *Club of Rome* forecasts, which proved to be even further off the mark. But I bought them at the time.

Bob Hanson, the manager of the new Trader Joe's in Santa Ana, which was off to a slow start, was a health food nut. He kept bugging me to try "health foods." After I'd read *Scientific American,* I was on board! Just how eating health foods would save the *biosphere* was never clear in my mind, or, in my opinion, in the mind of anyone else, except the 100 percent Luddites who wanted to return to some lifestyle approximating the Stone Age. After all, the motto of the *Whole Earth Catalog* was "access to tools," hardly Luddite.

Let's define health foods as foods grown with as few chemicals as possible, processed with as few chemicals as possible, and packaged as "ecologically" as possible. There was a notion that eating health foods, called "inner ecology" (inner to one's body), would somehow help the "outer ecology" (outer to one's body) of the biosphere.

## Some Bailey's Irish Cream on Your Granola?

We prepared to marry the health food store to the liquor store. This concept, obviously, was founded in schizophrenia. But it occurred to me that people who really thought about what they ingested, whether they were wine connoisseurs or health food nuts, were basically on the same radar beam. Both groups were fragmented from the masses who willingly consumed Folgers coffee, Best Foods Mayonnaise, *Wonder Bread*, Coca-Cola, etc. Both groups were the kind of people who, I was hoping, represented a breakup of mainstream consumption in America.

We began running experiments in Santa Ana. Alice and I went to San Francisco and walked Haight-Ashbury, then a hotbed of health food stores, and then University Avenue in Berkeley. I hired a young hippie woman out of the *University of California at Santa Cruz* to teach us the lingo. Leroy, Frank Kono (who had helped found the wine program and who was now the buyer for the chain), and I visited *Hadley's*, a tremendously successful dried fruit-and-nut store on the way to Palm Springs.

And by the spring of 1971, the caterpillar, Good Time Charley, had emerged from his chrysalis as Whole Earth Harry, a party store/cum health foods store.

Trader Joe's first private label food product was granola. We installed *Alta Dena* certified raw milk, to the disgruntlement of Southland, and within six months were the largest retailers of Alta Dena milk, both pasteurized and raw, in California. We began price-bombing five-pound cans of honey, and then all the ingredients for baking bread at home.

We installed fresh orange juice squeezers in the stores, and sold fresh juice at the lowest price in town.

By late in 1971, we were moving into vitamins, encouraged by my very good friend James C. Caillouette, MD. Jim spent a lot of time talking with the faculty at Cal Tech. He was convinced that Linus Pauling was on to something with his research on vitamin C. I set out to break the price on vitamin C. At one point, I think, we were doing 3 percent of sales in vitamin C!

Later, Jim forwarded articles from the British medical magazine *Lancet,* describing how a high fiber diet could avoid colon cancer. But where could we get bran? The only stores that sold it were conventional health food stores, who sold it in bulk, something that I have always been opposed to on the grounds of hygiene. And still am!

Leroy found a hippie outfit in Venice—I think it was called Mom's Trucking—which would package the bran. But bran is a low-value product. They couldn't afford to deliver it. Since they also packaged nuts and dried fruits, however, we somewhat reluctantly added them to the order. And that's how Trader Joe's became the largest retailer of nuts and dried fruits in California! Brilliant foresight! Astute market analysis!

By 1989, when I left Trader Joe's, we regularly took down 5 percent of the entire Californian pistachio crop, and we were the thirteenth largest buyer of almonds in the United States—*Hershey* was number one. There were times when we did 3 percent of total sales in cashews—the times, I guess, when we weren't doing 3 percent of total sales in vitamin C.

## The Big Move into Cheese

Cheese in those days was regarded as a health food by the Movement, just to show you how irrational it was. We went after cheese in a more systematic fashion than nuts. After experimenting with a conventional deli in one store, we jettisoned conventional thinking and designed our own way of buying cheese and merchandising it at store level.

Leroy ramrodded this whole program. He began investigating the minutiae of the federal regulation of cheeses. The United States is one of the most protectionist countries in the world when it comes to cheese, thanks to restrictive laws bought and paid for in the 1950s by the Wisconsin cheese lobby. Leroy dug into these regulations the same way we had dug into the Master Wine Grower regulations. We came up with more than our fair share of quotas and licenses to import cheeses like English cheddar, Cheshire, stilton, et al.; Italian cheeses like Fontina and all the Danish knockoffs of same, Emmenthal, various French hard cheeses, etc. As for some of our methods to get licenses, well, Senator Ervin's statute of limitations had, by then I hoped, run out.

But our big breakthrough was Brie. Because Wisconsin had no native Brie industry in the 1950s, it had neglected to shut off imports of Brie: there were no restrictions. We tore into this like we had torn into Fair Trade on imported wine and became the largest retailer of Brie in the United States. No other retailer was interested in selling Brie at a reasonable price. Hell, we sold it for less than Velveeta! We retrofitted all the stores with on-site cheese departments. This was no easy task given the stores' small size.

We also began packaging nuts and dried fruits in these departments.

By 1976, Trader Joe's, the Whole Earth Harry version, had evolved into a rather effective, very profitable retailer, but still small. We had a few private label food products outside of nuts and dried fruits (in which there is very little brand demand) and cheeses (ditto). We were still reliant on selling branded food products, bought in ordinary quantities, which made aggressive pricing unprofitable.

# Whole Earth Joe:
## How Much Goes On in a Man's Head!

Dear God, the things he thought and said!
How much goes on in a man's head!

–Margarethe, musing on her new lover, Faust,
in Goethe's *Faust* (Walter Kaufman's Anchor Books translation)

In the background, given my commitment to the outer ecology of environmentalism, I replaced all the company cars with diesels, which used less crude oil and lasted longer than gasoline engines. The diesel cars did pay off briefly during the Second Energy Crisis of 1979, but they gave us a lot of trouble in the long run because the diesel-powered *Oldsmobile* station wagons that *General Motors* rushed into production had nothing but a beefed-up gasoline engine (internal pressures are much greater in a diesel) and they were in the shop more often than on the road.

We aggressively redesigned the stores to conserve energy. To this day, Trader Joe's stores don't have very many windows, and all panes of glass are very small, an idea that had an accidental payoff in every subsequent earthquake and riot. As the young lady said back there in the God of Fair Beginnings chapter, I did the right thing for the wrong reasons.

I really went off the tracks in the first bloom of my conversion. In 1971, I set out to build a market using Buckminster Fuller's geodesic dome. Just how a new dome would help the environment . . . oh, well. I had a hard time finding a place where the zoning would permit it. Finally I purchased a Monterey Park location that violated every rule I had laid down for placing Trader Joe's. I even put out a memo to my colleagues saying that I thought it was a bad location; still I went ahead. Sigh. Note to self: pay more attention to your inner voice.

I encountered nightmarish problems with the geodesic dome. It was impossible to get washable ceilings required by the health department. I finally settled for a conventional building with the foundation outline of a geodesic dome; then the architect screwed up and located the store below the sewer outfall so we had to pump all our effluent uphill. We finally sold the store and property some years later.

I also wasted a lot of energy and time trying to design a new kind of store called Trader Joe's Biosphere, which would be a garden store cum pet store cum grocery selling only health foods. Its motto: "Good Foods for Humans, Plants, and Animals." Again, sigh. The best laid plans of mice and men.

The sharp 1974 recession combined with the stock market collapse gave me an excuse to cut back on opening more stores. In what was called the Green Movement, growth for the sake of growth was defined as a form of cancer. Growth for the sake of growth still troubles me. It seems unnatural, even perverted.

This helps to explain why I went from 1974 to 1978 without opening another store, something that could be viewed as inexcusable, given the success of Whole Earth Harry.

Again, however, I did the right thing for the wrong reason. When Fair Trade on milk and alcohol blew up in our face in late 1976, we were not locked into too many stores that had been built on the assumption that those 1930s laws would last forever.

Among other things, this saved us from having increased our huge investment in liquor licenses, which plunged in value when Fair Trade ended.

It left us in better shape to transition from Whole Earth Harry to Mac the Knife, a powerhouse that could draw people from twenty-five miles around, provided you leased stores with the boulevard access that would make that possible.

To keep sales increasing during the mid-1970s, we relied on new ideas implemented in existing stores. This was my favorite form of growth. I don't think that any given store ever fully realizes its potential. During those four years of no expansion in terms of number of stores, our dollar sales kept right on growing while the CEO of Trader Joe's struggled with trying to reconcile good business practice with the *Whole Earth Catalog*. Whole Earth Harry indeed!

In my private life, I had become an organic gardener. Few things have so enriched my life so much as my own personal conversion to organic gardening, something that I still practice except when the ants start raising colonies of aphids in my blood orange trees, and it's *Grant's Ant Control* to the rescue.

In any event, the schizoid marriage of the party store with the health food store was a great success for Trader Joe's, if not for the biosphere.

# 9

# Promise, Large Promise

Promise, large promise is the soul of an advertisement.

–Samuel Johnson in *The Idler*, January 1759

## The *Fearless Flyer*

The Fearless Flyer has attracted so much attention in both the U.S. and Canada that I'm devoting an entire chapter to it. It was known as the *Insider's Report* from 1969 to 1985. At that time, Dave Nichol, then President of the huge Canadian supermarket chain, *Loblaw's*, fell in love with the concept, and thanks to the negotiating skills of our attorney, he paid us $100,000 for the name. He began publishing Loblaw's own version, which was somewhat similar. Having sold the *Insider's* name, I renamed our magazine the *Fearless Flyer*. Dave then went on to create a line of private label products for Loblaw's, the *President's Choice*, modeled on Trader Joe's private label products. Dave has been most generous in giving us credit for all this.

The *Fearless Flyer* began life in 1969 during the Good Time Charley phase of Trader Joe's as the *Insider's Wine Report*, a sheet of gossip of "inside" information on the wine industry at a time where there weren't any such gossip sheets, for the excellent reason that few people were interested in wine. As of the writing of this book, 11 percent of Americans drink 88 percent of the wine according to contemporary wine gossip magazine the *Wine Spectator.*

In the *Insider's Wine Report* we gave the results of the wine tastings that we were holding with increasing frequency, as we tried to gain product knowledge. This growing knowledge impressed me with how little we knew about food, so in 1969, we launched a parallel series of blind tastings of branded foods: mayonnaise, canned tuna, hot dogs, peanut butter, and so on. The plan was to select the winner, and sell it "at the lowest shelf price in town."

To report these results, I designed the *Insider's Food Report,* which began publication in 1970. It deliberately copied the physical layout of *Consumer Reports*: the 8.5" x 11" size, the width of columns, and the typeface (later changed). Other elements of design are owed to David Ogilvy's *Confessions of an Advertising Man.* The numbered paragraphs, the boxes drawn around the articles, are all Ogilvy's ideas. I still think his books are the best on advertising that I've ever read and I recommend them. Another inspiration was Clay Felker, then editor of *New York* magazine, the best-edited publication of that era. *New York*'s motto was, "If you live in New York, you need all the help you can get!" The *Insider's Food Report* borrowed this, as "The American housewife needs all the help she can get!" And in the background was the Cassandra-like presence of Ralph Nader, then at the peak of his influence.

I felt, however, that all the consumer magazines, never mind Mr. Nader, were too paranoid, too humorless. To leaven the loaf, I inserted cartoons. The purpose of the cartoons was to counterpoint the rather serious, expository text; and, increasingly, to mock Trader Joe's pretensions as an authority on anything.

For artwork, I simply turned to nineteenth-century books and magazines, of which I built a large collection. I knew that (under the copyright laws of the time) works created prior to 1906 were no longer subject to copyright, so we were free to use the artwork. To create the cartoons, I would leaf through old sources until I found a cartoon that I thought would match the text.

Much later, I learned from Robert Graves's *The White Goddess* that what I was practicing was iconotropy, the deliberate misreading of images. Graves thought that a lot of myths had come from people misreading or twisting the meaning of the pictures on Greek vases.

I spent the next nineteen years iconotropically creating those cartoons. They were at once a chore and a relief from the pressures of running the business. Best of all, they caught on with the public, and played a major role of establishing Trader Joe's as a "different" kind of retailer, one that didn't take itself too seriously.

At all times I wrote the *Fearless Flyer* for overeducated, underpaid people. This required two mindsets:

1. There are no such things as consumers—dolts who are driven by drivel to buy stuff they don't need or even want. There are only *customers*, people who are reasonably well informed, and very well focused in their buying habits. (This caused me grief later in my career when I took over a chain that was so terrible it had attracted only dysfunctional shoppers. They did not respond well to my treating them as adults.)

2. We always looked up to the customers in the text of the *Fearless Flyer*. We assumed they knew more than they did; we never talked down to them. We did phoneticize the more difficult French words (I still can't pronounce *Bourgeuilor Maroilles*; I assumed that neither could my readers), but that was our only concession here.

3. Given the first two assumptions, we assumed that our readers had a thirst for knowledge, 180 degrees opposite from supermarket ads. We emphasized "informative advertising," a term borrowed from the famous entrepreneur Paul Hawken, who started publishing in the *Whole Earth Review* in the early 1980s. These informative texts were intended to stress how our products were

differentiated from ordinary stuff. Please see the chapter on Private Label Products for examples of claims we made.

Originally, we distributed the *Fearless Flyer* only in the stores and to a small but growing subscriber list. Doing a mailing to individual addresses, however, was a rotten chore: Americans move about every three years. In 1980, I attended a marketing lecture that taught me that, when someone moves, someone just like them is likely to occupy the same address. This proved to be correct. By mailing to addresses rather than to individuals—by blanketing entire ZIP codes—we were able to tremendously expand the distribution of the *Fearless Flyer.* The ZIPs to which we mailed, of course, were chosen on the basis of the likely concentration of overeducated and underpaid people.

This massive increase in the mailing massively increased our advertising costs in the short run. I don't believe, however, in advertising budgets that are based on a percentage of sales. You figure out the dollars needed to do the job right, and go ahead and spend them. As it turned out, the big sales generated by the *Fearless Flyer* dropped the cost of advertising as a percentage of sales after the fact. By the time I left Trader Joe's, we were mailing millions of copies five times a year.

The advent of the *Apple Macintosh* in 1985 made a tremendous improvement in publishing the *Fearless Flyer.* Using a piece of software called *Adobe® PageMaker*, we were able to dis-intermediate most of the printer's function and produce camera-ready copy entirely in our office. Pat St. John, whom Alice recruited for us in 1986 as head of advertising, made a great contribution here, cutting lead time by almost a week. Anyone who has been in advertising can appreciate the nerve-racking problems of products that are advertised but didn't arrive in time to cover the advertising. I would have had a coronary without the Macintosh, which had made it possible to expand the *Fearless Flyer* from twelve pages to twenty. This created all the more space to advertise products, but it also potentiated the coronary potential, and the almost-as-bad requirement for still more cartoons! Please remember: Trader

Joe's was a low-overhead operation with all of us wearing several hats. Sure, some of the above could have been done pre-Macintosh, but at vastly greater expense.

The expansion of the *Fearless Flyer* to twenty pages was an important factor in the jump of Trader Joe's sales after 1985. Down deep, the *Fearless Flyer* was an educational medium and hundreds of customers kept three-ring notebook collections of the issues so they could refer back to the articles. For years, we printed three rings on the cover.

Equally important, however, it was an educational medium for our employees:

1. A lot of our employees were under twenty-one; legally they could not have tasted the wines we were selling. So the *Fearless Flyer* was a sales tool for those employees.

2. As we got deeper and deeper into vitamins, and FDA got goosier and goosier about claims by the health food industry, I didn't want our employees to do any selling of vitamins and food supplements. When asked about a product, they were to refer to the *Fearless*, and a back copy file was kept at the store level for this purpose. (In 1993, Senator Orrin Hatch of Utah rammed a Magna Carta for health foods through Congress. The FDA hates the law, but all kinds of claims can be made now, which were impossible in my era.)

## Trader Joe's Pricing Driven by *Fearless Flyer*

One of the fundamental tenets of Trader Joe's is that its retail prices don't change unless its costs change. There are no weekend ad prices, no in-and-out pricing. In part this policy is made necessary by all those hundreds of thousands of *Fearless Flyers* that are out there.

But I have always believed that supermarket pricing is a shell game and I wanted no part of it.

I cannot stress too strongly that the success of the *Fearless Flyer* rests on the values in the publication, Samuel Johnson's "promise, large promise." Some people don't understand this. Early in the 1980s, some top marketing executives of a very famous airline came to see me. They wanted me to create a similar publication for the airline. After a few minutes I concluded that they had no special values to offer, that what they wanted was for me to baffle their customers with bullshit. I told them so. The airline later went into a richly deserved bankruptcy. Among other things, I begged them to offer nonsmoking flights. That probably convinced them I was an impractical weirdo.

## Radio Days

In 1976, there was a commercial radio station, *KFAC*, in Los Angeles that broadcast only classical music. My wife had become friends with the program manager, Carl Princi, as a result of her work in administering the *Metropolitan Opera*'s auditions for young singers. In 1976, Carl asked me to do a series of one-minute broadcasts on food and wine. When I left Trader Joe's twelve years later, I had done 3,300 one-minute broadcasts.

I wasn't paid for the broadcasts, but Trader Joe's got publicity from the opening line, "This is Joe Coulombe of Trader Joe's with a word on food and wine." We needed the publicity in those days, and KFAC was right on our target of overeducated and underpaid people. Between my wife's work in opera circles (she helped found the LA Opera in 1982) and my KFAC broadcasts, Trader Joe's got pretty much of a lock on classical music circles in California.

Mostly, however, the value of the broadcasts lay in my being forced to research and write all those broadcasts. It was a discipline that forced me to study the field of food and wine. Again, I must emphasize how ignorant I was even at age forty-six, nine years into Trader Joe's. I had a long way to go. (I still do.) So I tried hard never to repeat a given broadcast: as much as possible, each of the 3,300 scripts was unique. These broadcasts were in no way commercials. Here's a typical broadcast.

> **This is Joe Coulombe of Trader Joe's with a word on food and wine.**
>
> We're accustomed to hearing about ecological disasters these days. Some of these disasters occur when new animals or plants are introduced into a region where they had not existed before. Everybody knows what the introduction of rabbits did to Australia. Here in America, the introduction of starlings has been a disaster for grape growers.
>
> We also suffer from an invasion of carp. Carp are not native to America. They were brought here from Germany in 1876, and were considered a wonder fish for food, because for centuries the Europeans had farmed carp in ponds. In fact, our government distributed hundreds of thousands of carp to anybody who would grow them. These carp got loose in the environment, and now they're all over the United States.
>
> The problem with carp in the wild is that they feed by grubbing on the bottom. This stirs up mud, which reduces the amount of sunlight in the water, and that wipes out aquatic plants and plankton. As a result, many native fish have suffered from the introduction of carp.
>
> **This is Joe Coulombe, thanks for listening.**

Pedestrian? Yeah. But what do you expect from a guy who writes half the broadcasts on his shirt cuff, only he rarely wears cuffs? But I learned a lot.

I couldn't afford the time to crank over to Hollywood daily or even weekly to record; I would go only four or five times a year, recording fifty or sixty broadcasts in a session that left me pretty well burned out.

KFAC sold these "Words on Food and Wine." Airlines, banks, even supermarkets paid to have their commercials tagged onto these broadcasts. I thought this was droll; it certainly did no harm to our image. Otherwise, the advertising for Trader Joe's was confined to the *Fearless Flyer*, a very small scale newspaper program, and the lectures and wine tastings, which I gave throughout Southern California. In 1982, however, the success of the KFAC broadcasts was so apparent that I dropped all newspaper advertising and put the money into outright commercials for Trader Joe's. These were broadcast on demographically suited radio stations: mostly all-news or all-classical. This is still the pattern followed by Trader Joe's.

About the format of the sixty-second radio spots, which has attracted a lot of attention in media circles: I think that most radio commercials are terrible. They have too many "production values." Even worse, they issue commands to the listener: "Buy this!" "Shop now!" "Hurry!"

One should never use a mandatory sentence in addressing a customer; should never give orders. The subliminal message of a Trader Joe's commercial is, "We're gonna be around for a long time. If you miss out on this bargain, there'll be another. If you have the time and inclination . . ."

Most supermarket radio spots are paid for by cooperative advertising allowances from manufacturers. The supermarkets jam as many brands into sixty seconds as possible, because it maximizes their revenue. Information be damned! In sharp contrast, each Trader Joe's spot was devoted to a single product, about which we tried to develop a story. And we refused to accept any advertising revenue from any manufacturer. (The same was true of the *Fearless Flyer*.) These policies were absolutely unique in retailing and lent a quiet legitimacy to the advertising.

The tagline "thanks for listening," which has been so copied and admired, derived from the successful 1976 senatorial campaign of

S. I. Hayakawa. Hayakawa was a professor of linguistics at San Francisco State University (before he became university president). He knew how to use the English language. The calm manner of his radio commercials, his thanking the listener for staying tuned, really impressed me and, six years later, provided the chassis and the closer for Trader Joe's commercials.

We used the commercials to keep us in front of the public between editions of the *Fearless Flyer*. We didn't do both at the same time, or else the stores would have been overwhelmed with business. In short, the radio commercials were and are extremely effective. In the course of this, my voice became one of the best known in California.

## Public Television

The audience for Channel 28, the PBS station in Los Angeles, was demographically perfect for Trader Joe's. In those days, however, PBS did not accept overt commercials. Alice had been quite active as a volunteer at the station. Through her contacts, we made arrangements to sponsor reruns of shows that tied to Trader Joe's, such as the Julia Child shows, *The Galloping Gourmet*, and Barbara Wodehouse's series on training dogs, which proved very effective! These reruns were not expensive compared with sponsoring first-runs and they had very good audiences. All we got was a "billboard" announcing that Trader Joe's was sponsoring the show, but this was a cost-effective way of building our presence in the community.

Another way we promoted ourselves on public TV was to "man the phones" during pledge drives. Our employees, led by Robin Guentert who was running advertising at that time (Robin became one of the most important members of store supervision after 1982, then President of Trader Joe's in 2002), would show up en masse at the station. They loved being on TV, and we got the publicity.

# Promoting through Nonprofits

Most retailers, when they're approached by charities for donations, do their best to stiff-arm the would-be donees, or ask that a grueling series of requirements need to be met. In general they hate giving except to big, organized charities like *United Way*, because that way they escape being solicited by all sorts of uncomfortable pressure groups. At the very beginning of Trader Joe's, however, we adopted a policy of using non-profit giving as an advertising and promotional tool. We established these policies:

1. Never give cash to anyone.

2. Never buy space in a program. That is money thrown away.

3. Give freely, give generously, but only to nonprofits that are focused on the overeducated and underpaid. Any museum opening, any art gallery opening, any hospital auxiliary benefit, any college alumni gathering, the *American Association of University Women,* the *Assistance League,* any chamber orchestra benefit—their requests got a very warm welcome. But nothing for *Little League, Pop Warner,* et al.; that was not what Trader Joe's was about. (We did, however, quietly give food to homes for battered women, the regional food banks, etc. Whenever the freezers went down and we were concerned about the safety of the food, we gave it to the *Humane Society.*)

4. What we gave mostly was wine. Especially after we made this legal(!) by acquiring that Master Wine Grower's license in 1973. Most requests were made by women (not men) who had been drafted by their respective organizations to somehow get wine for an event. We made a specialty of giving them a warm welcome from the first call. All we wanted was the organization's 501c3 number, and from which store they wanted to pick it up. We wanted to make that woman, and her friends, our customers. But

we didn't want credit in the program, as we knew the word would get out from that oh-so-grateful woman who had probably been turned down by six markets before she called us.

5. Everybody wanted champagne. We firmly refused to donate it, because the federal excise tax on sparkling wine is so great compared with the tax on still wine.

To relieve pressure on our managers, we finally centralized giving into the office. When I left Trader Joe's, Pat St. John had set up a special Macintosh file just to handle the three hundred organizations to which we would donate in the course of a year. I charged all this to advertising. That's what it was, and it was advertising of the most productive sort.

## Giving Space on Shopping Bags

One of the most productive ways into the hearts of nonprofits was to print their programs on our shopping bags. Thus, each year, we printed the upcoming season for the *Los Angeles Opera* Co., or an upcoming exhibition at the *Huntington Library*, or the season for the *San Diego Symphony*, etc. Just printing this advertising material won us the support of all the members of the organization, and often made the season or the event a success. Our biggest problem was rationing the space on the shopping bags. All we wanted was camera-ready copy from the opera, symphony, museum, etc. This was a very effective way to build the core customers of Trader Joe's. We even localized the bags, customizing them for the San Diego, Los Angeles, and San Francisco market areas.

Several years after I left, Trader Joe's abandoned the practice because it was just too complicated to administer after they expanded into Arizona, Washington, etc., and they no longer had my wife, Alice, running interference with the music and arts groups. This left an opportunity for small retailers in local areas, and I strongly recommended it to them.

In 1994, while running the troubled *Petrini's Markets* in San Francisco, I tried the same thing, again with success, for the *San Francisco Ballet* and a couple of museums.

## Promoting through Personal Appearances

My staff gave dozens of wine tastings made legal by that 1933-issue Master Wine Grower's license, tastings that were key in building the reputation of an unknown retailer.

As the unknown retailer became better known, I was asked to give lectures, either on marketing or management or food and wine, at the rate of six or so per year, which I squeezed into my schedule. I still give lectures, even though I have no direct commercial incentive, but like the KFAC broadcasts, I don't like to do the same lecture more than once. The discipline of having to prepare for an audience forces me to pull together my current thoughts on a subject, whether the French paradox or The Little Ice Age or glass manufacturing, and make those thoughts more or less coherent. As I noted earlier, this book is the result of a talk I gave to the *Culinary Historians Society* in March 1998.

## Word of Mouth: the Power of True Believers

As everyone knows, word of mouth is the most effective advertising of all. Or, when in my cups, I have been known to say that there's no better business to run than a cult. Trader Joe's became a cult of the overeducated and underpaid, partly because we deliberately tried to make it a cult once we got a handle on what we were actually doing, and partly because we kept the implicit promises with our clientele.

I used to work every Thanksgiving Day in one of the stores. They only let me bag, because I had lost all my checker skills. One Thanksgiving, a woman came in and asked for bourbon. I told her that we had none, because we had not been able to make the right kind of deal (this was after the end of Fair Trade, when we were deep in the Mac the Knife mode). "That's all right," she exclaimed. "I know what you're trying to do for us!" Note the *us*.

There aren't many cult retailers who successfully retain their cult status over a long period of time. A couple in California are *In 'n Out Burger* and *Fry's Electronics*. But across America, in every town, there's a particular donut shop, pizza parlor, bakery, greengrocer, bar, etc., that has a cult following of True Believers. The old Petrini's of the 1950s and 1960s had that status when it came to meat. *Brooks Bros* had that status until the 1970s. *S. S. Pierce* in Boston was another. But all of them failed to keep the faith. Beware of ever betraying the True Believers! The fury of a woman scorned is nothing compared with that of a betrayed cultee.

# 10

## Hairballs

No one is ever held as an example of goodness or badness in
Shakespeare; He presents . . . a philosophy of wondering at
the world without looking for easy answers, looking for
some other easy way out. He shows us that there is none,
but that you can laugh just the same.

–Sir Ian McKellen, interviewed in the *LA Times*,
December 3, 1983

All businesses have problems. It's the problems that create the opportunities. If a business is easy, every simple bastard would enter it. In a sense, that was my problem with Pronto: the only barrier to entry in the "bantam market" field was capital. Anyone with enough capital could and did enter the field until overdevelopment caused the entire opportunity to crash and burn in the 1980s, leaving it in the hands of those with the most capital, like the oil companies.

The crash of department stores at about the same time was different. Department stores are complex creatures. More than just capital is needed for success, namely, management smarts. Only a few managements, those of Nordstrom's and *Dillard's* come to mind, were able to negotiate well the treacherous waters of retailing in the period 1986–1995. *Sears* barely pulled itself out while *Montgomery Ward* crashed and burned.

My point is that a businessperson who complains about problems doesn't understand where his bread is coming from. So by *hairballs* I don't mean those fundamental issues such as demand, supply, competition, labor, capital, etc., which create the matrix of a business. By hairballs, I mean those wholly unnecessary thorns that come unexpectedly. Their greatest danger is that they consume management stamina that is needed to deal with the Matrix Issues.

## The Department of Labor Audit

**Bureaucrats shuffle not paper but people.**

–Herbert Schlossberg, *Idols for Destruction:*
*Christian Faith and its Confrontation with American Society*

Here's an example of a hairball we choked on: a U.S. Department of Labor audit of our pay practices. There had been no employee complaint to the Department. We were paying the highest incomes in retailing. And yet, in October 1970, just as we were trying to solve the deep recession, which I described in the chapter "Uncorked!," an auditor suddenly appeared at our offices and demanded to see every document that pertained to wages and hours for the past three years!

Remember, we were still a tiny company in October 1970. We had not yet married the health food store to the party store. The *Fearless Flyer* had barely taken wing.

The fact that the audit came out of left field made us suspect that a competitor had a relative in the Department of Labor. This is not paranoia. Time and again when we tried to get a liquor license in a particular location, competitors instigated phony "protests" to the Department of Alcoholic Beverage Control. That sort of thing is so common that I consider it a Matrix Problem. But a Department of Labor audit is not common: they just don't have that many field auditors. I don't mean to imply that the auditor himself had special ties to competitors. The auditor just goes and does what he's told by somebody at HQ.

Briefly, during the previous three years, we had paid millions of dollars in wages. As a result of the audit, we wound up paying an extra $2,000 for some unrecorded time worked. So you can see we were really quite clean.

But first we had to persuade the auditor that the 1937 Supreme Court ruling—the one described in "The Guns of August" chapter—applied to our "nonexempt" employees; that is, the ones who must be paid by the hour according to the Fair Labor Standards Act. This was not easy. The poor auditor had never encountered this ruling before in his career. To this day, as Trader Joe's enters new states, the method of compensation has to be justified to the state authorities over and over again.

### Hairballs:
### Their greatest danger is that they consume management stamina that is needed to deal with the Matrix Issues.

*But*, even after accepting our 1937 Supreme Court method, the Department alleged that our assistant managers (First Mates) were "nonexempt" under the 1935 Fair Labor Standards Act. We considered them salaried, that is, part of management, and had not kept track of their hours or paid them by the hour. Although assistant managers are "exempt" in several fields of retailing, the California supermarkets had signed union contracts, which required that assistant managers be paid by the hour. Using this precedent, the Department claimed we were in violation of the law.

Please understand that, if anything, the assistants made more money under our system than if they had been "nonexempt." But if we were in violation of the law, treble damages could have been levied by the Department.

Thank God for our attorney in this matter. He taught me to calm down (I went ballistic—a term not yet in use in 1970) and read the regulators' own rule book. (That same year, in *Patton*, George C. Scott, beating the German tanks in Tunisia, cried, "I've read your goddamned book, Rommel!") Our lawyer read their book, comma by comma, on the definition of "exempt," and we began to build our case.

We went to a Senior Level hearing with the Department. I confess that I got overheated, pounded the table, and shouted that I would take the case to the Supreme Court, but it was Ray's meticulous work that won the day.

Months later, I happened to encounter the Department's field auditor in a coffee shop. We shook hands and he said very quietly, "We think you handled yourself very well in that matter." I consider this one of the most memorable compliments I have ever received. But had those treble damages been levied against us, we would have been brought close to financial failure. *Some hairball!*

After that I became somewhat of a connoisseur of the Fair Labor Standards Act, and of California's Labor Department's own interpretations of it. This knowledge has served me in good stead in all the companies I ran post–Trader Joe's and in all my consulting work.

Finally, in looking back on government regulators of those days, and on the fascist laws (see the first chapter on milk laws) they were sometimes called on to enforce, and on the sales managers of the corrupt creameries, I want to comment: I felt sorry for them.

Most of these men were in their fifties, born about 1900. They had spent their thirties in the Great Depression when jobs were hard to find, and if you ever got one you never left it. Now they were running out their terms, hoping to make it to retirement, "playing the game." They were a different kind of Willy Loman (also born about 1900) but more common and more real than Arthur Miller's character.

I remember one creamery sales manager so grizzled that he had lines on his wrinkles, a Dorian Gray with no surrogate in the attic. Young and bumptious, trying to make the newborn Pronto look good to Rexall, I asked for both illegal fixture financing and illegal discounts on milk. "You can't milk both ends of the cow, Joe," he replied softly.

When I was young, all the institutions were staffed with these Depression-scarred men—banks, utilities, railroads, most government bureaus, even letter-carriers. In many cases, they were overqualified for the work they performed and as a result the institutions tended to perform well. This is an aspect of the Truman-Eisenhower years—years that now seem islands of calm—that is overlooked.

# The Worst Hairball of My Career: The United Farm Workers' Secondary Boycott

Shortly before Thanksgiving, 1971, not long after the Department of Labor audit had been concluded and my blood pressure was slowly dropping, a representative of the United Farm Workers showed up unannounced at our office and delivered an ultimatum: either we drop the wines of the Napa Valley Eight wineries—wineries, he said, they were trying to organize—or they would picket our stores.

This had nothing to do with table grapes. We did not carry produce in our stores to any extent in those days, and I was totally opposed to selling table grapes, union or non-union, because table grapes are the largest single cause of slip-and-fall accidents in grocery stores.

The Central Valley was where, several years before 1971, Cesar Chavez set out to organize vineyard workers. His headquarters were in Delano, in the heart of the Valley. Most of the grapes grown there were "table grapes," mostly *Thompson Seedless.* Those Central Valley grapes, however, can wind up in three different uses: on the table, or as raisins, or as wine. Much of the cheapest California wine, especially cheap "champagne," is made from Central Valley Thompson Seedless.

Just two years before this UFW incident, I had heard Ernest Gallo give a fascinating lecture on the intimate price linkage among these three end uses. If, for example, the raisin crop failed in the Middle East, the price of California raisins jumped, leaving fewer Central Valley grapes to be made into wine or to be sold as table grapes.

If the UFW wanted to organize wine vineyards, the greatest single potential was those Thompson Seedless vineyards near Delano. In those days, that was the source of about 60 percent of all California wine. A secondary boycott of the wines that came from the Central Valley, therefore, would have had a real impact.

The grapes grown in the premium counties of Napa, Sonoma, and Mendocino have only one destiny: wine. Cabernet Sauvignon, Chardonnay, and Riesling make lousy table grapes or raisins because they have too many seeds and too little flesh: the berries are quite small. The typical crop is four tons to the acre, far too small for the efficient production of table grapes, which in the hot climate of the Central Valley and Imperial Valley runs more like fourteen tons to the acre.

Yet, here we get an ultimatum from a branch or perhaps a splinter group of the UFW: drop certain brands, because they were going to organize the wineries! Neither Cesar Chavez nor Dolores Huerta seemed to be directly involved.

On the face of it, the ultimatum was absurd, because some of the challenged wineries owned no vineyards. And the UFW was an agricultural union. Because farmworker unions were never covered by federal labor laws, it was okay for them to organize a "secondary boycott," which their picketing of Trader Joe's would be. If the UFW were an industrial union, it would not be legal for them to picket. Presumably they wanted to force the Napa Valley Eight to buy grapes only from UFW-organized vineyards. But at that time there were no such vineyards in the Napa Valley. There aren't very many even today.

Upon receiving the ultimatum, we called the Napa Valley Eight to find out what was happening. For some of them, this was the first they heard about the boycott! For others, the workers within the winery were organized by industrial unions—the Machinists or the Teamsters—whose jobs now were suddenly threatened.

It turned out that the attack on us was organized and led by young seminarians from the *Union Theological Seminary* in New York. This is why I will now put quotation marks around UFW. The whole thing was irrational and we told the UFW so.

Apparently the UFW decided to attack Trader Joe's because we were known for carrying the biggest range of branded California wines. We were so small, however, that the loss of our sales would hardly have been noticed by the biggest of the Napa Valley Eight like *Korbel* and Robert Mondavi. (Korbel and some of the others aren't even in the Napa Valley, but never mind.)

But the picketers showed up in force at each of our stores, just a couple of days before Thanksgiving, and tried to disrupt our sales throughout the entire, critical holiday season. They stayed through New Year's Eve.

And yes, there were incidents. Arson in the trash bins. Tires slashed. Employees being bumped, and bumping back. These clowns were threatening our high-wage jobs! Customers were bumped and assaulted with placards alleging that Trader Joe's products were "full of piss and pesticide," a term that, I regret to say, lingers in our family's lexicon. Customers shouted back. (One faithful customer, a ninety-pound blonde, made a point of crossing the picket lines every day, giving the International Sign.) We had no difficulty with Teamster deliveries, of course, because the UFW is not an industrial union.

Both we and the UFW began spending thousands of dollars on lawyers, depositions, photographic evidence, etc. Sales were hurting as we moved toward the crucial Christmas weekend.

# God Rest Ye Merry Gentlemen

At this time we lived in San Marino, a high-income suburb where we had moved because of the excellence of the public schools. In this town of four thousand upscale houses, the UFW roared through on motorcycles, scattering thousands of leaflets, which attacked me personally. What did they hope to accomplish? To say the least, San Marino was the wrong audience.

It was three nights before Christmas, 1971. Around our house were several dozen UFW picketers shouting and waving black eagle placards while the San Marino police watched uneasily but were unable, by law, to intervene. In our living room were two quite-polite young seminarians from the Union Theological Seminary. Only in part because of their brand-new, too-tight jeans were they crouched uneasily on our sofa, an ancient rattan object that Alice had found at a yard sale. The couch probably predated the dun-colored 1920s *Axminster* carpet in front of them, which I had bought at a bankruptcy sale for $50.

In the background, in the den, they could see our little kids coming and going, poking at the packages under this year's Living Christmas Tree, a sad, twisted specimen of Abies concolor. I, Whole Earth Harry, had bought that tree, sight unseen, from Boy Scout Troop 355 and was, uh, surprised when I came home and found it.

Clearly, the Evil Merchant Prince and his Bejeweled Consort (myself and Alice), who were sitting across from them, listening to their sermon on the evils of the Napa Valley Eight, fell short of their expectations. They had come to confront Ahab and Jezebel, but found only Fibber McGee and Mollie.

They should have suspected something was wrong on the way to the front door of this house, one of the more modest in this Capitalist Stronghold. Whole Earth Harry's front yard had been replanted with endangered California plants bought from the *Theodore Payne Foundation*, just what you would expect a Whole Earth Harry to do. One reason, however, that those plants were endangered is that they were not very physically appealing. Our neighbors tolerated this obsession of mine because at least it was tidier than the sunflowers that had filled the front yard the previous summer. They also tolerated the side yard, which sported the Living Christmas Tree left over from Christmas, 1970, my first Christmas after going Green.

Slowly, their argument about why I should drop wines from the Napa Valley Eight Wineries (oops! it changed to the Napa Valley Seven Wineries, because God had sent word they should not include that gentle man, Hans Kornell, in the vendetta) died down. They rose from the ancient couch, we shook hands, wished each other a Merry Christmas, and they departed. After they left, our neighbors came and serenaded us with Christmas carols, one of my warmest memories of the years at Trader Joe's.

Ten nights later, the picketers left our stores, after having spent six weeks trying to destroy our little company in an absurdly mismanaged endeavor.

Did we reach an accommodation with the UFW? Yeah, both sides signed agreements that dismissed the various lawsuits, sealed the depositions and all that expensive legal stuff. The UFW went off to picket *Bullocks*, a department store chain that then owned *Ralphs Supermarkets*. Another mismanaged effort, which lasted only a few days, and after that we heard no more about the Napa Valley Seven or any other effort to organize the premium wine counties, either the wineries or the vineyards.

The murmurs from the picketers, including speculations on the future safety of our children, didn't die away so quickly, however. We kept the kids under surveillance for the next six months.

The Living Christmas tree, that sad, twisted specimen of Abies concolor, still lives in the side yard of the house in San Marino. Twelve years after the Seminarians visited us, we sold the house to some very tolerant, cultured people who had lived for several years in Japan. Perhaps where I saw only deformity, they see a bonsai.

## Beyond Hairballs

In late autumn 1976, the entire legal foundation on which all California grocers had built their businesses blew up. And that blowup resulted in the next version of Trader Joe's, Mac the Knife.

---

# MAC THE KNIFE

# 11

# Mac the Knife

The economist, Joseph Schumpeter, was absolutely right:
Innovation is less an act of intellect than an act of will.

–Michael Schrage, former technology editor for the
*Los Angeles Times*, June 15, 1995

And so we come to the third version of Trader Joe's, the one that operated for at least the next twenty-one years. There is a lot of big, bold type in this chapter because we were sculptors taking the first big whacks off a chunk of extremely tough granite. The subtleties can come later. The creation of Mac the Knife was, above all, an "act of will" by my colleagues and me to survive. Late in 1976, we suddenly got two unsubtle surprises from the California bureaucracies:

1. The state would no longer mandate minimum retail prices on milk, starting January 1, 1977.

2. The state would drop the whole Fair Trade on alcohol program.

The end of Fair Trade on alcohol and of Retail Price Maintenance on milk in 1977–78 created shocks so great that many grocers didn't know what hit them. The radical consolidation of the supermarket industry during the next few years was the result of the lifting of those

1930s fascist laws, but it was an unwelcome lifting for grocers who could not adapt to the new realities.

For forty years supermarkets in California had operated on a simple formula: run weekend ads, promoting Best Foods Mayonnaise and Folgers coffee below cost to get the people in the door, and sell them full-profit milk and alcohol. Suddenly, well, they didn't know quite what to do. The guaranteed profit on milk was gone, sure, but they were slow in coming to grips with the end of Fair Trade on alcohol. Their sales began eroding, partly because Safeway, *Von's* and *Lucky* all tried experimental chains of discount liquor stores. (These all failed very soon except *Liquor Barn,* which lasted until *Kohlberg Kravitz Roberts*'s take-over of Safeway in 1986 caused it to be sold off. Later it went bankrupt.) Price competition was slow to emerge. Probably it was the Fourth of July Budweiser ads in 1978 that began to shake the industry.

The retail grocery industry went through the same kind of "bends" that the airlines suffered in 1981 when they were deregulated, or that the electric utilities had suffered. Freedom can be an unwelcome thing.

Within six weeks, our gross profit on milk went from 22 percent to 2 percent. Things like that tend to sober a guy. Fortunately, the end of Fair Trade on alcohol was being fought in the courts, and it was not finally abolished until 1978. This gave me time to develop the new operational parameters of Mac the Knife.

I had some idea of what had to be done, thanks to all we had been learning during the previous six years—from breaking Fair Trade on imported wine, developing private label California wine, and busting the price of health foods and cheeses. But to an extent we were just like a little kid running around while being kept from harm by a kiddie-keeper. We were "protected" by price controls on almost 50 percent of what we sold. Now we were ready to throw off the leash.

After chewing things over for two months with the key players— Leroy, Bob Berning, Gene Pemberton, and Frank Kono—I wrote a white paper in February 1977 outlining our answer to deregulation, a white paper I called the Five Year Plan '77.

# The Most Important Strategic Decision Was
# to Become a Genuine Retailer

The fundamental job of a retailer is to buy goods whole, cut them into pieces, and sell the pieces to the ultimate consumers. This is the most important mental construct I can impart to those of you who want to enter retailing. Most "retailers" have no idea of the formal meaning of the word. Time and again I had to remind myself just what my role in society was supposed to be. Many of the policy decisions for a retailer boil down to this: How closely should we stick to the fundamental retailing job?

**"Retail" comes from a medieval French verb, *retailer*, which means "to cut into pieces." "Tailor" comes from the same verb.**

The fact is that most so-called retailers don't want to face up to their basic job. In Pronto Markets we did everything we could to avoid retailing. We tried to shift the burden to suppliers, buying prepackaged goods, hopefully pre-price-marked (potato chips, bread, cupcakes, magazines, paperback books) so we had no role in the pricing decision. The goods were ordered, displayed, and returned by outside salespeople. To this day, supermarkets fight with the retail clerks' union to expand their right to let core store work be done by outsiders.

Whole Earth Harry's moves into wine and health foods had taken us quite a distance into genuine retailing. In our cheese departments we were literally taking whole wheels and cutting them into pieces. I took this as an analogy for what we should do with everything we sold.

Getting rid of all outside salespeople was corollary to the programs that would unfold during the next five years. In Mac the Knife, no outsiders of any sort were permitted in the store. All the work was done by employees. The closest thing to it that I see these days is *Costco*, which shares many features with Trader Joe's.

> We fundamentally changed the point of view of the business from customer-oriented to buyer-oriented. I put our buyers in charge of the company.

From 1958 through 1976, we tried to carry what the customers asked for, given the limits of our small stores and other operational parameters. Each store manager had great latitude in what was carried and from what supplier it was ordered. There was very little central distribution except for Trader Joe's labeled California wines or imports. Each store probably had access to ten thousand stock keeping units (SKUs), of which about three thousand were actually stocked in any given week.

By the time I left in 1989, we were down to a band of 1,100 to 1,500 SKUs, all of which were delivered through a central distribution system. The managers no longer had any buying discretion and there were no "DSDs," or direct store deliveries.

And along the way not only did we drop a lot of products that our customers would have liked us to sell, even at not-outstanding prices, but we stopped cashing checks in excess of the amount of purchase, we stopped all full-case discounts, and we persistently shortened the hours. We violated every received-wisdom of retailing except one: we delivered great value, which is where most retailers fail.

# Key Elements of Five Year Plan '77

What follows did not happen overnight. Among the guidelines set in February 1977 (remember, Fair Trade on alcohol was not finally ended until 1978):

1. **Emphasize edibles vs. non-edibles.** I figured that the supermarkets would raise their prices on foods to make up for the newly reduced margins on milk and alcohol. This would give us all the more room to underprice them. During the next five years we got rid of film, hosiery, light bulbs and hardware, greeting cards, batteries, magazines, all health and beauty aids except those with a "health food" twist. We began to cut back sharply on soaps and cleaners and paper goods. The only non-edibles we emphasized were "tabletop" items like wineglasses, cork pullers, and candles. It was quite clear that we should put more emphasis on food and less on alcohol and milk.

2. **Within edibles, drop all ordinary branded products like Best Foods, Folgers, or Weber's bread.** I felt that a dichotomy was developing between "groceries" and "food." By "groceries," I mean the highly advertised, highly packaged, "value added" products being emphasized by supermarkets, the kinds that brought slotting allowances and co-op advertising allowances. By embracing these "plastic" products, I felt the supermarkets were abandoning "food" and the product knowledge required to buy and sell it. But this position wasn't entirely altruistic. The plan of February 20, 1977, declared, "Most independent supermarkets have been driven out of business, because they stupidly tried to compete with the big chains in plastic goods, in which the big chains excel."

3. **Focus on discontinuity of supplies.** Be willing to discontinue any product if we are unable to offer the right deal to the customer.

4. Instead of national brands, focus on either Trader Joe's label products or "no label" products like nuts and dried fruits. This was intended to enable the Trader Joe's label to pick up momentum in the stores. And it worked.

5. Carry individual items as opposed to whole lines. We wouldn't try to carry a whole line of spices, or bag candy, or vitamins. Each SKU (a single size of a single flavor of a single item) had to justify itself, as opposed to riding piggyback into the stores just so we had a "complete" line. Depth of assortment now was of no interest. As soon as Fair Trade ended in 1978, we began to get rid of the hundred brands of Scotch, seventy brands of bourbon, and fifty brands of gin. And *slowly* (it was like pulling teeth) we dismantled the broad assortment of California boutique wines.

6. No fixtures. By 1982, the store would have most of its merchandise displayed in stacks with very little shelving. This implied a lower SKU count: a high-SKU store needs lots of shelves. The average supermarket carries about 27,000 SKUs in 30,000 square feet of sales area, or roughly one SKU per square foot. Trader Joe's, by 1988, carried one SKU per five square feet! Price-Costco, one of my heroes, carried about one SKU per twenty square feet. As much as possible I wanted products to be displayed in the same cartons in which they were shipped by the manufacturers. This was already a key element in our wine merchandising.

7. Each SKU would stand on its own two feet as a profit center. We would earn a gross profit on each SKU that was justified by the cost of handling that item. There would be no "loss leaders."

8. Above all we would not carry any item unless we could be outstanding in terms of price (and make a profit at that price per #7) or uniqueness.

By the end of 1977, we increased the size of the buying staff, adding one very key person, Doug Rauch, whom we hired out of the wholesale health food trade. Leroy, Frank Kono, Bob Berning, and Doug rolled out Five Year Plan '77, which for purposes of this history I call Mac the Knife. Back in those days we had no idea how sharp that knife would become! We just wanted to survive deregulation.

Everything now depended on buying. So here we go into the next chapter, Intensive Buying.

# 12

## Intensive Buying

> Jacques, Comte de Guibert's "Essay on Tactics" remodeled
> logistics, field artillery and military engineering, stressing
> mobility, irregularity, adaptability: all cardinal sins in the
> old rule books. In March 1788, he regrouped regiments of
> cavalry and infantry into combined brigades that were then
> trained together intensively for battle-readiness.
>
> —Simon Schama in
> *Citizens: A Chronicle of the French Revolution*

The rules of warfare seem to go in cycles alternating from neat rows—the Roman square, the French knights at Agincourt, the fixed battles of the early eighteenth century, the trenches of 1915–18, and the Maginot/Siegfried lines—to rules that stress mobility, irregularity, adaptability—Attila the Hun, the English longbowmen at Agincourt, the colonial guerrillas in 1776, both sides in our Civil War, the German panzers, the Viet Cong, and the Afghan guerrillas.

The mass retailers, especially the supermarkets and drug chains, have been practicing eighteenth-century buying and merchandising programs. They take rigid, fixed positions based on heavily branded and advertised goods. Each week we're treated to acres of advertising (either in newspapers or chain-published tabloids, depending on the city) in which the chains honorably blow each other out of the trenches with Coca-Cola, Budweiser, *Smirnoff*, Anacin, *Colgate*, Pampers, *Cheez Whiz*, Folgers Coffee; or in which the chains dutifully survey each other's prices on hundreds of brands, and declare victory on points. How gentlemanly! How bloodless! The only difference among the surviving market chains (most cities now have only three or four chains remaining) is whether they "double coupons"—that is, give you double the manufacturers' coupon value when you buy the product. This tactic, obviously, can have meaning only in the context of heavily branded products. The very merchandising could have been done by Frederick the Great: stiff shelves of merchandise, each item dutifully tagged with its UPC, cost per unit, and cost per ounce. Paper battles rage over slotting allowances and space allocation while the check stand scanners grind out more data than can ever be converted into useful information.

And then there was Trader Joe's, which, at that point, didn't even have scanning. In most of its stores, computerization in 1998 was still limited to a 1987 model Mac Plus. Yet it cuts a wide swath in food retailing thanks to Intensive Buying, which is what the 1977 Five Year Plan boiled down to, which I formally named by the end of that plan, and which stressed mobility, irregularity, and adaptability. Here's how Intensive Buying works:

## Honor Thy Vendors

- After all, these are the guys you're buying from. They should not be treated as adversaries. Five Year Plan '77 said, "Buying, therefore, is not just a matter of trying to beat down suppliers on price. It is a creative exercise of developing alternatives." Many of our best product ideas and special buying opportunities came from our vendors.

- Vendors should have prompt interviews. One of the most common complaints about chain store buyers is that their appointment calendars are booked weeks in advance.

- Buyers should be product-knowledgeable. Another of the most common complaints about buyers is that they are ignorant about what they buy. It tends to follow that "layering" in the buying organization should be discouraged, just as modern organizational theory (Peter Drucker) deplores it in the store field organization. I suggest that there shouldn't be more organizational layers between the CEO and the lowest buyer than between the CEO and the store manager. This can create problems in companies where the CEO is a lawyer or investment banker. But such companies are likely to have lots of problems anyway.

- Complementary to no "layering," the number of real buyers should be minimized. Buyers should buy, and be free of paperwork and routine reordering. Buyers need to be deeply knowledgeable about manufacturing, packaging, shipping, etc., but these aspects of vertical interference should be handled by assistants.

- Buyers should be well paid. Trader Joe's had the highest-paid buying staff in grocery retailing. Our super-competent buyers could handle tremendous workloads. Since I left Trader Joe's, one of my biggest problems has been to persuade clients to hire, and pay for, top buying talent. Most chains squeeze by with $50,000 buyers when they should be paying $150,000. Again, one of the basic distinctions of Trader Joe's was its high rates of pay.

- Rigid departmental splits between buyers should be avoided. It should be possible for two buyers to meet with one vendor at the same time. Most vendors have more than one product or product category to sell. Overt physical separation of buyers, especially private offices, should have vanished with Frederick the Great.

- Vendors should get prompt decisions. Some of our greatest coups were generated by our commitment to make an offer within twenty-four hours of a presentation. Desperate vendors knew they would not be strung out by a constipated buying procedure. They might not like the offer they got, but by God they got an offer. Conversely, our buyers shouldn't give time to vendor representatives who are more than one level removed from the final decision maker of the vendor.

- Vendors should be regarded as extensions of the retailer, a *Marks & Spencer* concept. Their employees should be regarded almost as employees of the retailer. Concern for their welfare should be shown, because employee turnover at vendors sometimes can be more costly than turnover of your own employees. And if a good salesperson leaves one vendor, follow that salesperson to the next place he or she works.

- Treasure entrepreneurial vendors and maintain entrepreneurial buying hours: on holidays, or very early or very late. Whenever a vendor claimed to be truly desperate, we offered to meet him at 6:00 p.m. on Friday night. That separates the wheat from the chaff! That's how Bob Berning made a sensational buy of magnums of *Chateau d'Yquem*.

- Vendors' manufacturing plants should be visited frequently, especially by your quality control people. Doug Rauch helped us recruit Patty Smith, a real health food devotee, to monitor the quality of everything we sold. Marks & Spencer is famous for its quality control people. Once I visited a Brie factory in France that supplied both M&S and Trader Joe's. That day the plant management was sweating blood, because the M&S quality control people were visiting. They were far tougher than the cheese company's own QC people.

> [Peter] Drucker was . . . an admirer of Marks & Spencer, the
> giant British retail concern which, while copying some of
> Sears' methods, notably in recruiting, training, and
> developing new executives, was imbued with a variety of
> objectives, perhaps more diverse than Sears' productivity
> and marketing, for example. It had also established
> "innovation objectives" as Drucker put it, by which "it
> rapidly built its quality control laboratories into research,
> design and development centers. It developed designs and
> fashions. Finally it went out and looked for the right
> manufacturer." The result was one of the world's best
> programs for private labels.
>
> –Isidore Barmash, *Macy's for Sale*, 1989

Sometimes it is the development of a complete recipe, sometimes it is specifying that a wine be left unfiltered, sometimes it is changing the unit weight. This is the complete opposite of dealing with *Procter & Gamble*, which presents the retailer with faits accompli. In developing our private label products, such as enchiladas, we worked with the manufacturers to adjust the product formulae to meet our health food criteria.

Up in Toronto, Dave Nichol established a wonderful product testing kitchen for Loblaw's, and worked with the University of Toronto Medical School in developing heart-healthy private label foods. He had a former vice president of Marks & Spencer on his staff. With Loblaw's resources, they could do things we couldn't.

- Trust the vendor: This is part of the genius of Marks & Spencer, which accepts deliveries from its long-established vendors without counting the cases. In the 1980s, I visited a cheese plant in England that was stocking wheeled carts with precut cheese for

M&S. Those carts would be rolled right through Marks & Spencer's distribution center on their way to the stores without ever being counted. Yeah, they were audited: if M&S ever found you cheated them, you were through.

- I adopted a rule: Screw me once, shame on you. Screw me twice, shame on me. The vendor who screwed us twice was through, forever. During all my years in the company, I can recall only a couple of instances of permanent banishment. One thing that never failed to astonish me was how well samples from vendors actually matched the delivered products.

Most people, even vendors, act well if you treat them decently. This knowledge—it's not just a belief—makes it all the more bitter when anyone steals from you. We'll discuss this dark side of retailing in a later chapter.

The progress of the internet and electronic interfaces is demanding new levels of trust between the retailer and the supplier. Under these new interfaces, the supplier automatically resupplies the retailer on the basis of scanning data, which goes online to the supplier without batch-by-batch purchase orders. Individual internet buying must also operate on severe rules of trust.

## Intense Intervention in Product Development

"Buying" in our context is not just a matter of negotiating for a chunk of well-defined product. Let's take coffee. The key to our program was finally discovered in nitrogen-flush packaging.

First, we began to study coffees as we had wines. Based on our newfound product knowledge about coffees, we made the decision that we did not want to deal in ground, vacuum-packed coffees for two reasons. First, the grinding of the beans releases too much of the volatile compounds that give smell and flavor. Secondly, we discovered that "vacuum-packed" is an illusion: if a true vacuum were drawn on those cans, they would collapse under atmospheric pressure. In short, "vacuum-packed" is at best a marginal way of preserving coffee flavor.

We decided to sell only whole coffee beans, a field that the supermarkets had almost abandoned in the 1970s. Furthermore, we would varietally label them just like wines. Peruvian *Chanchamayo*, Nicaragua *Jinotega*, Colombia *Excelso*, and so on. We started by selling roasted beans in paper bags, but those bags are even worse than "vacuum-packed" when it comes to preserving the volatile compounds. After visiting Athens, Greece, in 1980, where so many restaurants roast their coffee on the premises, I was ready to do the same. Many neighborhoods, however, would have objected to the odors generated by coffee roasting. And the process requires special conditions because the beans, for example, have to cool for twenty-four hours.

Then Doug Rauch came across a new process for canning coffee, which, instead of drawing a vacuum, flushed the can with the inert gas nitrogen, driving out the oxygen. This is still the way that Trader Joe's coffee beans are sold, and it's been a great success.

There is a drawback: the cans come in only one size, but different kinds of beans expand differently when they're roasted. You can't have a uniform weight for all beans, something that is foreign to the lockstep mentality of supermarkets, or the big brands of ground coffee. So we simply packed different weights, and explained it in the *Fearless Flyer*. It worked!

No effort was made, however, to always be in stock on say, Nicaragua Jinotega or Sumatra *Mandheling* beans. The buying was as opportunistic as in wines.

One of our greatest coffee bean successes was "genuine Swiss water process" decaffeinated coffee. I don't want to get mired in the politics of different methods of decaffeination. Suffice it to say that the genuine Swiss water process was desired by the health food customers. The big chains wouldn't mess with it because the supply was so small. We kept buying every container-load that arrived in San Francisco (the coffee roasting center for the West Coast) until finally the Swiss company stopped shipping for unknown reasons. The Swiss company finally started shipping again, and Trader Joe's enjoyed a near-monopoly because we were willing to buy the entire supply. Eventually, it disappeared again from Trader Joe's, I know not why.

Some of our great values in fruit juices were generated by getting the glass containers for cheap. Odd lots (though big ones) of glass containers show up from time to time. Let's say that *Sunsweet* prune juice tries an odd-shaped container and then drops it. The leftover inventory gets closed out at bargain prices. We'd buy up these odd lots and ship them to, say, our apple juice supplier. Since so much of the cost of fruit juice is in the glass container, we were able to reflect big savings in the retail price.

## Intense Legal and Financial Work

You must master the USDA, FDA, and BATF rules that impact labels such as vitamins, imported wines, imported meats, etc., *and* you may want to make your labels more informative than laws or trade practice require. Long before there was mandatory ingredient labeling, we went out of our way to make full disclosure.

I've already discussed how we studied the rules governing Fair Trade on wine, Master Wine Grower licenses, etc., and how Leroy mastered the Wisconsin-sponsored protectionist regulations on cheese.

We went on to assume the foreign exchange risk in buying imported wines, cheeses, mustards, candies, et al. All foreign vendors are willing to sell in U.S. dollars, but they charge a risk premium for doing so. We assumed the foreign currency risk and squeezed their premium out of the price. We didn't speculate, as soon as we issued a purchase order, we simply bought francs forward at whatever the same-day exchange rate was.

In bakery and dairy products, the key may be the willingness to absorb the spoils, so the vendors don't have to figure out the cost of returns.

I do not believe in keeping "spoils" in the back room until some salesperson comes by to pick them up. All they do is attract rats, ants, and cockroaches, and they take up valuable space. I believe that products should move in only one direction, never back up the supply chain. When a bottle was broken, a can dented, or a "short fill" was discovered, it went to the trash bin.

One way we got the cost down was to encourage manufacturers to increase their case pack from twelve to twenty-four, providing this didn't break our forty-pound-per-case weight limit (see the "Workers' Compensation" section in the "Supply Side Retailing" chapter).

We also dealt in "offset" goods from countries with weak currencies—those that wouldn't take U.S. dollars because of fluctuating exchange rates. Three-way deals were created. For example, Coca-Cola wanted to buy wine from Yugoslavia, which wouldn't take the U.S. dollar. So the company sold soda into Yugoslavia, and received dinars for it. Then they were able to purchase wines from Yugoslavia, with those dinars, and then sell the wines to American distributors for U.S. dollars.

Another element of our Intensive Buying was our willingness to pay cash on delivery. Few retailers are willing to do that. We simply computed our economic cost in paying COD and reflected it in our offer to the vendor.

# What Intensive Buying Is Not

1. **Eliminating the middleman.** Intensive Buying may accidentally eliminate middlemen, but this is not really the point: the problem is incompetent or overpriced middlemen. In fact, building a stable of competent middlemen can be considered a form of Intensive Buying.

2. **Buying power.** Any fool with cash has "buying power." What most people mean by "buying power" is actually selling power: the ability to move large quantities of goods. Selling power, however, is not a type of Intensive Buying, though selling power may be one of the results of successful Intensive Buying. There are other ways of getting selling power, such as by having good locations, or effective advertising, or low prices. The point where the "buying power" and "selling power" curves cross each other creates the magic physical thresholds. There are two magic physical thresholds that a retailer must achieve to be competitive: the truckload, and the oceangoing container load. These thresholds mark the limit of most economies of scale.

3. **Monopolism.** Buying the whole supply. Deciding not to buy, because you're afraid competitors will get some of the same product and undersell you, is an admission that Intensive Buying cannot be applied to the product.

4. **Limited to branded closeouts and private label.** A substantial amount of the Intensive Buyer's merchandise is going to be private label, or "closeout," branded products like those sold by the *99 Cent Stores* and *Pic 'N' Save*. Many products, however, simply don't fall within the branded/private label dichotomy. You have to handle these products as private label, or no label, or not at all.

Many products are either unbranded (oat bran) or with only weak national brands (maple syrup, olive oil, pasta, dried fruit, dried beans, whole bean coffee, rubbing alcohol, Epsom salts). The Frederick the Great–style retailers, who are accustomed to dealing primarily in branded goods, tend to lack the skills to exploit the other types of opportunities.

For example, Leroy, Doug Rauch, and Bob Johnson virtually invented a product category new to California: frozen, packaged, unbranded seafoods. Supermarkets tend to sell all seafoods from their meat departments, usually in thawed (so-called *fresh*) form, sometimes packaged, sometimes in bulk from a service case. In their frozen food departments, you find only branded seafoods: seafoods that have been value added, like breaded fish sticks, stuffed crab, etc., from *Mrs. Paul's* (*Campbell's Soup*), *Van de Kamp's*, etc. The Watson/Rauch/Johnson approach allowed Trader Joe's to become a prominent retailer of seafoods in only three years, because we could sell (profitably) at much lower prices than the supermarkets, simply because of Intensive Buying of frozen seafoods. To achieve this, Trader Joe's had to learn about seafoods and often interfere in the packaging, transportation, etc. of the products. But we became the No. 1 retailer of Black Tiger Shrimp in the country this way.

## How Did We Create Those Bargains?

That's the question I'm asked so often. People assume that the only way we created "those bargains" was by cutting our gross profit—or even by selling below cost. The "default condition" assumed by those people is that there is only one wholesale price for a given product, and that retailers compete by shaving their profit based on that sole price. Intensive Buying assumes *no hay precios fijados* (there are no fixed prices).

# How Did We Set Our Prices?

This is the question other retailers most often ask. Usually they ask, "What percentage margin did you aim for?" Which always launches me into my tirade about how you pay your bills with dollars, not percents. This seemed to be a concept that was pushed aside in the traditional supermarket environs.

Your buyers always want to make their workload easier by applying uniform percentages for any given product category. (As a grocer I think in terms of gross profit percentage, which is your profit divided by your retail. Department store people think in terms of markup, which is your profit divided by your cost. Thus, if your cost is $1.00 and your retail is $1.25, your gross profit is 20 percent and your markup is 25 percent.) Grocery buyers love to apply a uniform percentage gross profit to everything, but that is bad practice.

During my tenure, Mac the Knife happened to run on a gross profit of about 23 percent after all distribution costs and what is euphemistically called "shrinkage." But that was an after-the-fact result. We never aimed specifically to hit 23 percent. Our approach, when the buyers followed it, was to find out what the going price was for a given SKU and then undercut the market. At the same time, they were to consider how many dollars we made on each sale.

Thus, at the time, I was willing to make only 13 percent on a $20 bottle of champagne, because that was a $2.60 profit. For a $2.00 item, however, I wanted to make a much greater percentage. Actually, we persistently got rid of anything that sold for less than a dollar. We stopped selling individual cans of soda and beer, for example, as I didn't want that kind of trade in the store. When I left Trader Joe's, our average sale was around $30, and that was pretty close to the median, too.

The fact that we wound up with 23 percent is irrelevant. What was relevant was that each SKU was a profit center after considering all the costs of handling it. Thus, spoilage (or stale-age) of bakery products and cheeses must be considered.

Intensive Buying stops short of actually manufacturing the product and may even stop short of physically handling the product at any point before it reaches the distribution center. Intensive Buying is a program of vertical interference and supervision, but not vertical integration. Vertical integration is what finished off A&P.

Guibert's mobility, irregularity, and adaptability are at the heart of this vertical interference. These are risky strategies, however, unless you have deep product knowledge. Without that, it is better to abstain from selling the product at all, or abdicate your functions to Procter & Gamble.

# 13

## Virtual Distribution

His slowness of perception bothered him at times. "At the
start I see my subject in a sort of haze. I know perfectly well
that what I shall see in it later is there all the time, but it
only becomes apparent after a while. Sometimes it is the
most important things that come out last."

—Jean Renoir in *Renoir, My Father*, the warm memoir
of Auguste Renoir. Here he discusses how
Auguste created a painting.

That's not a bad take on how I came to perceive the crucial role
of distribution as we unrolled Five Year Plan '77.

Intensive Buying can't work unless you have a way to receive container loads and truckloads in one location and distribute the goods to the stores, a process of which we were quite ignorant. The problem with Five Year Plan '77 was that as of 1977 we were wholly reliant on third parties to deliver goods to our stores.

During the next twelve years under Mac the Knife, we not only radically changed the composition of what we sold; we totally centralized the distribution into our own system, ending *all* direct store deliveries by vendors! To get a better handle on what we did, please look at the following page's table of the Composition of Sales in 1976 vs. 1988.

During Whole Earth Harry, Bob Berning had created a system of third parties who warehoused and then distributed the container loads of bargain imported wines and the truckloads of bargain Trader Joe California wines. Most of these third parties were alcoholic beverage distributors who also sold us "regular" goods. Bob leaned on them to add the distribution of our bargain wines. But such promotional wines were only about 8 percent of our sales.

## WHOLE EARTH HARRY'S ~ 1976

| CATEGORY | % SALES |
|---|---|
| Dry groceries | 10 |
| Alta Dena milk & ice cream | 10 |
| Cigarettes | 10 |
| Wines—Promotional | 8 |
| Liquor | 8 |
| Cheeses & butters | 8 |
| Beer | 7 |
| Wines—Fair Trade | 6 |
| Packaged deli | 6 |
| Bread, cupcakes, cookies, Fritos, chips | 5 |
| Eggs | 4 |
| Soft drinks | 4 |
| Hardware, hosiery, photo, health & beauty | 3 |
| Fresh orange juice squeezed on premises | 3 |
| Frozen foods | 2 |
| Nuts, dried fruits | 2 |
| Vitamins | 2 |
| Sandwiches made on premises | 1 |
| Produce | 1 |

Bob then went on during Mac the Knife to master the intricacies of different-sized oceangoing containers (sometimes it's cheaper to use twenty-footers than forty-footers) and truck back-hauls in bringing products from Northern California.

## MAC THE KNIFE ~ 1988

| CATEGORY | % SALES |
| --- | --- |
| Wines—Promotional | 22 |
| Dry groceries | 12 |
| Nuts, dried fruits | 12 |
| Frozen foods | 11 |
| Cheeses & butters | 10 |
| Bread, cupcakes, cookies, Fritos, chips | 8 |
| Alta Dena milk & ice cream | 6 |
| Fresh juices shipped with milk | 5 |
| Coffee beans | 5 |
| Vitamins | 3 |
| Beer | 2 |
| Eggs | 2 |
| Liquor | 1 |
| Hardware, hosiery, photo, health & beauty | 1 |
| Cigarettes, soft drinks, OJ squeezed, Wines—Fair Trade, packaged deli, sandwiches, produce | 0 |

As we moved deeper into nuts and dried fruits and health foods, Doug Rauch and Leroy lined up some people who not only warehoused and distributed products for us, but also packaged products for us. Slowly, painfully, we began to get a handle on distributing all products that could be shipped at ambient air temperatures. At one point we had as many as eighteen different warehouses with three different trucking companies. I was partly responsible for our having so many warehouses: I was deeply concerned about earthquakes after the 1971 Sylmar quake, which not only knocked down some warehouses, but knocked down so many freeway overpasses that it was impossible to get trucks in or out of some places. Also, of the eighteen warehouses, there were "only" four or five principal ones, each of which were selling their own goods, and lacking space for expansion.

## Major Logistical Challenges Ahead

### Frozen and Refrigerated Foods

All of our frozen foods were branded products delivered by our wholesaler, *Certified Grocers*. In the early stages of Mac the Knife, I had little hope that we could create our own stable of frozen products *and* create a frozen distribution system, because our sales were so small. Furthermore, still wearing my Whole Earth Harry hat, I projected that electrical costs would continue to go through the roof. Five Year Plan '77, therefore, contemplated getting rid of all frozen food cases to make room for more displays of room-temperature and refrigerated products. Fortunately, I was dissuaded from this by my colleagues and we didn't pull out the frozen food cases.

Leroy and Doug worked out a system of warehousing frozen products in a public warehouse in Pasadena that needed business, then shipping frozen products in Styrofoam chests on the same trucks that delivered nuts and dried fruits and other products.

Cheeses and similar refrigerated products were still shipped by the various local cheese suppliers from whom we purchased them. We still were not making direct purchases from Europe, Vermont, et al. Cheese wholesalers, like *Peacock* and *Dairy Fresh*, worked with us because it was in their interest.

As Leroy got further along in mastering the cheese import regulations, we began doing more direct buying, then warehousing the cheeses at the biggest cold storage plant in Los Angeles, *U.S. Growers*. As this volume grew, we were able to get truckers with refrigerated trucks who could distribute both refrigerated and frozen products.

By 1986, Mike Campbell, owner of *M&C Trucking*, had made such progress that we were able to take over the distribution of milk from Alta Dena with a "cross-dock" system. Since milk has to be delivered much more frequently than cheeses, however, we needed still more physical volume. That's when we stopped squeezing orange juice in the stores, a popular but hard-work program, and went to fresh juices squeezed in a central plant. Our volume in fresh juice was so high, not only in orange juice but in carrot juice—of which we became the largest retailer in California—that the combined milk-juice program could be put in place in 1986.

The ability to make only one purchase of milk per day from Alta Dena also got the Bureau of Milk Control off of Alta Dena's back. Only consumer prices had been decontrolled in 1977. Wholesale prices were still controlled, and the Bureau was objecting to the uniform prices that Alta Dena was charging us for store-door delivery, because the milk sales from one store to another varied so much. Had we not gone to this central delivery, furthermore, we would not have been able to expand to San Diego in 1986 and to Northern California in 1988. Starting in 1987, when I brought him in from the field as a principal buyer, Bob Johnson did brilliant work in dealing with the complicated logistics of the refrigerated/frozen products. Additionally, he perfected the distribution of . . .

## Bread and Bakery Products

By 1981, we had made so much progress in logistics that we were willing to consider going into our own bakery program. The trade thought we were crazy. While all the supermarket chains had their own bakeries, delivered by their own people, none of them had dropped the outside bakers like *Continental*, *Langendorf*, and *Interstate*

*Bakeries.* Everyone predicted that we would eat so much "stale" that we'd drop the program.

Our concept was to line up several small "health food" bakers, have them deliver to a central dock, and hire a trucker to distribute the bakery products from there. As we fleshed out this project, I hired Lori Tannenbaum Latta, who had studied baking in Paris, and who had been pastry chef at several prominent Los Angeles restaurants. Her expertise made a great contribution over the next five years. (She resigned to get married, then returned to Trader Joe's about 1994 and made further contributions to the company.)

The new bakery program was an instant success. And our rate of "stale" was so small that finally we stopped keeping track of it. As of 1988, we were selling eighty-five SKUs from seventeen small bakeries. Having very recently emerged from the small business category ourselves, we went out of our way to encourage small suppliers.

The bread program, and the other distribution programs, however, would never have been adequate for our requirements had the third challenge not been met.

# Computerization:
# Never Buy a Computer You Can't Lift

In 1980, my son, Joseph Steere Coulombe (Young Joe), after having worked on computers for two years at one of the Grandes Ecoles in Paris, got his BA in communication theory at *UC San Diego* and won a fellowship for a master's program at the Annenberg School of Communications at the University of Southern California. This brought him back to Los Angeles, where he introduced us to Apple I and Apple II and, in 1984, the Macintosh. Young Joe was a certified Macintosh programmer. The Apples were the first computers in the office. Payroll and general ledger were, at that point, still done on an ancient IBM punch card machine, which required constant attention.

Dave Yoda manually made out the quarterly operating statements from information generated by the IBM antique.

Our first efforts at distributing bread were being done in a most painful and inefficient manner with paper, pencil, and an adding machine. Telephone calls had to be made to all the stores, asking how many loaves, etc. they wanted of each product. The orders were totaled and each baker was called and told how many loaves to bake. It was a nightmare, especially since bakers started work about 2:00 a.m., and they needed to know by midnight what we wanted from them.

In 1982, we employed an Apple II to do most of the number crunching. That was a big help, but it didn't solve the problem of the nightly communication to the bakers. Young Joe rigged up one of the first voice-activated computer systems in the U.S. to take the orders from the stores. It was daring and full of bugs, but it began to teach us about electronic ordering. Furthermore, Joe indoctrinated us with a concept that fit our mindset perfectly: never buy a computer you can't lift. After life with IBM, we were ready!

I was serving on the board of *Denny's Restaurants* at the time. I was appalled at the cost, both initial and in maintenance, of its mainframes: mainframes that had a lifetime of about twelve months before they were obsolete. Not only did the mainframes eat electricity, but they generated so much heat that high-load air-conditioning was required. The whole massive system was housed in a seismically correct concrete bunker with huge diesel generators to provide backup power in case of emergency. I was also impressed by an article in *Scientific American* (again!) that showed that the "cost per million instructions" would collapse, giving desktop computers the power of mainframes. No way did I want to own mainframes. I still don't.

Leroy, therefore, found an outside (mainframe) computer service bureau, *Lundberg*, which, for the rest of my time at Trader Joe's, did the major number crunching for us.

In the meantime, we installed desktops in the office: I started on an *Otrona*, which ran on a language you have probably never heard of, called

CPM. We also bought *MS DOS* machines, IBM being the principal provider, but Young Joe saved us money by buying "clones" from *Corona*. The storage of these primitive machines was enhanced by *Corviss* hard drives whose storage capacity—20 megabytes—is a historical joke today.

When I was put in charge of the $3.4 billion Thrifty Corp. in 1992, one of the first appalling things I discovered were the mainframes. They were all in the basement of Thrifty's eleven-story office building (in itself, a barrier to efficient communication among the office staff). There was no backup power, as the city wouldn't let us keep a diesel generator on the premises, so power for the computers and their air conditioners was continually at risk. Even worse, there was no documentation of the software programs, which had been patched and repatched to meet the changing needs of the business. We immediately took steps to decentralize as much computer work as possible to the five subsidiaries like *Big 5 Sporting Goods* and *Pay 'n Save Drugstores* in Seattle. And we began to look for a service bureau, so that we could outsource the whole mess. The subsequent owners of Thrifty got this done about two years later, as outsourcing such a monstrosity cannot be done overnight.

Then, in 1994, when I took over *Provigo* in Northern California, I found another terrible office facility. The mainframe computers were in infinitely better shape than at Thrifty, but I couldn't move out of the mis-located, mis-designed office building because of the complexities of moving the damn mainframes!

The real breakthrough, however, came with the Macintosh. As soon as it appeared, we noticed that some employees were bringing their own Macs to work to use instead of the Corona/MS DOS machines. We dumped the Coronas and installed a Mac on almost every desk. The ability of our office people to create their own spreadsheets and write their own correspondence was astonishing. It certainly helped me as well, since, as I have commented earlier, I have never had a secretary. And, as I have commented in the chapter "Promise, Large Promise" it was a breakthrough in producing the *Fearless Flyer.*

Young Joe created a payroll system that could be run on the Mac (we'd had a poor experience with an unliftable computer from another vendor). This was a system, by the way, which foresaw the Year 2000 problem, and which was used until the early 1990s when the payroll simply got to be too big for the program.

That's something to be remembered in this distribution discussion: we were not dealing with a static problem. The company was growing 20 percent per year (doubling every 3.6 years). And the more efficacious the distribution program became, the more our sales increased.

Macs were installed in all the stores. Leroy, Robin Guentert, and Joe (until he stopped consulting for us so he could get a master's in management from Peter Drucker at Claremont) created an electronic ordering system on the Macs that fed into Guy Lundberg's computer service. This was an enormous breakthrough.

You need to understand that we were outsourcing not just the mainframe number crunching but the printing of the documents that it generated. High-speed printers were a big choke point. They had to spew out "picking" documents for the warehouses, "receiving" documents for the stores, and summaries for our Accounting Department. In short, "never buy a computer you can't lift" does *not* apply when it comes to buying printers for our heavy-duty application.

One of the major advances in 1987 at Trader Joe's was outsourcing the printing of our computer-generated reports to a professional warehouse company. Lundberg would electronically transmit the data to the warehouse, which had the picking documents printed and ready for the warehouse crew when they came to work. That eliminated sending the documents from Lundberg to the warehouse, a distance of forty miles in Los Angeles traffic. I'm going into this detail as an example of how you keep trying to make a business work better. And also as a reminder that computers have not eliminated paperwork in our society.

As I slowly learned some of the ramifications of computers, I suddenly realized that a given SKU, regardless of its physical size, occupies the same electronic space. A fifty-cent candy bar occupies the same electronic space as a twenty-five-pound bag of kibble. This was one more justification for the radical down-SKUing of the number of SKUs in the system: it helped the computers work better.

## Pulling the Distribution System Together

By 1996, it was obvious that we needed more professional help in making this edifice work. With young Joe leaving for Claremont and Leroy—who had no formal computer background at all—overloaded with all his other work, I hired a computer expert. Being an expert, it was difficult for him to accept don't-buy-a-computer-you-can't-lift. When he planned to buy and install an unliftable *Wang* mini-computer, we parted company with him. I was sort of at my wit's end, and data processing and distribution were not the only management issues with which I was struggling.

There comes a time in the evolution of any company when the people who built it need reinforcement, not necessarily replacement, with broader-scope managers.

The next year I made the biggest organizational change I ever undertook: I hired a new President, John Shields. John had been two years behind me at Stanford. We kept in close touch during all the years that we struggled in our respective careers, mine entrepreneurial, his corporate. I could talk with him because I felt that he was an entrepreneur mis-employed in the corporate world.

After getting his MBA, he went to work for *Macy's San Francisco*, where his father-in-law was chairman, and specialized in logistics. It was John who discovered that Macy's could not afford to sell mattresses because the cost of delivery far exceeded the gross margin on the mattresses. After about ten years at Macy's he migrated to *Mervyn's Department Stores*, where he worked with its great founder, Merv Morris, with whom I have had the pleasure of serving on the board of *Cost Plus World Markets* during the 1990s; and then with Jack Kilmartin, with whom I served on the advisory board of *Canned Foods Grocery Outlets*. (I have profited from my time with both of these astute retailers.) At both Macy's and Mervyn's, John was primarily involved in logistics as opposed to merchandising. Logistical help was what we needed.

Merv sold to Dayton Hudson, and later, Jack retired. John, at age fifty-five, decided to take early retirement. He moved to the desert and found himself starting to vegetate. When I called him in July 1987, he was ready to go back to work. I was ready to have him come work.

I asked John to start as a management consultant and analyze the way Trader Joe's worked and how we could improve it. He immediately did a great job of untangling knots in our distribution system—he even talked me out of my earthquake fears and we began consolidating the eighteen warehouses into one. In October 1987, I hired him as President and Chief Operating Officer. We'll resume this discussion in the chapter on my resignation and the appointment of John as my successor.

## Summary

For people who didn't know anything about distribution, Leroy Watson, Bob Berning, Doug Rauch, Bob Johnson, Robin Guentert,

Lori Tannenbaum, Diane Tennis, Gloria Reynolds, Mary Genest, and young Joe created one of the most remarkable systems in America. We owned no trucks, no warehouses, and no mainframe computers. I used to call it Leroy's Lighter Than Air Distribution System. Today I can call it "virtual" and you'll all get the point. John Shields pulled it all together in 1987–88, and when I left Trader Joe's it was running quite well, even with the logistical challenges of shipping products at four different temperatures from Los Angeles to San Francisco.

One of the most important decisions we made back in 1977 was to ship to the stores only in whole-case quantities. This is central to the efficiency of the system. The downside is that expensive products like wines, liquors, and vitamins don't sell equally well in all stores. You wind up with excessive inventory in dollars and cubic inches. That's why many chains let their stores order liquor in single-bottle quantities. I saw this at both Owl Drug and Thrifty Drug and it's a bloody mess. But to execute a high-SKU assortment policy you almost have to adopt single bottle shipments. Our 1977 decision to cut back on SKUs made it possible for us to go with the full-case-only practice.

When I left in 1989, the biggest unsolved problem, apart from managing the ever-growing volume of shipments, was the paperwork. The receivings in the warehouses, and the deliveries to the stores, were batch processed by Lundberg instead of continuously (online) processed. This made Mary Genest's job harder than it needed to be and delayed the critical balancing of store inventory results. Store inventories need to be taken often and the results determined at once: said results have a lifetime similar to that of fresh fish. I left before that problem was solved.

# 14

## Private Label Products

Cheerfully adorn the proudest table,
Since yours it is to bear the glorious label.

—Rose Fyleman

**W**e started in 1967 with no private label merchandise except the obligatory, non-differentiated vodka, gin, etc., most of which we dumped as soon as we knew what we were doing. Today, the great majority of products in Trader Joe's are private label or unknown label like the fish roe, many of the olive oils, etc.

Our first private label wine came in 1969. Joe Heitz, the celebrated winemaker in the Napa Valley, had made a batch of Ruby Cabernet that he didn't want to put his name on. Low on the learning curve of wines, we eagerly bought it under the Trader Joe's label. The wine was not very good. And here's a problem with private label wine: it goes into customers' wine cellars. They keep opening the stuff over a long period of time, and getting sore all over again. In this sense a wine re-tailer is more like an art dealer than a grocer. The latter's mistakes didn't linger more than a few days in the household.

As we kept learning more about wines, foods, and, above all, our customers, the private label program really got going under Whole Earth Harry.

**A Guideline:** No private label product was introduced for the sake of having private label.

This is 100 percent contrary to the policy of supermarkets. The supermarkets try to have a private label copy of every branded product, which they usually sell for less, but in these days of double coupons, "customer loyalty programs," and God knows what else—who can tell? Even when we dropped all branded bakery products in 1982, we did not, for example, introduce a Trader Joe's "balloon loaf" of white bread, nor hamburger buns, nor hot dog buns. We simply did without these products.

> **The willingness to do without any given product is one of the cornerstones of Trader Joe's merchandising philosophy.**

It is important to remember that our product knowledge commenced with wines—foods came later. So a lot of what we had learned about merchandising wines was carried over to foods, of which the most extreme example was Trader Joe's *Vintage Dated Canned Corn*. This corn, grown in a specific field in Idaho, isolated so it wouldn't be cross-pollinated from other fields, was the best in the world. Our biggest problem was wrestling the crop from the Japanese, who tend to buy the very best, whether it's coffee, fish, or Bordeaux. Each year the label bore the date of that harvest, and when that was gone, that was it, until next year. This is very vinous thinking, but it illustrates the principle of discontinuity in merchandise, which we embraced wholeheartedly.

As we got into Whole Earth Harry, every private label food product had to meet the current shibboleths of the health food movement: no monosodium glutamate, no added sugar, no added salt, no artificial coloring. And as we moved into frozen seafood, no sulfites.

## How to Differentiate Products

Here are some of the claims we made besides vintage-dating. They can be classified as: obvious wine merchandising applied to foods, obvious health-food appeals, medical news, ecological appeals, rarity, and gourmet.

**Wine merchandising:** Pineapple from the island of Maui (as opposed to just "Hawaii"). Concord grape juice from the 1981 harvest.

Above all: Because almost all of our purchases of wines were in limited, or at least delimited, quantity, we always announced how many cases we had. This carried over to all other products in the *Fearless Flyer*. We always announced how much we had bought. This also ties to the rarity appeal below.

**Health food:** Molasses without sulfur, made from sun-ripened cane. Prunes without preservatives. Did you know that most dried prunes are preserved with sorbates? I didn't until Doug Rauch gave me the background to write up.

> **Each private label product, therefore, had to have a reason, a point of differentiation.**

**Medical news:** Solder-free cans. In the early 1980s, the dangers of lead in soldered cans were publicized and we took advantage of the news. Vanilla extract with no alcohol; low sodium baking powder. We also campaigned against aluminum in deodorants because of suspicion in the medical community in 1986 that it was linked to Alzheimer's. This has since been borne out as false, but nevertheless . . .

Most of the *Trader Darwin* vitamins were introduced in response to specific medical news. For example, we introduced Trader Darwin's Metamorphosis for special needs children based on a *Medical Tribune* story in 1981.

**Ecological appeals:** Albacore caught on long lines (instead of nets). Phosphate-free detergents. (We were one of the first grocers in America to promote this.)

**Gourmet:** "Unfiltered" is a powerful claim to make on wines. Winemakers don't like to do it because it creates the potential of a (bad) tertiary fermentation, so they bottle unfiltered wines with extra care. We applied the same claims to apple cider vinegar reinforced by the claim that it was made from whole apples, not concentrate. Handmade tamales, handmade berry pies.

**Rarity:** Cold pressed peanut oil. Hey, there's one you don't see every day! The only Extra Prime Whole Bean Kona coffee in Los Angeles. Eighteen-month-old Longhorn cheese. Unfermented Zinfandel grape juice.

No bulky products like paper towels or sugar, because the high-value-per-cubic-inch rule still prevailed.

There was a particular angle to the naming of our products. I wanted to create a silent conspiracy among the overeducated, underpaid people in town, so that as they moved down the aisles they would read secret messages on the products.

During the first years of Trader Joe's, we continued to carry a convenience-store's assortment of basic branded items, including toilet paper, five-pound bags of sugar and flour, branded detergents, etc. Finally, one day, Frank Kono, who was supervising half the stores by then, came to me and said that these ordinary groceries just weren't selling, they were taking up valuable shelf space, and we dropped them all. We simply went out of business on the "bulkers" and did not replace them with private labels.

## Selling Branded Products under Our Label

Once the virtual distribution system started working, its logistics were so good that we could buy some branded merchandise and sell it for less than the supermarkets, partly because we were willing to exchange one low landed cost for all the bells and whistles of ad allowances, slotting, etc. Sometimes the supermarkets got upset because we were underselling them, and held the manufacturers' feet to the fire. Always gentlemen, we accommodated our vendors and sold the same stuff under our label.

A prime example was *Wolfgang Puck's* frozen pizza. To avoid a direct comparison with the product in the supermarkets, they made a smaller-diameter size for us. This had the unanticipated advantage of fitting in toaster ovens!

The same desire to hide their light under a bushel afflicted winemakers, and many of Trader Joe's private label wines were from very famous wineries.

## Individualized Labels Aimed at the Overeducated

Instead of having a one-size-fits-all private label like the supermarkets, we tried to individualize each label to each product.

Wherever I could, therefore, I used artistic, or musical, or literary, or historical, or scientific allusions in the product names. Thus, when we got into private label baked goods, we had the *Brandenberg Brownies,* the *Sir Isaac Newtons, The Bagel Spinoza, The Peanut Pascal, Disraeli & Gladstone's British Muffins,* etc.

My favorite of all the private labels was *Heisenberg's Uncertain Blend* of coffee beans. At the coffee roaster they process different batches of beans and some fall off the conveyor. Periodically they would sweep these up, roast them, and sell them to us for very little money. The blend, from batch to batch, was literally uncertain. And the label gave the *Encyclopedia Britannica's* explanation of Werner Heisenberg's Nobel Prize–winning 1927 discovery, one of the keystones of modern physics. How many customers had ever heard of Heisenberg? Not many. But the ones who understood the joke were literally bonded to us forever. And the price of the coffee was so cheap that non-initiates bought it.

Some of my other favorite names are *Trader Darwin's Vitamins* (for the survival of the fittest), *Little Cat Feet* dry cat food (pace Carl Sandburg), *Habeas Crispus* potato chips, *Eve's Apple Sparkled by Adam, Trader Cleopatra's My Salad Days* vinegar, *Trader Gainsborough's Blue Boy* blueberry syrup, *Great Expectations* kibble for puppies. Oh, we did had fun!

**I believe in the wisdom that you gain customers one by one, but you lose them in droves.**

Often, however, the light of inspiration failed to shine and we fell back on some useful naming devices:

- All Mexican products were Trader José's.

- All Japanese products, Trader Joe-San.

- All Italian products were Trader Giotto's, a cultural allusion that overrode the correct translation of Joe, Giuseppe.

- All products associated with New England: cranberry juice, maple syrup, et al., were Pilgrim Joe's.

All baking products were named for my two daughters, Madeleine and Charlotte, something that I fear has haunted them into later life. Trader Charlotte and her wine cake recipe, which appeared in the *Fearless Flyer* each year, has frozen her in time at eleven years of age, something that her colleagues at the *Getty Museum* have not let her forget.

Finally, the same nineteenth-century art that we used for the *Fearless Flyer* was deployed on the labels. Since there was very little four-color art in the nineteenth century, I especially prized those plates when I found them in used bookstores. We used them on several of the coffee bean cans (a view of Rome on *Espresso di Roma*, Indonesian art on *Sumatra Mandheling*), and a beautiful plate of Egyptian art adorned "*Secrets of the Psyllium*"—how else can one romance a proctologic product? Again, the art work was aimed at our well-traveled, well-educated clientele.

# Summary

As the private label program grew, its growth was given additional stimulus by a hysteresis or feedback loop among the private label products. Confidence in one product led to purchases of another. As you will find in the next chapter, From "Discrete to Indiscretions," I wound up wishing we sold nothing else, the "Brooks Bros." strategy. But that was with the value of hindsight in 1987, after having built the Trader Joe's brand for twenty years.

## 15

# From Discrete
# to Indiscretions

You know, my friends, with what a brave carouse
I made a second marriage in my house;
Divorced old barren reason from my bed,
And took the daughter of the vine to spouse.

—Omar Khayyam

## Continuous vs. Discrete

I cannot repeat too often that Trader Joe's entered the City of Foods (foods as opposed to groceries) by way of the Wine Gate. We took the daughter of the vine to spouse.

Our first real product knowledge came when we learned about wines; that indoctrination flavored everything we subsequently did in foods. The foremost character of wines (note my repeated use of the plural) is that each vintage, and each batch within a vintage, is separate, unique, discontinuous, discrete. Discrete means distinct, different, disjunctive. It is the opposite of continuous. Early in Whole Earth Harry we dropped Gallo wines because (at least in that era) they were as continuous as Coca-Cola. The space was diverted to small wineries' products.

This philosophical approach put us in conflict with the mainstream of American retailing, which emphasizes continuous products. Thus, when a supermarket promotes Coca-Cola it doesn't have to explain that Coca-Cola is a secret formula for a soft drink created a century ago in Atlanta, which originally was based on cocaine but was cleaned up decades ago, "Coca" being a regrettable artifact of its origins. All the supermarket has to advertise is "Coca-Cola," the size, and the price.

Look at any supermarket ad. You'll learn precious little about the provenance of any product in it; you'll see only name, size, and price. Partly this is because the grocers themselves don't know anything about the provenance of what they sell, and they don't want to bring up the subject of individual differences. How are you going to cover an ad for three hundred supermarkets if you don't have uniform products? In a way it's the Extra Large Egg choke point that we discovered in 1962 with Pronto Markets visited over and over again.

Back in 1967, Good Time Charley made a bet that rising levels of education would fragment the masses, that a small but growing group of people would be dissatisfied with having to consume what everybody else consumed. By dumb luck we blundered into the one product field that fit this new pattern: wines. *Wines have not been popular in America because, intrinsically, they are not continuous products.* You can't just order up some more sugar and chemicals and make another batch. Every major conglomerate that tried to capitalize on the boutique wine boom lost its shirt, including Coca-Cola, *Hunt-Wesson*, and *Pillsbury*, each of which made mistaken bets on California wineries in the 1970s. Discontinuity is not their game. This has two implications:

1.  Americans have been trained since *Amos 'n' Andy/Pepsodent* in 1930 to select a brand and then stick with it. That's the way they buy their toothpaste; that's the way they buy their catsup; that's the way they buy their gin. That's the way they'd like to buy their wines but they are continually frustrated.

2. This inherent discontinuity makes it hard for the mass merchants to promote wines.

That's one reason why (as I write this) 88 percent of the wines are consumed by only 11 percent of Americans (and you can bet that most of them are Trader Joe's customers or would be except for geography). The wine boom of the late 1990s is focused on the most discontinuous, most discrete, most expensive wines, the wines most unlike Pepsodent—the wines hardest for mass merchants to sell. Even Gallo has shifted its focus from (continuous) jug wines to vintage dated, varietally named wines from premium wine counties like Sonoma. On a gallonage-per-capita basis, however, wine consumption in America has been falling since the mid-1980s.

Because of our wine background, we liked and embraced discontinuous lots of foods. This worked well when it came to vintage-dated canned corn and maple syrup under the Trader Joe's label. When we began dealing in closeouts of branded foods, however, we got some real headaches.

## Trader Joe's: A Closeout Store?

During 1971–76, while we were living it up with all the wines being closed out by wholesalers' liquidations, our competitors put out the word that all Trader Joe's sold was "closeout" wines. The leading wine guru of Los Angeles sniffed that "Trader Joe's sells *Akron* rejects." (*The Akron* was a low-end but high-style discounter selling 99¢ wines that went bankrupt.) The great majority of customers paid no attention to this, obviously, but the "closeout image" stuck, and we didn't do anything to help it with some of our biggest food promotions during Mac the Knife.

As we moved into more Intensive Buying of foods with Mac the Knife, the middlemen who specialize in solving manufacturers' inventory problems began offering us closeouts of branded foods. These products are discrete only in the sense that they are onetime closeouts. There are usually three reasons for this: discontinuance of an entire line, like *Sara Lee* exiting the ice cream business; or a flavor or size that proved unpopular like *Libby's Pear-Passion Nectar*; or an inventory imbalance that had to be solved by the end of a manufacturer's fiscal year.

You may wonder how these great bargains became available. Most of the big food manufacturers have "product managers," young MBAs who are put in charge of first one brand and then another as they're moved along the "career ladder." Quite often they make big mistakes: a recipe that proves unpopular, or a production run that was too big. Confronted with such a dilemma, they would "barter" the surplus product to a middleman in return for advertising space, "bought" at an inflated price to cover up the mistake in inventory. The product manager was gambling that he'd be moved to another product line before the barter scheme unraveled. Most of the deals we made were "advertising media barter."

These are the same kind of discrete deals that are offered to retailers like *Canned Foods Grocery Outlets, MacFrugals*/Pic 'N' Save, *Odd Lots, 99¢ Stores*, etc. We began buying them because they offered great value, and because they sold like crazy. The real excitement started when the frozen food offerings began coming in.

The light bulb went on: we and Canned Foods Grocery Outlets (on whose advisory board I served for four years after I left Trader Joe's) were the only "closeout" retailers in America with frozen food cases! The other closeout merchants couldn't participate.

Doug Rauch and, later, Bob Johnson led us to some sensational frozen sales: *Certi Fresh* seafood entrees, Sara Lee ice cream, *Johnston Frozen Pies, Armour Dinner Classics, Mrs. Paul's Seafood Entrees, Pillsbury Cheesecake, Pillsbury Microwave Popcorn, Gloria Vanderbilt Tofu, Perdue Cornish Game Hens, Budget Gourmet* entrees, *Frusen Gladje* ice cream, *Breyer's* ice cream.

Sometimes we'd gamble a million dollars on a single promotion, which was still big bucks for us. On the other hand, we were one of the few retailers who could tie up a million bucks in a warehouse. Once again our strong cash position played a key role in making us a powerful retailer.

But these deals were nerve-racking. We'd publish a *Fearless Flyer* and the product wouldn't show up in time. Or the product would show up and we'd reject it because it was out-of-code. Or not all the flavors that we advertised actually were there.

The products were discrete only in the fact that they were one-time-only quantities of intrinsically continuous products. We did try to observe our health-food criteria, in the sense of avoiding overt MSG, food coloring, etc. But our "due diligence" in some cases matched that of an investment banker on the trail of a hot IPO.

Anyhow, as promised in the Trader Joe's Sampler chapter, here are some indiscretions we committed as we wobbled our way to fame:

- **Famous Name Bologna:** In 1977, Leroy got a special deal going with one of the major meat companies for bologna that the cryovac machines had improperly wrapped. I explained this in the front-page *Fearless Flyer* article. We didn't hide the provenance. Our price was sensational; the product, however, left Whole Earth Harry bleeding on the sidewalk. Undaunted, we next sold famous name improperly wrapped hot dogs and various lunch meats.

- **Closeout Vitamins:** In 1982, *Schick* (the razor company) pulled out of the vitamin field. We closed out their vitamins, and then *Carnation*'s failed program in 1984. We never should have done this. It compromised sales of *Trader Darwin* vitamins.

- **Feast for One:** Sometimes what we did was inexcusable. In 1984, we bought a closeout of wonderful *Feast for One* gourmet entrees. But the quantities were too small to cover the ad properly. Yet we were afraid that if we didn't put it in the *Fearless Flyer*, it wouldn't sell. Cowardice prevailed.

1958.
Pronto Market #1:
Pacific Palisades, California, the first Pronto Market!

1966.
The first Trader Joe's, just before it opened!

1973.
Joe and Bob Berning's daughter
Christina stomping juice from grapes
in Trader Joe's short-lived winery.

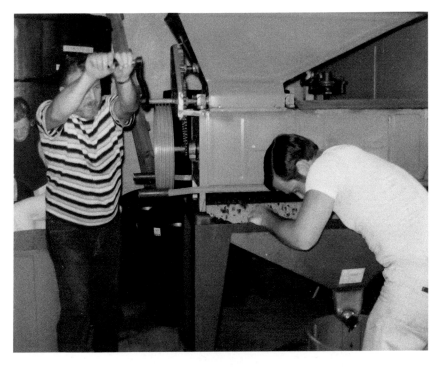

1973.
More wine-making!
Bob Berning (left) drops the grapes
from the hopper, while Leroy Watson
keeps everything flowing smoothly
into the barrels.

1975.
Joe poses with a wheel of
"Closed Eye Baby Swiss"
in the cheese aisle.

1975.
The zig-zag method of displaying wine bottles showed
more faces than flat rows and created more open space.
These displays, called "concave shelving," were made by hand
from 4' × 5' sheets of plywood with a large semicicle cut out by
store workers during their off-hours.

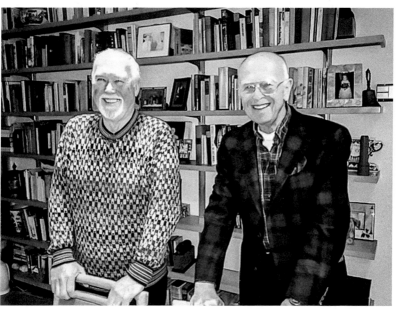

Lifelong friends and business buddies, Leroy Watson (left) and
Joe Coloumbe get together in 2013 to spin tales about the old days
of Trader Joe's and reminisce about their accomplishments.

1975.
Joe visits one of his stores.

2010.
Joe and his wife, Alice,
in their backyard.

2014.
Joe poses with a portrait he painted
of himself with his grandchild
napping peacefully on his lap.

I could continue this list but it depresses me.

## The Brooks Brothers Strategy

After an especially awful experience with the promotion of some branded frozen food in 1987, I began to lose my zest for that game. I took a survey of the 1,500 SKUs in the stores and realized that, excluding wines, about 80 percent of them were continuous in supply. They were mostly private labeled, including breads and Alta Dena dairy products.

They were differentiated by their qualities, yes, but from chocolate chip cookies to black tiger shrimp they were more or less continuous in supply. They could be replicated by our competitors, but our competitors either weren't aware of their volume potential (maple syrup) or were too engaged in other competitive battles to try to match us. Jarlsberg was a good example. The supermarkets knew perfectly well the sales potential of Jarlsberg if they matched our price, which they did once in a blue moon for a weekend, but they were too tied up in their own knots to follow us.

In November 1987, I outlined to the buyers where I thought we should go:

1. "We *want* continuous products. Any sane person does. The trick is to have continuous products which are profitable without creating a high-price image."

2. To create such products, they needed to be differentiated at least in order to avoid direct price comparison. Of course there was no price comparison for almond butter (it was our exclusive) except vs. peanut butter.

3. Products in which we had an absolute buying advantage. For example, we were the largest seller of cheap Bordeaux blanc in the United States.

4. I was willing to continue to indulge in the spectacular "closeout" sales of branded products, but I wanted to do so in the context of much greater overall sales, principally generated by continuous products, most of them private label. In other words, I wanted those branded promotions to be as big in absolute dollars but a smaller percentage of our sales.

Please remember, I was writing the preceding outline in the shadow of the October 1987 stock market crash. I was anticipating very tough times ahead, and those closeouts of branded products had helped us through the turbulent 1980s.

My shorthand for this strategy of developing more continuous, private label products was "Brooks Brothers." Brooks Brothers had created a chain that sold only its own products, and those products were a very good value.

Brooks Brothers began to slide in the 1970s. Part of this was a sea change in the way Americans dressed, a trend to the casual. In the context of Trader Joe's, it would be like our clientele massively shifting to junk food.

Also, however, I think a big part of the Brooks Bros. slide was that it lost its vision of quality in relation to price. As long as one holds on to that vision, I think that Brooks Brothers (the original Brooks Brothers) is a good metaphor for an exclusively Trader Joe label store, as long as you don't create private label just for the sake of private label. As long as "Brooks Brothers" doesn't copy *Jockey* shorts just to have shorts in the store.

# On the Other Hand . . .

There's a "treasure hunt" appeal in a closeout retailer, to borrow a term from Steven Read, co-owner of Canned Foods Grocery Outlets. We got the "treasure hunt" image right along with the closeout image starting with our great wine bargains in 1970. The closeouts of foods added real excitement to the stores, and customers liked them. They were rotten to administer, they cast a shadow on our overall reputation, but they sure did generate profitable sales. A Brooks Brothers store can be damn dull.

# 16

## Too, Too Solid Stores

O! that this too, too solid flesh would melt,
Thaw and resolve itself into a dew.

—*Hamlet*, Act I, Scene 2

**W**ould that could happen to stores! That's where the too, too solid flesh gets a bullet from a bandit. That's where the too, too solid flesh pulls its back out, or herniates its guts. That's where the too, too solid flesh gets turned on to cocaine and starts to steal because wages, no matter how high, after being taxed at something close to 50 percent by federal and state income taxes and social security, cannot possibly afford that habit. And when the flesh goes from mere solidity to outright tumescence, in June 1998, the Supreme Court issued a sexual harassment decision that would inspire me, as an employer, to put saltpeter in the stores' water supply. (But of course, this was merely a passing figment.)

It's easy to see the attraction of the internet for retailers, and there's nothing in that semantic definition of retailing back there in the Mac the Knife chapter that says you must have physical stores.

But, until *United Parcel Service* and *FedEx* make the next quantum leaps in delivery technologies, you gotta have stores, at least in the food business with its four different temperatures. All the Intensive Buying, all the private labels, all the discrete and indiscreet buys, all the virtual distribution: worthless. Until the goods are physically received and sold by the stores.

So how do you attempt to manage the problem? The keys to management are strong locations with good people.

## Leasing Locations

### How Many Stores?

With our heavy investment in leasehold improvements for electrical and plumbing, we had to sign long-term leases, usually fifteen years. Those leasing decisions are not reversible if something bad suddenly happens. It can be a change in street patterns or in the demographics of a trade area, or a change in the laws, which prevailed when you leased the store. Think of the liquor stores that existed only by virtue of Fair Trade.

**People often ask me, how many stores did we have at such-and-such a time? It's the wrong question to ask. What's important is dollar sales. For example, from 1980 to 1988, we increased the number of stores by 50 percent, but sales were up 340 percent.**

I believe in having enough stores so you're hedged against getting wiped out by a single fire or earthquake or flood control project (the Culver City Pronto Market fiasco in 1962). But my preference is to have a few stores, as far apart as possible, and to make them as high volume as possible.

With Mac the Knife we could draw people from twenty-five to fifty miles away. When we opened Ventura in 1983, 30 percent of our business came from Santa Barbara.

Sales per store, sales per square foot: those are the measures I look at. Trader Joe's sales were $1,000 per square foot of total area. The supermarket average is $570, but they use "sales area" not total area. And yes, there is a difference.

Beware of that "sales per square foot" calculation. "Sales area" excludes back room area, thereby shrinking the denominator and pumping up the "sales per square foot" figure. I can't justify not counting back rooms. If you don't need that back room, why did you lease it? Let's take *Stew Leonard's* in Connecticut, the highest volume supermarket in America. "Sales area" means nothing without that giant warehouse where they land those great buys because they have no distribution facilities anywhere else. And part of their "sales area" is a milk bottling line! Even in a normal store, it's hard to draw a sharp dichotomy between selling area and back room area.

Too many stores, too many irreversible leases, too much geographical saturation was a recurrent theme in the failure of American retail chains in the twentieth century. When I took charge of Thrifty Drug, I estimated that half of its 650 stores needed to be closed. It was the same story in 1991 when most of the department stores in California went bankrupt; or in 1974 with *W. T. Grant*, or in 1930 when Rexall itself went bankrupt as a result of unwise leases.

Retail square footage per capita in the United States had doubled in the twenty-eight years since we had started Mac the Knife in the mid-1970s. In 1998, retail square footage per capita kept climbing to new heights while the internet challenge was yet in its infancy. Put in the most hifalutin' terms, over-storing is a mis-allocation of society's resources; certainly it raised the hackles of Whole Earth Harry. We'll return to the question of store density a bit later on.

I want to brag about something here: in thirty years we never had a layoff of full-time employees. Seasonal swings in business were handled with overtime pay to full-time employees, and by adjusting part-time hours. The stability of full-time employment at Trader Joe's was due in part to caution in opening new stores, and insisting on high-volume stores.

### The Key: High-Volume Stores with Correct Leases

*Ancient Mariner Retailers* claim that "volume solves everything." If it's profitable volume, they're right. Things always go the most sour in the lowest-volume stores. It's like riding a bicycle: the faster it goes, the more stable it is.

The "normal distribution" of most chains is 20 percent dogs, 60 percent okay stores, and 20 percent winners. (At Thrifty Drug the distribution curve was wildly skewed: the top 5 percent of the stores generated 60 percent of the profit.) I believe in ruthlessly dumping the dogs at whatever cost. Why? Because their real cost is in management energy. You always spend more time trying to make the dogs acceptable than in raising the okay stores into winners. And it's in the dogs that you always have the most personnel problems.

# Under Mac the Knife
## Here's How We Leased Stores

### Location Criteria

1. I believe that the sine qua non for successful retailing is demographic coherence: all your locations should have the same demographics whether you are selling clothing or wine. We looked for our

demographics: there are lots of overeducated and underpaid people in Southern California. That's why most Trader Joe's were located near a major institution of learning: *Long Beach State*, UC San Diego, *UCLA*, and hospitals like The Huntington in Pasadena or *Long Beach Veterans'* and high tech corporate offices like *TRW* in Manhattan Beach, which probably has more PhDs than most colleges. The second most important group of customers were retirees (old folks are top consumers of liquor, candy, high fiber foods, and vitamins) so I paid special attention to retirement villages and trailer parks.

I won't go into the technical details of how I measured the potential of a given location; suffice it to say I was looking for our core clientele in sufficient numbers based on our experience in existing stores. The ideal was the trading area around the West Los Angeles store.

The last thing I wanted was a brand-new tract of $400,000 houses. Those people are the poorest of the poor, even though census data says they have high incomes. Sure they have high incomes—that's how they qualified for those monster mortgages! Strapped by the mortgages, saving for college for their kids, they should shop only at Costco and *Walmart*.

I liked semi-decayed neighborhoods, where the census tract income statistics looked terrible, but the mortgages were all paid-down, and the kids had left home. Housing and rental prices tend to be lower, and more suitable for those underpaid academics.

Related to this, I was more interested in the number of households in a given area than the number of people in a ZIP code. Trader Joe's is not a store for kids or big families. One or two adults was just fine.

Given the number of households, I would judge the degree of suitability based on my experience since 1954 in looking at California real estate, and then based on driving the area thoroughly. I would never trust a broker's judgment. If I saw lots of campers and speedboats in the driveways, I'd ax the location. People who consume high levels of fossil fuels don't fit the Trader Joe's profile.

Computerization has radically upgraded the statistics available; I'd probably do it more formally now. But there's no substitute for "driving" a location to ferret out the traffic problems. And do it at night, too. And either I or one of my colleagues would drive the location all over again just before we actually signed the lease.

Generally speaking, I would not look at any trading area with fewer than forty thousand households likely to contain "core" customers. So you might have sixty thousand residences but if only 66 percent were judged "core," I'd rank it at the threshold level of forty thousand. West Los Angeles had about ninety thousand "core" residences, I estimated.

I hardly need to mention that a trading area is rarely determined by a radius. It's determined by geographical barriers, boulevard access, and where the demographics lie.

Here's a sin I committed early in Pronto Market days. I put a store right between the towns of Fullerton and Placentia, in the city limits of Fullerton, but on Placentia Avenue. How do explain that location on the radio?

2. We wanted excellent boulevard access to large numbers of "our" people. Do you want freeway access? Sure, but here's a worry: holdups are most common in stores that are closest to freeway on-ramps, because it's easier to make a getaway.

3. Preferably, freestanding locations. Co-tenants get in the way of a powerhouse like Trader Joe's.

4. I was willing to pay extra for a loading dock. You'll recapture the extra rent in labor savings and workers' compensation premiums. But in many locations it simply isn't possible to get a dock.

### That's it? What about competition? Friends, Mac the Knife *has* no competition. That's why I called it Mac the Knife!

My years at Pronto Markets convinced me that where there is no competition today there will be tomorrow. Except for rare geography and even rarer honest city councils, you must assume that competitors will open all around you.

The answer is to design a store that has no competition. That's why Mac the Knife should not carry any SKU in which it is not outstanding. Management should remember that Captain MacHeath was finally brought down not by competition, but when he betrayed one woman too many. You can read that as: one customer too many, and you'll go back to reviewing every SKU in the store.

After 1978, I paid no heed to nearby supermarkets, liquor stores, health food stores, or anything else.

Well, then, you say, let's go back to the question of number of stores. How do you space them? Here are some parameters:

1. You need to have enough stores in a trading area to economically amortize the radio advertising. Since you don't do any newspaper advertising, you don't have to worry about that. Your print ads, the *Fearless Flyers*, come through the mail. Radio radii are big so you don't have to jam stores together.

2. You need enough stores in an area to have a large enough pool of employees. This was a real problem when we first opened in Northern California and caused us to bend the site selection rules a little in leasing Concord (which fortunately worked out okay though a little short of the forty-thousand-residences threshold).

3. My rule was that distance between stores should not be measured in miles but in driving time. I wanted no less than twenty minutes between stores. That pretty much avoided the dread word, cannibalization.

Could a given trading area support more Trader Joe's? Almost certainly! I figured we could break even at ten thousand core residences. But I wanted super-volume stores. If the credo that super-volume stores have the fewest operating problems is valid, then the overall health of the chain, in the long run, is maximized. (If the credo is invalid, of course . . .) For one thing, the spoilage of bread, cheese, and dairy products in super-volume stores is zilch. For another, you can afford to make more deliveries per week so out-of-stocks are reduced. And, given our policy of shipping merchandise in only full cases, inventory turnover is improved by having only high-volume stores.

Okay, then. How many trading areas should you enter? As long as you can preserve the culture of the company, and as long as logistics don't kill you, go ahead. In the case of Trader Joe's, we had a formidable problem in continuing the wine program if we crossed state lines, as I discussed in "Uncorked!"

## The Lease Terms

Never, never, *never* sign a lease with a "continuous operation" clause. That clause means you must stay open—you can't "go dark" and just pay the rent. When I got into Thrifty Drug's leases in 1992, I was horrified to discover that half of the leases had continuous operation clauses. *Cost Less Markets*, the nightmare I took over in 1994, had those suicidal clauses. After we sold it to the Kohlbergs, they simply closed those black holes and dared the landlords to sue! Some did.

The forty-page lease form itself was one of the most valuable assets I got from my years at Rexall, along with a leasing education from

Rexall's legal department during 1954–61. That lease form was, as they say, "tenant-oriented." I never would have dared to ask for things that Rexall took for granted. Yeah, we gave up a lot of them, but we wound up with more than if I had started without that form.

If you're a key tenant in a shopping center, like Thrifty or Cost Less, and your closure happens to coincide with a general failure of the shopping center, the landlord can enlarge the damage suit, alleging that you caused the co-tenants to fail.

The real job of lease negotiations, however, was "outsourced" to Leo Orsten, starting in 1963, even before we went into Trader Joe's. Leo, who had been an attorney in Czechoslovakia both before and after World War II, takes a unique, shrewd view of leases. His negotiating skills had been a major factor in the success of Trader Joe's. I never met with the principals, which was part of our negotiating tactics.

There's no way I can cover all the important terms of our leases. Because of our cash-rich position, we could be really generous about spending the money for leasehold improvements, and this took a lot of pressure off landlords who otherwise would not only have to raise the money but carefully monitor the expenditures. Virtually all of the locations we took were in existing buildings so this was an important negotiating point. Eighty percent of all the stores we leased were existing structures. (Whole Earth Harry smiles as fewer trees are chopped down.)

All the stores were at least marginally profitable, and only two were sold: the "geodesic dome" in Monterey Park (where I went off the intellectual rails in 1971, as was painfully described in the "Whole Earth Harry" chapter) and in Alhambra, where after fifteen years the demographics shifted radically against us.

## The Store People

To repeat the statement in "The Guns of August" chapter, the most important single business decision I ever made was to pay people well.

The quality of the people recruited, and retained, so dominates the way the stores were run that I might close the discussion here. But I'll flesh out those earlier statements a little.

## Compensation

The following specifics are out of date, but they are still pretty impressive:

1. In 1988, median family income in California was $32,000. The average full-time employee at Trader Joe's made $34,000, excluding any bonuses or overtime pay (that is, pay in excess of the basic forty-eight-hour week) or triple time for Thanksgiving. The range was $18,000 per year for the newest beginners (who had to be eligible for promotion within ninety days or they were out) to the $44,000 of the Captains.

2. The Captains had that salary plus a bonus that theoretically had no limit. The bonus was based on Trader Joe's overall profit, allocated among the stores based on each store's contribution. Sure, we massaged the numbers to avoid perceived unfairness, but that was basically the system. In 1988, several Captains made bonuses of more than 70 percent of their base pay. And our 15.4 percent retirement accrual applied to bonuses as well as base pay! I don't believe in bologna-slice bonuses. Unless a bonus system promises, and delivers, big rewards, it should be abandoned. I keep thinking about the *Mars Candy Co.*, which pays absolutely top salaries but no bonuses. Perform or you're out! That's much better than a bologna-bonus system that pays maybe 5 percent of base salary.

3. My ideal, often stated to everybody, was that Captains should have the chance to make more than executives in the office. In a traditional chain store, managers aspire to become bureaucrats with cushy, high-paying jobs in the office. I wanted to kill such aspirations at the start.

4. Part-timers. There is no such category except on the dumbed-down basis of hours worked. We had many part-timers who were graduate students, probably smarter than some of the full-timers. They were certainly more adept at getting the Macintosh systems installed. At a time when the minimum wage was $4.35, we often paid $13.00 per hour because these people were worth it. A distinction between full-time and part-time is a false dichotomy, when it comes to productivity.

In 1967, Dave Yoda, our Controller, and I innovated what has since become fairly common in the industry under the name "The Leave Bank": no distinction is made between sick leave and vacation time; and your Leave Bank account never expires just because you fail to take time off. I consider the Leave Bank as one of my innovations as great as Trader Joe's itself. Employees drag themselves to work, with a 102-degree temperature, because the less time they're sick, the more time they have for vacation! With a Leave Bank, there is no absenteeism! And it's denominated in dollars, not hours, so it's much more computer-friendly.

We instituted full health and dental insurance back in the 1960s when it was cheap. When I left, we were paying about $6,000 per employee per year! Why? If the employees are stressed by medical bills, they may steal. That's one good reason for Trader Joe's generous health and dental plans. On the other hand, we were cheap, cheap, cheap on life insurance. Nobody steals because of an inadequate life insurance program. Our insurance brokers did a brilliant job of meeting the special needs of Trader Joe's.

One of the most important employee benefits that I installed back there in 1963 was Income Continuation Insurance. It's one of the smartest things I ever did. It took the monkey off our back if an employee got sick for a protracted period of time.

Finally, as Trader Joe's became famous, the employees began earning something else: prestige. To be part of Trader Joe's brought them instant recognition from their friends and families.

# What Are They Doing Out There?

When we started Good Time Charley, I envisioned the Captains as super salesmen who would spend a lot of time outside the stores giving wine tastings, and a lot of time inside the store selling. This was a bad idea, and I dropped it as we moved into Whole Earth Harry.

By the time we got into Mac the Knife, we didn't want the employees to sell at all; all we wanted was to keep the store running. This laid-back attitude was part of the "culture" of Trader Joe's just like the radio commercials: no hard-sell. If you, the customer, want to know something, we'll try to tell you. *You* are best judge of what you want.

We did want to foster the climate of product knowledge. To this end, we sent every Captain and spouse to Europe to make a three-week grand tour of wine and cheese regions in Germany, Switzerland, and France. This was very expensive and very productive. They could take along their kids, too, if they paid the extras.

Sure, some of their meals were given to them by our vendors. But that was it. That applied to Bob Berning, Leroy Watson, and myself in our buying trips to Europe. Except under very unusual circumstances, we paid for our own lodging and most of our meals. We wanted every dollar of cost to be reflected in the product, not in the entertainment of ourselves. Yes, we did have some magnificent lunches. But this was in the context of the corporate culture of France: part of the compensation of those French salespeople was to lunch very, very well. You deprived them of their compensation if you insisted on pizza (which I did, while still green in the trade!).

How do you judge a Captain? It's simple. Good Captains don't have bad inventories. A bad inventory usually means employee theft. But this good, gross result is always the result of meticulous micro-care in running the store, especially in the indoctrination and training of part-timers.

Each full-timer was supposed to be able to perform every job in the store, including checking, balancing the books, ordering each department, stocking, opening, closing, going to the bank, etc. Everybody worked the check stands in the course of a day, including the Captain. Nobody got stuck there all day long, as it is part of "The Human Use of Human Beings" discussed in "The Last Five Year Plans" chapter.

The people in the stores were long-tenured, partly because most of our full-timers had risen from the ranks of the part-timers; and partly because of the slow growth of the number of stores, so there weren't scads of promotion opportunities. Was that a downer?

Well, at some point, a chain must stop expanding just for the sake of creating new positions. What a crazed objective of expansion that would be! All of the full-timers were so well paid and had such good working conditions that the attraction of promotion was not as great as in the typical chain where the only guy who makes money is the manager. Furthermore, the Trader Joe's non-management people made at least as much money as the managers of most non-food outlets!

As for those *skunks in the office* . . .

# 17

# Skunks in the Office

## Central Management

Here's how the office was organized: I was inspired by Tom Peters's story of *Lockheed's Skunkworks*. A *skunkworks* is a group of people brought together to work on a project. When the project is completed, you dissolve the group and transfer the individuals to other projects. I wanted to instill this feeling of transience, to keep the organization loose. God knows we have had to repeatedly shuffle people as we moved through the various stages from Pronto to Mac the Knife.

Central Management was divided into three parts: Skunkworks I, Buying (why use "purchasing"—it has an extra syllable); Skunkworks II, Sales, which included the stores and what is now called Human Resources; and Skunkworks III, Accounting. I had signs made with these titles to be hung in each department. Over my door was the sign "Chief Skunk."

To further the transient mentality, all the titles were based on projects. The principal buyers like Bob Berning were Senior Project Directors, as were the regional supervisors; the next rung down was Project Director, etc. After all, these people were being moved among jobs and even among Skunkworks all the time. Those titles indicated a range of pay, a rather narrow range. There wasn't much difference between what Gene Pemberton and Bob Berning were paid.

The top thirteen people were in the Central Management Bonus Pool. They voted each year how it would be divided among themselves and they usually voted to split the pool evenly, so Leroy got the same bonus as Doug Rauch or our Controller, Mary Genest. Like the Captains' bonus pool, the bonus pool was determined by profit before taxes, and after the Captain's bonus had been paid. It was rich, typically 40 percent of a Senior Project Director's salary. As I recall in 1988, the typical salary and bonus came to $120,000.

# Skunkworks I:

## Buying

We have sufficiently discussed Skunkworks I: Buying. It takes so much of this book because that's what really put Mac the Knife over the top. The three principal Senior Project Directors in the last years were Bob Berning, Doug Rauch, and Bob Johnson. They reported on paper to Leroy. But I interfered directly with them hourly. John Shields, when he arrived in 1977, said I was the de facto General Merchandise Manager. Leroy also was in charge of the Virtual Distribution System.

# Skunkworks II:

## Sales

With all that pay and all that tenure, we had very competent Captains when it came to running things. Sure, you needed supervisors to install new computers, but the most serious store issues were human, the problems of too, too solid flesh.

The principal job of the field supervisors, what we called the regionals, was to be field psychiatrists, analogous to field surgeons— and those operating rooms can get pretty bloody. And nobody can handle the human problems of more than ten stores and remain sane. That's what really drives the issue of "span of control."

As part of field psychiatry, the Regional Project Directors conducted those six-month interviews I described in the "Guns of August" chapter. They hated the job but knew how vital it was.

The man who logged more years as a "M.A.S.H." psychiatrist for more stores was Gene Pemberton. He came to me in 1958 saying he wanted to graduate from a *Royal Crown Cola* route to Pronto Markets. He was eighteen and newly married. He spent his first years with us debating whether to stay or quit to pursue a career as a professional softball pitcher. After Gene had spent years as a manager, I relieved Leroy of store supervision duties and turned them over to Gene and the late Frank Kono, whom I will eulogize in the chapter "Goodbye to All That." They both reported directly to me. So there was only one organizational "layer" between me and the Captains.

Frank and Gene had assistants, battle-hardened managers like John Epp, Russ Penfold, and Steve Haro, graduates of the Frank Kono School of Management. And Robin Guentert who, after a spell in the office, was shipped off to organize Northern California.

The person keeping all this running was Rosella Moore, who worked with all the Regional Project Directors. She was the real heart of field supervision, the Keeper of Secrets.

Dave Hetzel, who was in charge of fixtures, maintenance, and utilities, worked for Frank and Gene. The equipment wears out from the sheer traffic and tonnage, the compressors blow up, the power fails, the floor drains back up, the roofs leak, etc.

As part of store administration, starting with Pronto Markets, we had two employee parties a year, one in the summer and one at Christmas. Because the stores were always open, each party ran two nights so everybody had a chance to come. The parties were always held in our house until crime raised its head (see the "Supply Side Retailing" chapter) and the company got too big for our house and we moved the venue to various places like the *Hollywood Bowl*, the 1984 World Cup soccer games, and various restaurants.

I found these parties great sources of information from the people in the stores and a wonderful way to pull everybody together. People who had worked together, but now were in different stores, people who were now in the office, and so forth. Those parties helped knit the occasional un(?)raveled sleeve back together. Encouraging social gatherings is often an essential ingredient in maintaining good—great—morale.

# Skunkworks III:

## Accounting

These people had two terrible jobs: running the accounting system for the Intensive Buyer and Virtual Distribution Systems, as I've described, and balancing the inventories taken in the stores. Most of this burden fell on Mary Genest, especially after we made Dave Yoda Treasurer, where he concentrated on the increasingly massive retirement accounts, insurance policies, and lease administration.

I want to give special credit to the people who created Trader Joe's cost accounting system as we got deeper and deeper into Intensive Buying. We had plunged into the *Twilight Zone* of vertical integration without any accounting-system forethought. For example, Whole Earth Harry got us into buying bags of nuts and then contracting for them to be repackaged into consumer sizes. This requires bags, labels, and cartons for the repacks. Later we bought frozen shrimp in bulk and had them repackaged. If you get conversion factors wrong, it can play hell with your bookkeeping. We bought blocks and wheels of cheeses. While nominally forty pounds apiece, they actually vary quite a bit.

Diane Tennis was the first to face up to these complex problems. The system, however, was really forced into functionality by Mary Genest, our head of Accounting whom I promoted to Controller in 1987. Mary was strongly supported by our auditor from *Peat Marwick*, Sandra Bane. Sandy is a brilliant woman who was Trader Joe's auditor from the early 1980s until 1998 when she had to give up the account. Reason: her husband, Dan Bane, who had been CFO of *Certified Grocers*, was hired as President of Trader Joe's West. (As of this writing, Dan Bane is the President of Trader Joe's.) If these people hadn't created a workable accounting system, the supply-side constraints would have severely compromised our demand-side appeal of outstanding prices, because our costs would have been out of control.

The store inventories, however, were the most critical control in the company. Taken on the Retail Accounting System (one reason Thrifty could never be brought under control was that it lacked such a system) and taken every three months, they told us whether theft might be occurring in a store. They had to be reconciled as quickly as possible. The Coronas and then the Macintoshes were a quantum advance here.

One of the great advantages of getting rid of all direct store deliveries was that everything could be shipped to the stores at its retail value. Cost didn't appear on the receiving documents. This tremendously increased our control of the enterprise and reduced "phantom" losses due not to theft but to paperwork.

Believe me, the highest repetitive drama in the chain was reading those inventory results and then deciding whether to go in over the horns and "correct" shrinkage. In any event, we got shrinkage down to 0.6 percent of sales and held it there.

## Sell the Mail Room

Six months after I left Trader Joe's, Peter Drucker wrote a seminal piece in the July 25, 1989, *Wall Street Journal* called "Sell the Mail Room." Every executive should take it to heart. It described what we had been doing since we shifted to the Mac the Knife mode in 1977: getting rid of all functions except those of buying and selling. We got rid of our own maintenance people, we sold off almost all the real estate we had acquired during the 1970s, we never took mainframe computing in-house, etc. We tried to stay out of all functions that were not central to our primary job in society: namely, buying and selling merchandise.

> Some choice quotes from Dr. Drucker:

> In-house service activities have little incentive to improve their productivity. . . . The productivity is not likely to ramp up until it is possible to be promoted for doing a good job at it. And that will happen in support work only when such work is done by separate, free-standing enterprises.

Corollary to this is that the size of central management at Trader Joe's was reduced, making the enterprise easier to manage.

## Double Entry Retailing

At this point I'm going to break stride and enter into a discussion of operating decisions and policies (a policy is a "standing decision," as I was taught at Stanford) in the context of retailing and especially Trader Joe's. There's a short introductory chapter, "Double Entry Retailing," and two long ones on the demand side and the supply side.

# 18

## Double Entry Retailing

Tyger, Tyger burning bright,
In the forests of the night,
What immortal hand or eye
Dare frame thy fearful symmetry!

—William Blake

The game only runs out when you run out of money.

—Robert Amman, President of Western Union,
quoted in the *Wall Street Journal*, October 13, 1989

Shortly before Christopher Columbus sailed to the New World, another stay-at-home Italian, namely Fra Luca Pacioli, revolutionized the concept of business by inventing the system of double entry accounting. This system was later adopted and perfected by the Medici Bank, the largest in western Europe during its heyday.

The principle of double entry is that, on the left-hand side of the ledger, you show the assets of the business: cash, accounts receivable, inventory, machinery, real estate, etc. On the right-hand side you show the financial claims on those assets: the claims of suppliers (accounts payable); the claims of the governments (taxes due); the claims of the banks; the claims of bondholders; and finally the claims of the owners, the stockholders. Double entry accounting was one of the great intellectual advances of mankind (and has been the source of five hundred years of obscene jokes).

In 1966, while I was still trying to conceptualize the Good Time Charley version of Trader Joe's, I had to prepare a lecture for Stanford Business School. In trying to figure out how to explain to the students the problems I was wrestling with, I hit on the idea of using double entry accounting as an analogy, what I call Double Entry Retailing.

On the left side of the ledger is the business in terms of how its customers see it: I call this the Demand Side. On the right side of the ledger are the factors that limit or determine the retailer's ability to satisfy those demands: the Supply Side. I developed this analysis further for lectures given at Australian grocery conventions in 1972 and 1975; it was invaluable in helping me keep my head through all the changes at Trader Joe's.

All businesses, whether manufacturing, wholesaling, services, etc., have William Blake's fearful symmetry of both Demand and Supply sides. And all businesses are subject to the ultimate supply-side constraint of cash cited by Amman: you can do anything, no matter how stupid, within that fearful symmetry, as long as you don't run out of cash.

From my view, the Demand Side of Retailers can be analyzed in terms of five variables:

1. The **assortment** of merchandise offered for sale.

2. **Pricing:** stability (weekend ads?), and relative to competition.

3. **Convenience:** geographical, in-store, and time.

4. **Credit:** the accepted methods of payment.

5. **Showmanship:** the sum of all activities that result in making contact with the customer, from advertising to store architecture to employee cleanliness.

Here are factors on the Supply Side:

1. Merchandise Vendors

2. Employees

3. The way you do things: "habits" and "culture"

4. Systems

5. Non-merchandise vendors

6. Landlords

7. Governments

8. Bankers and investment bankers

9. Stockholders

10. Crime

As in double entry accounting, the change in any factor must be matched by a corresponding change in another factor.

For example, a decision to increase geographical convenience (Demand Side) obviously involves some change of policy with land-lords (Supply Side) including the amount of rent you're willing to pay. Consider how *Barney's* paid through the nose because they thought they had to offer the geographical convenience of being in Beverly Hills. How big a factor was this in Barney's subsequent bankruptcy? Was it Demand Side success at the price of Supply Side failure?

As for that Supply Side player, the government: in California, you can't sell alcohol from 2:00 a.m. to 6:00 a.m. So, a twenty-four-hour liquor store, which might make sense from the Demand Side (hours, convenience), doesn't make sense because of the Supply Side: they'll put you in the slammer if you sell liquor twenty-four hours a day.

The lists above aren't much different from other businesses. What distinguishes retailing is the asymmetry of the fearful symmetry: the huge number of customers (Demand Side) vs. the number of suppliers. This is the exact opposite of a government defense contractor.

This lopsided butterfly may cause a retailer to act as if the only people they have to "sell" are customers: the Demand Side. That's a major mistake. All the people on the Supply Side have to be sold, too.

The next two chapters, "Demand Side Retailing" and "Supply Side Retailing," try to expand the double entry approach. It's sort of like watching a tennis match, except that you have to move your head not only side to side but up and down, because some of the most important decisions are made intra–Demand Side or intra–Supply Side. The most critical decision we made in Mac the Knife was the intra–Demand Side decision to forgo breadth of assortment for outstanding prices.

You may get a stiff neck from reading the next two chapters, but you'll also get a sense of what it is like to run a business day in, day out, as I did for thirty years.

# 19

## Demand Side Retailing

As well ask whether the metric system is true and the avoirdupois system is false; whether Cartesian co-ordinates are true and polar coordinates are false. One geometry cannot be more true than another; it can only be more convenient. Geometry is not true, it is advantageous.

–Robert Pirsig, *Zen and the Art of Motorcycle Maintenance*

I hope you will take this "geometry" of demand-side retailing in this light: advantageous but not always necessarily true.

## Assortment

Some of the obvious promises made by retailers to customers about assortment include:

### Biggest or Most Complete Variety in Town

That's where we were with liquor (seventy brands of bourbon) in Good Time Charley. That's definitely not where Mac the Knife is.

Indeed, one of the biggest operational issues for limited-SKU retailers like Trader Joe's is: What SKUs do you drop to make room for new ones? Mostly we did it on the basis of dollar value of sales. We made no effort to have a complete assortment, which was one of the hardest concepts to put across to the troops. No sugar, salt, flour, *Mrs. Penny's White Sauce*, etc., unless we could be outstanding in it, and make a sufficient number of dollars from it. For example, we tried selling some excellent whole wheat flour at a great price, but the stuff has such a low value per cubic inch it could not justify the space it took in the store.

The real limit on what range of products we could carry was our product knowledge. I believe that the greatest advantage of a limited-SKU retailer is that the employees at all levels can become truly knowledgeable about what they sell—a Supply Side factor.

There are some product categories, however, in which it was impossible to become *outstanding* (the fundamental commitment of Mac the Knife): soft drinks, beer, and cigarettes. All are products that are available in infinite supply.

As will be discussed under Supply Side Retailing, Coke, Budweiser, et al., refused to deliver to our warehouses. That violated my policy of no direct-store deliveries. It's just as well: there is no way to make money selling Bud and Coke, even if they did permit warehouse shipments, if you want to be outstanding. We kept them in the stores at the insistence of our managers, at not-outstanding prices, until finally I was able to sell the troops that we no longer needed them. And worse, they were damaging our overall price image. We dropped them in 1985.

That same day, one of the most satisfying of my life, I dropped cigarettes. I didn't want to be outstanding in cigarettes. The only way you can do that is to bomb the price, and when you do that on a product that is available in infinite supply, there's no bottom to that game. That violated my principle that each SKU should be profitable. Secondly, well, how would you like to go home at night and brag that you sold a thousand cases of cigarettes that day? Whole Earth Harry smiled at this discontinuation.

Our dropping cigarettes raised a furor. I was interviewed on the TV news channels, etc. But it had a very positive response from the public, even from smokers.

> We got a bonus from dropping cigarettes: burglaries of the stores stopped cold. Most burglars enter and exit through the roof, because they have to boost the booty back up the way they came. Cigarettes, with the highest value per pound, are the target of choice.

Sometimes you can be outstanding for what you don't sell. We were one of the first to drop *Zig Zag* papers once it became apparent they were no longer being sold to roll tobacco. I was also happy to get out of the girlie magazine business. This had been one of the major props in getting Good Time Charley into orbit, but I had repeated controversies with PTAs who wanted me to censor the assortment of magazines we carried. I don't like censorship, but there was no way for me to determine the difference between *Playboy* and Helen Gurley Brown's *Cosmopolitan*.

Finally, I got a letter from a priest, a polite letter. He said that he bought all of his wine from us, but he didn't like having to look at the magazine covers (*Cosmopolitans*?) while he stood in line. That did it, so we dropped magazines altogether, which also have some rotten Supply Side features, which I don't care to describe here.

One of the hardest things to drop was the assortment of California boutique wines. We hung on to about 250 of them until my last year at Trader Joe's in 1988. My problem wasn't so much with the customers as with our employees, most of whom had now logged twenty years as premier retailers of these wines. They felt the loss of many long-term relationships with the old wineries, and they felt the removal of a group of products for which they held a comfortable knowledge base. It was, therefore, primarily a Supply Side issue of employee morale and was handled as such.

## Exclusively at Our Stores

In Good Time Charley we strove to be the exclusive retailers of certain (fair-traded) California boutique items. This proved to be a fool's errand, since the exclusives were honored in the breach, and I was glad to get out of that rat race as soon as Fair Trade ended.

## First or Newest in Town

We repeatedly promoted the first-of-season pistachios, dried fruits, etc. But what really drove sales on these products was our prices. For example, anyone who buys Beaujolais Nouveau in November should know something: the wine is flown in at vast expense. Trader Joe's always waited until the oceangoing containers arrived in January, then sold Nouveau at one-third the price of the November arrivals.

Fashion, at least in apparel, can be an appeal that falls in "first or newest," but this is too superficial a reading of Trader Joe's assortment. *Fashion* derives from the Latin *facere*, "to make," and implies something of only outward substance without real foundations (except, possibly, foundation garments). Granted, wines, especially expensive wines, are trendy; health foods, too. But we caught those waves well before their peaks and stuck with them through their successive ups and downs. Our promoting them stemmed from our genuine belief in them.

In the case of wines, the growing volume of medical evidence has justified our faith in wines but it didn't explain it. We never sold it as medicine, but as a component of quality of life. It was satisfying to see Americans switch massively from white wines to red wines as a result of the 1991 CBS *60 Minutes* show on the French paradox (red wine sales went up 150 percent). But in my opinion, they switched for a misplaced, medical reason instead of the aesthetic ability of red wines to enrich most foods, starting with fish and chicken.

What so many would-be competitors didn't understand is that Trader Joe's was never a store of far-out "gourmet" foods, but a store of basics: oils, breads, cheeses, coffees, canned fish, nuts, jams, chocolate. Sure, within these basic categories some trends come and go. For example, safflower and sunflower oils are no longer favored because, apparently, they lower high-density lipoproteins. Olive oil, canola oil, and grapeseed oil are "in." But these shifts are grounded in medical research, not rootless "fashion."

*Fashion* derives from the Latin *facere,* "to make," and implies something of only outward substance without real foundations (except, possibly, foundation garments).

Rather, I challenged our buyers to find a certain number of additional basic products each year that would sell so well they would force us to drop other products. Out of the 1,500 SKUs, there was no requirement that, say, 400 be wines or 100 be bakery products, or 75 be cheeses. There were no allocations of SKU-counts by category. If various kinds of apple juice would take all the space in the store, so be it, especially if each of those apple juice SKUs outsold the products they displaced. At least that's what I alleged to the troops, knowing I was in no danger of getting an all–apple juice inventory. The only allocation was that which was forced by refrigeration: We had a limited amount of cubic feet of refrigerated and frozen. We had to keep them filled.

After I left Trader Joe's in 1989, cheeses fell out of favor with the public because of their high fat content. Dollar sales fell, and Trader Joe's appropriately cut back the cheese assortment. Those cubic feet of refrigerated space are now filled with many other refrigerated products, which, in turn, had to justify their continued presence.

Since I left Trader Joe's, the buyers have done an outstanding job in following major developments in vitamins (like saw palmetto, gingko biloba) and substitute milks, like rice milk, soy milk, and coconut milk, the latter a reflection of the growing Asian influence in our culture, but hardly "fashion."

## Physical Condition of the Product

Some other retailers promote "Coldest beer in town," "Rail-hung aged beef, no cryovac," and "Photographic film—kept refrigerated." We couldn't make any legitimate claims except one: our high sales of cheeses, vitamins, nuts, and dried fruits *automatically made our products fresher* than our low-turnover competitors.

One of the criticisms most often leveled at Trader Joe's is that our wine displays were not temperature-controlled. We admitted it. It's a question of trade-offs: most people went for our prices. (Supply Side constraints here included the cost of special air-conditioning, separating the wine department physically, which can create shoplifting problems, etc.)

Freshness has a powerful appeal. When Whole Earth Harry introduced orange juice that was squeezed on the premises, it was a great Demand Side success. But it was also a total nightmare to administer because of the Supply Side issues of fresh orange juice, which include: the great variation in sweetness of oranges over the course of a year (Valencias are great but are available only four months; navel juice goes bitter after twenty-four hours, etc.); how do you keep the employees from setting the machines to squeeze too much (thereby raising "yield" per case of oranges) so the bitter rind oils get in the juice; and what the hell do you do with all the leftover rinds? Still, we struggled with it for twelve years and dropped it only because it helped us take over the distribution of milk. The day we announced no more squeezed orange juice, the Captains cheered.

Another "freshness" project that we struggled with for years was making sandwiches. Once we had installed the cheese shops in the stores, we had all the equipment and health department clearances needed to make sandwiches. But we never could master the art. Basically the problem was that we could not be outstanding in this field and we finally gave up.

The only "on-site manufacturing," as I called it, that we kept was cutting cheese on the premises and, when the equipment was idle, bagging nuts and dried fruits on the premises. Like orange juice, this had tremendous Demand Side appeal, especially when we sampled cheese fresh from the cutting board. Also, I liked the "theater" created by these on-site activities.

About three years after I left, my successors folded on-site cheese cutting. I regret it, but I understand why. The cheese departments were overwhelmed by a Supply Side factor: personnel. None of the men wanted to work in the cheese shops. The Captains, whether men or women, felt it was an inappropriate use of their time except for the really top-notch Captains. This left it to the "cheese girls." The cheese departments were creating a caste system within the stores! This problem was building as I left Trader Joe's; I can understand why they no longer cut cheese on the premises.

## Retailer Screening of Product

"Laboratory tested for . . ." Well, God knows we built the business on blind tastings of foods and wines, which were amply reported in the *Fearless Flyer* and, I guess, honored by our customers. We did, in fact, submit samples of products to independent laboratories to verify manufacturer claims, but we rarely published the results.

## Positive Negatives

"We sell no products with MSG, or animal-tested, etc." This is a very big factor in the health food business, and we resorted to it daily.

## "Always in Stock" or Rain-Check Promises

*Ha!* We made a point of going out of stock to encourage the customers to "buy while it's still there." A group of wine customers would show up in a van, buy a bottle of each wine that looked interesting, sample them in the van, and go back in the store and buy cases of the ones they liked. This happened all the time.

# Measuring Assortment

Retailers seem to be falling into two distinct SKU modes: those with under 4,000–5,000 SKUs and those with over 25,000 SKUs.

In the low-SKU class we find Costco. Stew Leonard's in Connecticut, the highest-volume supermarket in the U.S., carries only 850 SKUs. In the high-SKU class, we find all supermarkets, chain drugstores, Walmart, etc. Curiously, the "Over 25,000" retailers rarely assert the superiority of their assortment in any department.

The SKU dichotomy is echoed by another division among retailers: those who feel they must carry certain brands and types of products (most chains), and those who feel they don't have to carry any particular brand or type of product (Costco, Stew Leonard's, Trader Joe's), unless it provides value for the customer, and is profitable for the retailer.

In general, Trader Joe's has stayed in the mostly edible assortment of Mac the Knife with the notable addition of fresh fruits and vegetables. We struggled with produce for all thirty years I was at Pronto and Trader Joe's and could never make it work. The new plastic films and gas-flushing technologies developed in the 1990s, however, have put

Trader Joe's into produce for the first time. Today, more than half of all the lettuce sold in supermarkets in California is the precut kind in sealed plastic bags. My wife calls it "the housewife's revenge."

# Pricing

1. **Stability of price levels within the store.** There is a dichotomy between conventional retailers who cut prices and advertise for a limited period of time (usually weekends) and the one-price retailers like Costco and Trader Joe's. Department stores, supermarkets, and chain drugstores have become totally committed to the first mode. "We never change our prices" is one of the foundations of Trader Joe's success. No shell games.

2. **Price levels vs. competition.** "Price comparison advertising" is at an all-time high. Many retailers, especially in electronics, offer to meet or beat competitors' prices. Such a policy seems intellectually feeble to me. You should price a product where you think it should be in terms of the market and stick with it. *We never cut a price to meet a competitor.* If we had done our job of Intensive Buying correctly, and a competitor undercut us, that was their decision.

We never had "closeout" sales. What a terrible practice! You train your customers to wait for the "sale." Any product that failed to sell was given to charity. We were developing new products all the time; sometimes they didn't pan out. So we gave them away.

I do not believe in "market testing" new products. Each year, 22,000 new products are introduced to the grocery trade, most of them from big guns like Procter & Gamble or Colgate, who have conducted elaborate test marketing before going nationwide. Ninety percent of these new products fail. Our approach was to run an experimental batch: If it sold, we ordered more. If it didn't, charity got it.

Another practice I avoided was "day-old bread." We gave all out-of-code bakery products to charities. Each manager lined up a church or a Salvation Army or Food Bank, which, each day, received the out-of-code product.

3. **Coupons.** Doubling the value of manufacturers' coupons has become an important form of price competition at supermarkets, drug chains, etc. As we moved away from branded products, coupons had no relevance to Trader Joe's.

As for how we set our prices at Trader Joe's, please see the Intensive Buying chapter.

4. **Senior discounts.** Giving discounts to people over sixty is, to borrow a phrase from Charlie Munger, "a type of dementia I can't even classify." Here you have the fastest-growing, most affluent part of the population, and you give them a discount? If anyone should get a discount, it's the shrinking workforce, which subsidizes the old folks through their income and social security taxes. Now that I'm over sixty-five, I eagerly take advantage of all such discounts: I know, Charles Darwin smiles every time.

## Convenience

### Geographical Convenience

In general, all of the U.S. is overpopulated with all kinds of stores. Population per supermarket stabilized in Southern California in the late 1980s (at about ten thousand per store). Population per department store stabilized during the early 2000s. As a result, geographical convenience, making your stores accessible to the public, is not a serious issue for most chains. Only newer chains with new, apparently successful formulas, like Costco or pet supply warehouses, still have this issue.

Trader Joe's has yet to hit this barrier. I used to get at least one call a week from different communities begging to get a Trader Joe's.

Home delivery, of course, is the ultimate form of geographical convenience, and the internet is radically exploiting this opportunity. Down deep it's just mail-order retailing. I don't think that the internet grocery store will successfully invade food retailing because you're dealing with four different temperatures: dry grocery, refrigerated products, frozen products, and ice cream when you try to home-deliver foods. Significant advances will have to be created in order to solve this problem. It will impact, however, non-foods sold by supermarkets. Consider how the greeting card industry has been impacted, because users can design and send them over the internet. Shoes and clothing can both be returned easily. But food, not so easily.

The competition between "fixed site" retailers and virtual retailers is coming to a showdown. One of the first legal showdowns will come over state laws that prohibit internet sales of wines across state borders. Sooner or later, I think this will be struck down. If Fair Trade violated the Interstate Commerce clause, the wine barriers do so in spades.

The whole issue of state-level sales taxes vs. buying by mail order or over the internet is in the process of being resolved, but we may see more state-level income taxes to take the place of lost sales tax revenues. Amazon.com is located in Washington, a no-sales-tax state. Avoiding sales tax at least compensates for the delivery charges. The internet is a direct attack on what I call the "tyranny of geography." Encryption, anyone?

In general, geographical convenience is no longer a way to differentiate yourself from your competitors, with the notable exception of stores located in the euphemistically named inner cities, where few chains operate.

### In-Store Convenience

The trend toward sixty-thousand-square-foot supers results in less convenient stores, in terms of in-and-out speed. Many chains have countered with promises to keep express lane check stands open, promises mostly honored in the breach. And all chains have gone to scanning, which speeds up the check stand, unless the electronic "deck" has failed to include the price of a SKU in which case all the wheels stop.

These "super" supermarkets do increase overall convenience for the customer through the "Assortment" appeal discussed above, most notably with the addition of pharmacies, because the customer has to visit fewer stores. With the growing population of retired Americans who have lots of time, however, I question this concept; it simply goes against one of the two most fundamental demographic trends in America, the other being Hispanification.

**When you deliver value, you don't have to worry about in-store convenience.**

At Trader Joe's we never worried about in-store convenience. The check stands are still not flow-through: I think that seeing a row of check stands when one enters a supermarket is about as attractive as seeing a row of urinals.

## Time Convenience

In 1958, when I started Pronto (7:00 a.m. to 11:00 p.m. seven days a week, 365 days per year), most supermarkets closed at 9:00 p.m. weeknights, and 7:00 p.m. on Sundays. And they were closed during all seven triple-time union holidays including Thanksgiving and Christmas. That was part of the core opportunity for "bantam" markets as I presented it to Rexall. By the time I bought out Rexall in 1962, however, the retailing depression that started in 1960 caused scads of chains to go bankrupt, and caused the remaining supermarkets to match our hours, except for the union triple-time holidays. And then the supers started opening on those days, too, by 1975. Now most supers are open twenty-four hours a day, seven days a week.

We stayed open every Christmas Day until 1980. We finally gave it up because Christmas Day proved to be a lousy wine day: we had stayed open in order to move inventory, that is, convert it into cash, even though we paid our employees the equivalent of triple time.

We continued to stay open—limited hours—on Thanksgiving Day, because it's a much bigger wine day than Christmas (which is, appallingly, a very good hard liquor day). All members of Central Management, including myself, worked in the stores those days as a matter of morale for the troops.

I have mentioned my friend James Caillouette frequently in this book. We got to be friends because we were the only two men in our circle who worked every Thanksgiving and Christmas: the grocer and the obstetrician. So our families have had their holiday dinners at night on those holidays, a tradition that began in 1966.

Today it is impossible for a retailer to achieve differentiation through long hours. Again, we're seeing a dichotomy between conventional retailers, who now operate extreme hours, and retailers like Costco and Trader Joe's, with very limited hours. Value retailers don't have to have long hours! After I left Trader Joe's, they closed on Thanksgiving, too. It was a correct move, long overdue.

# Credit, or Accepted Methods
# of Payment

As discussed earlier, Trader Joe's was one of the first grocers to accept Visa and Master Charge; now it's commonplace. It's interesting to see department store chains pushing their own charge accounts, just like in the 1930s; it was also interesting to see Sears take a big write-off in 1998 from the same practice.

Food stamps were an important alternative method of payment in markets; I dropped them early in Mac the Knife, partly because so many customers objected to seeing food stamps cashed in at Trader Joe's for "luxury" products. There was never a murmur about our dropping food stamps. (This was twenty years before the SNAP program replaced food stamps with debit cards, and Trader Joe's does accept SNAP now.)

I was very proud of the four years I served on the Advisory Board of Canned Foods Grocery Outlets, a hundred-store closeout chain that delivered great nutritional value to food stampers. And while I was consulting for Thrifty Drug Stores, I tried hard to persuade them to apply for food stamps for the two hundred stores that were in low-income neighborhoods. Do you know one reason why they wouldn't? Because the managers of those stores didn't want the social stigma associated with being a "food stamp" store. Tragic! A Supply Side choke point similar to the "cheese girls."

I also tried to get Thrifty to get their managers to stop wearing those miserable neckties. For one thing, they are a workplace hazard: they can get caught in store equipment like balers. But the managers wanted the neckties—a badge of distinction. Pitiful.

# Showmanship

This is the sum total of all efforts to make contact with the customer. It's the most ephemeral, the most difficult, and the most important of the Demand Side activities.

## Employees

Perhaps the most important element of showmanship, the efficacy of employees (vis-a-vis customers), has been deeply compromised by the twenty-four-hour operations noted above under "Convenience." As a supervisor of one twenty-four-hour supermarket chain once told me, "I don't want to know what goes on in the stores after midnight!"

"Efficacy" can be defined different ways. Since few employees like to work midnight shifts, the wheat inevitably migrates to the day shifts; the chaff to the late-hour shifts. One of the smartest things we ever did was to cut the hours of Trader Joe's. This is mostly a Supply Side question, but the quality and attitude of the employees handling your customers is a Demand Side factor.

"Efficacy" can also be defined as product knowledge. I believe that the decline of the department stores commenced in the late 1960s when they began opening on Sundays and later at night. Before then, there were a lot of knowledgeable people on the sales floor, whether in appliances or wedding registry.

Nordstrom's practice of letting a single employee sell from every department in the store to a customer was, in my opinion, a breakthrough in department store retailing. This is a definite Demand Side appeal, but, like Trader Joe's, it demands high-quality people, a quality that its competitors are too cheap to hire. Is this Demand Side or Supply Side? It's some of both.

The physical appearance of the employee is critical: clean fingernails, tidy hair, etc. Employers are usually the worst offenders here. They put all the employees into uniforms of the same color. They might as well cram all their feet into one shoe size.

## Uniforms

Since Trader Joe's furnishes the Hawaiian shirts to its employees, we had to start buying them not only in four sizes but in four shades to match the seasons. It's a pain but one of the subtle things that makes Trader Joe's what it is.

## Advertising

I've already devoted a chapter to Trader Joe's advertising. Advertising is a critical component of showmanship.

## Merchandising

**Advertising moves the people to the product;
merchandising is what moves the product to the people.**

–Charles Luckman

Mr. Luckman, the man who saved Pepsodent in 1930 by going on network radio with *Amos 'n' Andy*, is an authority to whom I paid a lot of attention, even though he had been known more as an architect than a merchant for at least fifty years.

At Trader Joe's, after Good Time Charley was laid to rest in 1971, we didn't pay any attention to merchandising. The store layout is driven primarily by shoplifting concerns and physical stocking concerns. All the research on whether people turn to the left or the right, or whether you can "force" people to the rear of the store, is irrelevant if you're a value retailer.

Fixturization, of course, is closely linked to merchandising: I wanted as few fixtures as possible. The flexibility of display in value retailers like Stew Leonard's or Costco, flexibility made possible by a paucity of fixtures, stands in startling contrast to the rigidity of most mass merchants. Like Costco, Trader Joe's uses warehouse shelving. It's cheap, it's pretty good seismically (no cantilevered shelves), and it's inexpensive to change. Our own employees could assemble and disassemble the fixtures easily. This is not true of the fixtures you see in most supermarkets.

---

**To thine own self be true.**

–William Shakespeare, *Hamlet*, Act I, Scene III

**Form follows function.**

–Frank Lloyd Wright

---

My feeling about fixtures is that they are fixed in expense, an invitation to bankruptcy, and fixed physically; sooner or later they get in your way and have to be replaced before you've fully depreciated them. I have been unconvinced of the selling power of fixtures, per se, since the failure of some elaborate "gourmet" markets in the 1960s.

Fixtures certainly can identify the nature of a retailer. Stores can be divided into two classes: those stores in which the first thing you see is merchandise (department stores, boutiques), and those stores in which the first thing you see is check stands. Many customer preconceptions flow from this simple dichotomy.

What's really hard to find is good signage on products. I failed to get really good, informative signs in Trader Joe's. As of 1998, my in-store signage heroes are *Crate 'n Barrel* and *Brookstone*.

## Architecture, Signs, and Lighting

*McDonald's* Golden Arches are a great example of showmanship through architecture, even though most cities won't let them build the actual arches anymore. The tiny, symbolic arches to which McDonald's is restricted in most locations have almost a gestalt quality to them.

The architectural beauty of Bullock's Pasadena (1947) undoubtedly was a factor in the store's upscale success; the same goes for Bullock's Wilshire (1929). The warehouse atmosphere and industrial racks of Costco are true; therefore, effective in terms of showmanship.

Lighting, I think, is one of the key elements in successful retailing. Dick Richard's celebrated *Lido Isle Market* in Newport Beach (c. 1959) was a triumph of lighting in both foot candles and choice of spectra. Basically Dick put light only on the merchandise. And he used warm spectra. Many stores are lit in the blue end, which chills out the merchandise and, worse, makes your female customers look corpselike. Dick, one of the truly creative grocers of the mid-twentieth century, flattered both his goods and his customers. The aisles were so dark you almost stumbled. This really attracted me in my Whole Earth Harry days: it cut energy usage. But your eyes were never blinded by the overhead lighting, because after all, you aren't selling the ceiling.

Paint goes along with lighting. The same is true of floor covering, but the Demand Side has to be compromised by critical Supply Side questions, like "Can you drag pallets over it?" During the first years of Good Time Charley, I carpeted the stores using the new carpet material just developed for the hospital trade. There were advantages. When bottles fall, they bounce instead of break; and dust gets trapped in the carpets instead of on the merchandise. Unfortunately, when the Santa Ana winds blow in Southern California, the humidity goes to zero and static electricity builds in your customers as they tread the aisles. When they reach for a metal shelf: *Zap!* What with static electricity, chewing gum, and ground-out cigarettes, carpets didn't prove out.

Clean parking lots are also part of showmanship. Time and again people would complain that our "parking lot is dirty." Late in my tenure at Trader Joe's, I would snarl in reply that the parking lot was clean; it was our filthy customers who dumped their ashtrays on the tarmac. Obviously it was getting to be time for me to move on.

Given the need for long leases, landlords and tenants are trying to outguess each other about the objective future (for example, the business cycle, as opposed to the subjective futures of the parties, the commercial success of the tenant, the demand for the space offered by the landlord).

Programs of collaboration should focus on offering some form of relief to the landlord if the objective future runs in the tenant's favor, while maintaining some degree of protection for the tenant if it runs against the tenant. This is obvious, but mass hysteria usually dominates real estate markets. California plunged from a leasing frenzy to what amounted to a leasing moratorium from 1989 to 1994. In 1998, it was frenzy time again. The point is this: tenants who enter into negotiations with the idea of beating the landlord at the objective future game usually get the kind of landlords they deserve. And vice versa.

In conclusion, a very real part of the success of Trader Joe's stems from the excellence of its locations and the shrewdness of the language of its leases. "Occupancy expense" in its broadest definition (which I won't go into, because it's not straightforward) ran about 2 percent while I was there.

# 20

# Supply Side Retailing

"But we cannot say that our modern system is 'based on
private ownership.' That is pure fable and myth.
The modern capitalist world is only one-half ownership;
the other half is creditorship."

—Richard Dana Skinner, *Seven Kinds of Inflation*,
the best economics book I ever read, written in 1937
just after the pit of the Depression

H ere are factors on the Supply Side. In varying degrees of truth
we are debtors to them all:

1. Governments

2. The way you do things: "habits" and "culture"

3. Systems

4. Non-merchandise vendors

5. Merchandise vendors

6. Landlords

7. Bankers and investment bankers

8. Stockholders

9.  Employees

10.  Crime

You may notice that the sequence here is different from that in the introductory chapter on Double Entry Retailing. I didn't want to scare you off so I listed the Supply Side factors in somewhat conventional order like vendors first. I prefer the above sequence, however. Employees come near the bottom of the list, only because I chose to end this chapter with the *Dark Side of the Moon* of retailing: employee theft and the atmosphere of crime in general. Yes, crime is an important Supply Side constraint.

# Governments

If you're going to enter a business, the first question you should ask is the extent to which governments—federal, state, and local—intervene in its affairs. Among businesses that are relatively free of government regulations are bookstores, apparel stores, hardware stores, music stores, appliance stores, etc.

Grocery stores, by contrast, are heavily impacted by state laws and regulations (milk, alcohol, weights and measures), and local laws and regulations: health departments; building departments, whose rules may conflict with the health departments; zoning, which among other things may restrict hours of operation; and the dread catchall, conditional use permits. Cities and counties regulate alcohol as well as the state itself. As you know by now, some of my most serious business problems were created by government regulations, both the nationwide regulations like Fair Labor Standards Act, which had me choking on the hairball Department of Labor audit, and state regulations on milk and alcohol.

For years after the federal government had deregulated interstate trucking rates, California's bureaucracy clung to anti-competitive intra-state rates, which forced Trader Joe's into all kinds of acrobatics to stay legal in its contracts with independent truckers (the fiction of "dedicated equipment"). At the same time, thousands of "coyote" truckers operated with drivers who didn't even have chauffeur licenses. They were never detected unless their routes took them past a truck-weighing station, and they knew better than anyone where those stations were located.

The governments are suppliers. That must always be kept in mind. I hate to admit it but the inspections by health departments and weights and measures departments save the conscientious grocer from having to do the same thing. Generally, I think that occupational and safety regulations, bizarre though they may sometimes be, are constructive. Sometimes they don't go far enough.

For example, one reason I dropped sugar in Mac the Knife is that five-pound bags of sugar come packed twelve to the bale. That's sixty pounds in a very awkward, floppy shape and promises lots of back injuries. After we made a deliberate effort to employ women full-time in the stores (c. 1975), we made an effort to get rid of any single case that weighed more than forty pounds (champagne and milk are the heaviest cases in Trader Joe's). Otherwise, the male employees get turned into beasts of burden: many women have difficulty with the heaviest cases, and there is still a reservoir of male chivalry out there, especially when you hire people of the quality of Trader Joe's employees.

Governmental intrusion can be considered as a Supply Side opportunity. The retailer who masters the skills of dealing with the regulatory authorities erects a threshold that his competitors will have to cross. There are several facets to this opportunity, excluding "La Mordida."

Except for the occasional zealot, the "Programme of Collaboration" for most public officials is to avoid rocking the boat. They may back down if challenged. Many of them don't understand their own rules anyway. However, be gracious when you're nailed. Don't win Pyrrhic victories. The same mentality that doesn't want to rock the boat also tends to hold onto its job. You'll encounter those guys again and again!

Try to help them do a good job; make them feel important; and make them feel that you're Playing the Game, not trying to abolish it.

## The Way You Do Things

This is what most management authorities like Tom Peters and Peter Drucker are writing about. What is the smell of the organization? It's ephemeral, but no less real.

Peter Drucker has said, in the context of troubled companies, that it's impossible to change a company's "culture" but you can change its "habits." "The Way You Do Things" is the most limiting Supply Side factor in any company: Are you entrepreneurial or "corporate"?

I want to make it quite clear that I called the shots. I reject management by committee. I think, however, that my regime was somewhat short of despotic. I like this quote about Pierre Monteux, the great conductor of the *San Francisco Symphony* while I was attending Stanford.

---

**Monteux never tried to get a performance out of an orchestra. He was always giving one with them.**

*–Los Angeles Herald Examiner,* 1988

---

## Systems

Whether your "System" for cash is a cigar box or detailed scanning online with the office, it is one of the defining factors in the way you conduct the business.

Believe me, you have a system for everything that has to happen in your business—you just may not be conscious of it. And you probably have still other systems that are not needed. That's why *The Winning*

*Performance* calls for a "constitutional contempt for business as usual." To practice "constitutional contempt," you have to arrive at work every day with the attitude, "Why do we do such-and-such that way? Better yet, why do we do it at all?"

Usually the answer is, "We've always done it that way," "That's the way we did it at my last job," or "All our competitors are doing it."

It was in that mood that Dave Yoda and I created the Leave Bank, which had the radical feature of combining vacation leave and sick leave, and in accruing it in dollars instead of hours.

Starting back in the 1960s, when no receiving document bore the retail value of the shipment, we were among the grocery pioneers in the Retail Accounting method. So Dave and Bernice Cliff ground out all those numbers on our Friden calculating machine, a sixty-pound mechanical wonder that couldn't print a tape, so you had to run all calculations twice to make sure you hadn't made a mistake! I've paid tribute to the Retail Accounting system in the "Skunks in the Office" chapter.

When we went to Northern California in 1988, we seriously considered accepting only credit cards: no cash, no checks. It would have eliminated all bad checks and the systems used to avoid them; it would have ended all trips to the bank for cash or to pick up back checks; and it would have radically simplified cash accounting at store level; it would have ended most bank statement reconciliation work, etc.

I felt that the cost of credit card fees would be more than offset by these advantages, especially in the context of Trader Joe's clientele, virtually all of whom had credit cards by 1988. (Eighty-two percent of all households had Visa in 1989, according to *Chain Store Age*.) In the end we chickened out. Trader Joe's would be an unknown quantity in Northern California. We wanted to enter the market with all guns blazing. In other words, we were afraid that we would lose too much in terms of the Demand Side factor of "method of payment accepted." But it was an exercise in constitutional contempt for doing business as usual.

# Non-Merchandise Vendors

"Systems" and "Non-Merchandise Vendors" often cross paths, especially in the current trend toward outsourcing. Some of the non-merchandise vendors like trash companies, radio stations, and utilities don't interface on a personal basis very much (though the deregulated utilities may change). Other non-merchandise vendors are very much extensions of Trader Joe's and should be treated as such. Just like the merchandise vendors we encountered in the "Intensive Buying" chapter.

Since we owned no trucks, no warehouses, etc., I asked our people to keep track of the outsourced drivers and to do their best to see that our contractors were paid reasonable wages with reasonable working conditions. Turnover is the most expensive labor expense!

Physical inventories were always taken by outside services like *Washington* or *Blue Chip*: I wanted them to send the same crew to the same stores inventory after inventory. I asked our regional supervisors to take *Polaroid* pictures of the counters so we could learn which ones could count (not all of them could).

# Insurance Carriers

## Workers' Compensation

Workers' comp carriers' "Programme of Collaboration" is to find clients who don't have losses. The design of the retail enterprise must take this into account: design to avoid accidents. Trader Joe's tried to eliminate any case that weighs more than forty pounds. We closed the sandwich departments because that was where the most injuries occurred, like knife cuts. We stopped selling keg beer because of back injuries. Workers' comp is a real Supply Side constraint on Demand Side assortment.

When you operate in several states, like some of the companies that I ran after leaving Trader Joe's, you learn that workers' comp laws vary greatly from state to state. While I was on the advisory board of *Liberty Mutual*, the biggest writer of workers' comp insurance in the U.S., it seemed that Texas had the worst laws of all.

## Health Insurance

As usual, the carriers' Programme of Collaboration is to have no losses. The best program you can offer an insurance company in California is to have a workforce with no females over thirty-nine, and no males over fifty-four. And of course even if you wanted to pull that one off, you run smack-on to another Supply Side constraint, the government.

The above is true of all businesses. What is special about retailing is that so many employees have access to cash and cash-convertible merchandise. As I've explained earlier, security problems give the retailer special incentive to have good health insurance plans.

## Product Liability

Dealing with so many merchandise vendors, many of them small and shaky, creates an exposure. Accordingly, we insisted that every vendor furnish a certificate of product liability insurance, and that the carrier had to notify us of any lapse or change in coverage. Time and again important purchase orders were held up until we were satisfied that the vendor had proper insurance. So this can be a Supply Side constraint that leads to your being out of stock. In the most extreme cases, it can mean that you can't "cover" an ad. This is one reason why the Macintosh was so important to the *Fearless Flyer*: by shortening the lead time before we went to press, we could pull products from the issue if we still didn't have proper product liability insurance.

We carried our own product liability insurance, too, but some claims we settled ourselves, such as claims for "broken teeth." We simply treated this as part of the cost of selling nuts, and we settled such claims without troubling our insurance company. Some retailers, however, feel this is such a Supply Side constraint that they limit their nut program to totally branded products like *Planters*.

"Slip-and-fall" claims are a built-in feature of fixed-site retailing, one more factor driving retailers to the internet. I know of one supermarket chain whose stores were located in areas notorious for slip-and-fall claims. They treated slip-and-fall payoffs like a normal expense, such as trash collection. Of course they reflected the cost in their retail prices.

## Merchandise Vendors

I've discussed these worthies at length in the "Intensive Buying" chapter, but only the ones who play ball with Intensive Buyers. There are other vendors who won't—or can't—play ball.

## Underpricing Highly Branded Products

One of my early experiences was with the American distributor of a cork puller made in Europe. I found the device in a *Hoffritz* store in New York in 1969, and thought it was excellent. We ordered a large quantity and cut the price, which, of course, we advertised in the *Fearless Flyer*. When we went to reorder, mysteriously our orders never arrived.

We didn't get sore, we got even. There was nothing patentable about the cork puller. I knew a couple of engineers who'd been laid off in the great 1970 aerospace recession, turned them loose on it, and broke the price permanently on that design of cork puller.

I could understand the problems of vendors whose strongly branded products showed up in our stores at greatly reduced prices. Our competitors accused them of selling to us at lower prices, which was not true (for a given quantity). Part of the problem lies in the "costing" prices of supermarkets.

For example, by the time I left Trader Joe's, we were selling 45 percent of all the Jarlsberg cheese sold in California. Our price was $3.49. The going price in the supermarkets was $6.00. The "cost" of the supermarkets into their stores, however, was about $3.49. Why? Because the supermarkets insisted on advertising allowances, which were credited to the ad budget; cash discounts, which were credited to General Administration; promotional allowances, which were credited to revenue, etc. The apparent cost was inflated by all these accounting decisions. The fact is that most supermarkets don't know what their true cost is for Jarlsberg because their buyers want to look good. They are incentivized by the amount of revenue and ad allowances they generate.

While I was consulting for Thrifty Corp.'s sporting goods chains in 1990, I discovered that they had no idea what the true cost was for thousands of items because they "recognized" profit on products before they were ever shipped out of their warehouses. For example, if the "normal" cost of a volleyball was $6.00, but they got a special deal for $5.00, they "booked" a cost of $6.00 into the warehouse, and recognized $1.00 of profit long before the volleyball was ever sold.

Trader Joe's buying objective was to get just one, dead-net price, delivered to our distribution centers. This was quite similar to the policy that Sam Walton was developing at about the same time, a practice called "contract pricing."

## Direct Store Vendors
## Who Won't Ship to Warehouses

Because of territorial franchise agreements, Coca-Cola, *7-Up*, Budweiser, *Coors*, *Miller's*, et al., won't ship to your warehouse and let you distribute their products because it would upset the territories they have granted to individual distributors. If you want to see fireworks, just get some out-of-state Coke into your warehouse! When canned Coke first appeared, they made the mistake of letting our wholesaler, Certified Grocers, sell this new container to its members. Canned Coke became the No. 1 item at Certified until Coke cut them off in 1981. There is no way to intensively buy such products.

The same vendors also won't let you distribute their product because they want to run your store. All the potato chip and corn chip guys, cupcake guys, cracker guys, etc. The curious thing is that the supermarket chains welcome these vendors, because they provide "free" labor. What the vendor salesmen are actually doing is fighting over shelf space, physically shoving competitive products aside.

One of my grand objectives in Five Year Plan '77 was to eliminate all outsiders from our stores and to halt all direct store deliveries. This was one of the most radical features of Trader Joe's, vis-a-vis the rest of the grocery industry.

## Why Did I Want to Get Rid of
## This "Free" Labor?

1. Some of those guys steal. They steal by doing "fast counts" with your receiving clerk (some of those route men should be dealing blackjack in Vegas). That's one big reason why the supermarkets went to "electronic receiving." They also steal by putting high-value items in the "empty" cases they take back to the trucks. That was one reason I welcomed *L'Eggs* in its egg-shaped containers in the late 1960s: it was harder to hide L'Eggs in an empty soft drink case than flat-pack hosiery. Ask any grocer about this.

2. The bread and cupcake guys are under heavy penalties if they bring too much "stale" back to the bakery. So they pick up out-of-code product from one store and "roll" it into the next.

3. As the drug culture developed in the wake of Vietnam, route men evolved into natural distributors of the stuff.

4. You never know when they're going to arrive at the store: this makes labor scheduling difficult. Related to this . . .

5. They always show up in your parking lot when it's jammed. Or have you never been blocked from a parking space by a beer truck?

By eliminating all direct store deliveries, we:

1. Improved security.

2. Made it possible to schedule labor to coincide with the arrival of (our) trucks.

3. Freed up our parking lots for customers.

But these Supply Side policies obviously impacted our Demand Side Assortment.

## Have Lots of Vendors!

Certified Grocers, an ancient and honorable retailer-owned cooperative wholesaler, is critical to the existence of independent markets in California because it is almost their only source of dry groceries, delicatessen, and frozen products. Starting about the time of Mac the Knife, in the late 1970s, however, economic pressures forced Certified to impose increasingly high physical and dollar minimum load requirements. Many small markets simply didn't have the storage capacity to handle the minimum loads. Ergo, they were frequently out of stock on important items, because they were not ready to digest another minimum-quantity load.

This is what we saw in the late 1970s. Our stores had deliberately been built with almost no back rooms: a real Supply Side constraint! Time and again we had to order extra cigarettes (high value per cubic inch) just to make a dollar minimum. When Coke withdrew canned Coke from Certified (see above), that was the end; we just couldn't make the minimum. So our exit from conventional groceries was partly driven by this Supply Side constraint, which has only worsened since then.

A related problem is getting cut off from trader information. Even independent chains who have fairly large stores are increasingly "out of the loop." The big grocery manufacturers have radically reduced their field sales forces so the independents are no longer called on by them— and those office calls can be quite important in terms of knowing about deals and what's happening in the trade. By 1994, when I was in charge of Market Wholesale, this problem was becoming acute for our small grocery customers and even the not-so-small ones. I didn't foresee this particular problem in the 1970s, but Trader Joe's, fortuitously, avoided it by going outside conventional channels.

## Landlords

I've discussed our leasing practices in the "Too, Too Solid Stores" chapter. Here's a somewhat larger context. Most landlords fall into one of two classes:

1. Landlords who have the financing in place for a new building, or who have already existing space. These Class 1 Landlords are interested in maximizing rent from your particular store space or, if it's a multi-tenant development, in getting tenants who can draw traffic in a manner that maximizes total revenue from the shopping center.

2. Landlords who desperately need a strong tenant on a long-term lease, to secure the financing for the real property.

In the 1950s, the Rexall Drug Company had a very strong financial statement, but its Demand Side programs were such dogs that only Class 2 Landlords were desperate enough to lease space to it. By contrast, Sav-on was a relatively weak, relatively new company, but its Demand Side programs were so great that Class 1 Landlords always preferred it over Rexall. As a result, Sav-on tended to get the best locations.

Trader Joe's is able to drive hard bargains partly from its willingness to take existing structures (and do the tenant improvements itself), as I've discussed, and partly because of its strong Demand Side programs, something that I learned from Sav-on.

Also, Trader Joe's has no need for co-tenants. In fact, co-tenants just get in the way. That's why we didn't insist on "co-tenancy" clauses, something that landlords don't like.

Most problems in leasing are created by the need to deal with the future: the longer the lease, the more significant the problems in negotiating the lease. This may seem obvious, but:

1. Retailers who are desirable because of their financibility must sign long leases; otherwise, they have nothing to sell the landlord.

2. Retailers who have big leasehold/fixture investments must sign long leases in order to amortize their investment. This investment is partly a function of store size, but mostly it's a function of intensity of fixturization. Trader Joe's, like all markets, has intensive fixturization in refrigeration, etc. (The opposite would be the Halloween stores, which could move in and out of empty stores each fall season. They could have the same time horizon as a floating crap game, because their leasehold investment was about the same as a floating crap game. Most gift stores, toy stores, dress stores, etc., don't have time horizons that are much longer.)

Given the need for long leases, landlord and tenant are trying to outguess each other about the objective future. For example, the business cycle, as opposed to the subjective futures of the parties, the commercial success of the tenant, and the demand for the space offered by the landlord.

Programmes of Collaboration should focus on offering some form of relief to the landlord if the objective future runs in the tenant's favor, while maintaining some degree of protection for the tenant if it runs against the tenant. This is obvious, but mass hysteria usually dominates real estate markets. California plunged from a leasing frenzy to what amounted to a leasing moratorium from 1989 to 1994. Then 1998 was frenzy time again. The point is this: tenants who enter into negotiations with the idea of beating the landlord at the objective future game usually get the kind of landlords they deserve. And vice versa.

In conclusion, a very real part of the success of Trader Joe's stems from the excellence of its locations and the shrewdness of the language of its leases. "Occupancy expense" in its broadest definition (which I won't go into because it's not straightforward) ran about 2 percent while I was there.

## Bankers and Investment Bankers

Bank of America people were almost part of our management team even after I no longer owed them any money. They gave us tremendous support, even when we started writing all our checks on *First Union National Bank* in North Carolina in order to get the "float." Ah, those pre-electronic banking days! A bad snowstorm at O'Hare could delay the clearance of checks in North Carolina by four days! ("Remote disbursement" was the polite term for geographical float.)

In the publicly owned companies for which I later worked, I became well acquainted with investment bankers. With the public boards on which I serve, they are very much a part of the scenery. I mention them here only because top management people of publicly traded companies spend an inordinate amount of time with investment bankers, to the detriment of the "real" business. This is a real and tangible Supply Side constraint.

# Cash

I might as well discuss the ultimate Supply Side constraint, cash, here. Criticism of my ultra-conservative cash policy is justified, especially with the benefit of hindsight. Please remember that we were damn near bankrupt in 1962; please remember that I saw at least twenty supermarket chains go bankrupt from 1959 to 1970. (I used to keep an "honor roll" of bankrupt chains on my desk, as a constant reminder, and to show salespeople.)

My cash policy was this: we would always have cash at least equal to two weeks' sales. (I think this is called an "heuristic" decision in business school.) Any month we didn't meet the test, I would borrow from Bank of America on a five-year term loan ostensibly secured by store fixtures. But I wasn't borrowing for fixtures and inventory, as I took pains to explain to Bank of America. If I had enough cash to buy fixtures, I didn't borrow. After 1975, I never borrowed again.

This must seem hilarious to investment bankers who, in judging return on equity, subtract "surplus" cash from the balance sheet. But the resultant cash position gave us the ability to make those killer deals in Intensive Buying. (I should add it also created a big potential problem if the IRS ever adjudged that I was unreasonably accumulating earnings. Every year we carefully stated in the corporate minutes why we needed all that cash.)

# Stockholders

As controlling stockholder of Trader Joe's, I ran scared, too scared after our success in Whole Earth Harry in 1971, because every dime we had was in the company (I kept my salary low partly to maximize profit in the company, partly because I would have been in a marginal 73 percent tax bracket back in those pre-Reagan days). The Albrechts, to whom I ultimately sold Trader Joe's, were totally absentee and did not become a Supply Side factor until the last year of my tenure.

Since all the companies I ran after I left Trader Joe's were (a) publicly held and (b) in deep trouble, stockholder concerns about low stock prices were a real constraint. But from my point of view, this was a positive, because it wound up giving me all that work.

# Employees

Generally, labor expense in grocery retailing is relatively small, compared with manufacturing or the professions or restaurants. This was one reason I could get away with Trader Joe's high compensation policies. Cost of Goods is the dominant expense. The funny thing is that grocers seem to spend more effort squeezing payroll than squeezing Cost of Goods Sold, though there is at least five times more opportunity to save money in the latter.

Another way of looking at our high compensation policy: it was an effort to loosen the Supply Side constraints created by the nature of human beings. By attracting the more competent people, and keeping them, you can gain some degrees of freedom.

A large percentage of the population is qualified to work in most stores. Because as we proved, you don't need college graduates at any level. It's relatively easy to train people for the work, as opposed to the professions, a lot of modern manufacturing, etc.

And there's the element of enthusiasm. As soon as we got into Whole Earth Harry, we started to attract health food nuts who probably believed more in what we were doing than we did. To a considerable extent, they kept us on the straight and narrow: management was policed by its own employees! I noticed the same phenomenon when I began consulting for sporting goods chains, and when I ran *Sport Chalet*. In both Sport Chalet and Trader Joe's you run the danger of having employees who are too far into the products they sell, and not wanting to sell anything else.

# Crime

So many Demand Side things that you'd like to do are so constrained by crime that it must be considered a major Supply Side constraint.

### Internal Crime

The opportunity for internal theft at all levels regrettably distinguishes retailing:

1. A chain that leases a lot of locations is exposed to corrupt dealings in the real estate department. There is no such thing as a low-paid, and honest, employee in charge of leasing. I've seen some real horror stories.

2. As in many other kinds of business, the accounting/buying people can set up false vendors in the computer; the merchandise buyers can be on the take even with genuine vendors. The old rule in retailing used to be that a buyer could accept anything he could eat or smoke in a day, a rule mostly honored in the breach.

3. The warehouses receive and disburse a lot of very liquid merchandise (if customers don't want it, you shouldn't be stocking it). Bud Fisher prolonged the life of the Owl Drug Co. by slapping body searches on the workers as they left the warehouse and by locking up film, hosiery, etc. A bonus of our virtual distribution system was the key decision to ship only in full cases. That discouraged a lot of theft. And private label merchandise is harder to fence, although now and then we'd get word of a swap meet where Trader Joe's label nuts were being sold. (Those big swap meets are important in moving goods into the economy. Too bad

they aren't included in the official Gross Domestic Product figures.)

4. The truckers sometimes have interesting rendezvous on the way to the stores. One reason companies install those electronic recorders on trucks is to see what unplanned stops were made along the way. This was one of the few productive things they had done at Thrifty and Market Wholesale.

5. The store people have extraordinary access to cash as well as merchandise, and so do their "sweethearts." To "sweetheart," a verb that should be in the dictionary, means to ring a lower price than the one marked when your sweetheart goes through the check stand. Or in the case of scanning, to apparently scan but actually avoid the laser beam. When I was working on *Pay 'n Save* drugstores in Hawaii in 1991, we found one clerk who was taking us for $500 an hour. She had lots of sweethearts!

All of these problems were exponentiated in the post-Vietnam drug-ridden culture, a culture that rose at the same time as Whole Earth Harry and kept growing. But pre-Vietnam, in the so-called good old days, it was horses or women: they all consume large amounts of after-tax dollars so the men turned to no-tax dollars. In the '60s, I wanted to burn down the *Santa Anita Horse Race* track.

In short, theft is mostly a too, too solid flesh affair. Through our health insurance and income-continuation insurance, I think we pretty much pre-solved the problems of family health and living expense bills, problems that, very arguably, could "excuse" theft. No, most employee theft is oriented to drugs, gambling, and extracurricular sex. As a poet once said, "It takes a lot of money to support two women."

One of the few business-oriented thieves was a store manager who always liked to work the late shift and close the store by himself, so that he could load his station wagon with products to sell in a store he owned on the side. Leroy staked him out and caught him one night.

As I discussed in the "Skunks at the Office" chapter, we had employee parties in our house twice a year. Time after time that same manager had come to our house, eaten our salt, broken our bread, and yet the son of a bitch stole! That incident was followed by a purse theft. After that, we held the parties away from home.

Because of internal theft, one of the most important non-merchandise suppliers may be a detective agency. It is very hard to find effective agencies. The nature of the work tends to attract unstable people. I often suspected that the operatives were worse than the criminals. But shop around and get referrals, because they can be worth it.

## External Crime: Eine Grosse Crime Musik

Shoplifting is chump change. All veteran retailers agree. Frozen shrimp is the #1 problem at Trader Joe's. It has a high value per cubic inch, and it is easy to fence; the thieves usually operate in teams.

Customer theft through the media of bad checks and fraudulent credit cards costs more in dollars. The highest income areas like Pacific Palisades, where our first Pronto was located, tended to be the worst. Today, a variety of electronic verification procedures reduce bad check and credit card crime, but those came too late for my tenure. Where you really get wiped is by good customers whom you know so well you just take their checks. Then they decide to divorce and both spouses become hyperactive in seeing who can clean out the joint bank account first.

Although employee theft is the greatest dollar problem, the most traumatic is robbery. We averaged about one holdup every three months. I became a Mozart fan in 1971, listening to Mozart's *Eine Kleine Nachtmusik* while driving home at midnight from a store robbery to which I had been summoned. It's a hell of a way to make one's progress toward Mozart.

**All life, I suspect, consists of a progress toward Mozart.**

–Bernard Levin, *London Times*, 1976

You defend against it with multiple safes, frequent bank deposits, cameras. And still the drug culture arrives at your door. Having a bigger store with lots of employees is no defense. Some sensational supermarket burglaries occur every year. Who pays the price of the War on Drugs? The people who work in stores, restaurants, and banks. Even if they never get shot at, even if they never get locked in a refrigerated walk-in box, the stress they suffer when weird people enter the store takes a toll. Do I agree with Milton Friedman? Yes.

Burglaries are less traumatic, but only by a little. As I explained in Demand Side Retailing, our burglaries dropped off sharply after we dropped cigarettes. Having floor safes instead of above-ground (portable) safes is a big deterrent, too.

During my thirty years at Pronto and Trader Joe's, I suppose there were a couple of hundred robberies and burglaries.

The combination of internal theft, vendor theft, bad checks, armed robbery, and burglaries can be overwhelming at times. An entire chapter, "Crime Side Retailing," could be written because that's how I spent half of my time: dealing with crime with before-the-fact controls, and after-the-fact with detection and action.

This is one reason why the management function of Control is so critically important to retailing. Retailers like *Aldi* and Costco may commit many sins on the Demand Side, but their bulldog tenacity on Supply Side Control makes them profitable in spite of it. Ask not what you can do for your customers, but what your employees, vendors, customers, and druggies can do to you.

One of the most important Supply Side constraints is the stamina of the Chief Executive Officer. I haven't listed it above, but it's there. And the sort of thing that wore down this CEO was year after year of employee theft. Back in 1966, dealing with the first major case of betrayal, I almost quit the business. I made up my mind, however, that it was part of the "matrix" of retailing and gritted my teeth. After thirty years, however, one could get lockjaw. But fortunately, Mozart does more than Milton can, to Justify God's ways to man!

And malt ain't so bad either.

This is a dark note on which to end this chapter but, as Ahura Mazda would say, "Without darkness there can be no light."

# 21

## The Last Five Year Plans

The designed reshaping of existing situations into preferred
ones [is] the objective distinguishing the professions—
engineering, medicine, law, business, and architecture—
from the sciences, which seek not so much to alter
as to explain the world as it is.

*—Smithsonian*, Spring 1990.

**W**e continued to make formal plans as opposed to winging it:
that's the real message of this chapter. In order to begin writing this book, I had to blow the dust off all those plans, going back to 1958, and reread them. I cringe, cringe, cringe as I see how often I was wrong in my forecasts. At least, however, I had put down on paper what I thought was going to happen, and went public with it to my closest colleagues, and sometimes to all the employees.

## Five Year Plan 1982:
## Design for Human Use

Five Year Plan '77 had been a great success. We had accomplished, I estimated, 80 percent of FYP '77. We had survived the deregulation of the grocery business and wound up a rather powerful retailer. We also survived my lack of foresight on the issues of distribution. In 1982, sales had more than doubled from 1977; profit before taxes had tripled.

By the Five Year Plan '82 (written in July 1982), we were ready to flex our muscles. "The fact is that we are one of the most efficient food retailers in Los Angeles. . . . We are ready to play the kind of hardball that will be needed to survive in the early years of the 1980s. We are the leaders in catering to the tastes of the newly educated masses. They may lose part of all of their incomes, but they will retain their new tastes: They will be all the more ready to recognize value in the things that we sell best."

Actually that could have been the script for the 1990–94 recession. Many of our customers were laid off in the aerospace crash; lots of doctors got hurt by new medical plans; there was a gross surplus of lawyers; and many of these overeducated and newly underpaid professionals started shopping at Trader Joe's. So I was wrong by eight years.

I was expecting really hard times in the 1980s. The stock market was crashing in 1982 as I wrote FYP '82. Interest rates were sky high. I was wrong: Reagan's Cold War defense program poured billions into Southern California, and the strength of the dollar, recounted in the "Uncorked!" chapter, played right into our hands.

## Design as the Major Issue

The world does not have an economic problem, but a design problem.

–Buckminster Fuller, sometime in the 1970s

The following quotes are by Frederick P. Brooks Jr., architect of the *IBM 360* system, in his insightful 1982 book, *The Mythical Man Month*, one of my favorite books on management.

"I will contend that conceptual integrity is the most important consideration in system design. It is better to have a system omit certain anomalous features and improvements, but reflect one set of design ideas, than to have one that contains many good but independent and uncoordinated ideas."

"Conceptual integrity in turn dictates that the design must proceed from one mind, or from a very small number of agreeing resonant minds."

"To get a good design, therefore, the Number One consideration is to have integrity of design, and you can't get integrity from a committee."

"The purpose of a programming system is to make a computer easy to use."

"All my own experience convinces me that the conceptual integrity of a system determines its ease of use."

"Ease of use is enhanced only if the time gained in functional specification exceeds the time lost in learning, remembering, and searching manuals."

"Because ease of use is the purpose, this ratio of function to conceptual complexity is the ultimate test of system design. Neither function alone nor simplicity alone defines a good design."

"For a given level function, however, that system is best in which one can specify things with the most simplicity and straightforwardness. Simplicity is not enough."

"Simplicity and straightforwardness proceed from conceptual integrity. Every part must reflect the same philosophies and the same balancing of desiderata. . . . Ease of use, then, dictates units of design, conceptual integrity."

## Computers and the Discrete

Bottom line: FYP '82 recommitted us to the Discrete vs. the Continuous, because we had proven it was our key to differentiating ourselves from all the other grocers.

We were learning, however, that all those batches of discrete products were tough to administer without real computing power, especially as we kept opening new stores. The problems of ordering bread that I discussed in the Virtual Distribution chapter were hitting home as I worked on FYP '82.

We wound up betting the farm that computers would bail us out and achieve Frederick Brooks's "ease of use." And it did pretty much work out that way. Of course I didn't argue with "Conceptual integrity in turn dictates that the design must proceed from one mind."

## The Human Use of Human Beings

This inspiring phrase had been in my vocabulary since 1954, when Norbert Wiener ushered in the Information Age with his book *Cybernetics*. In 1982, the employees were very uneasy, what with the threat of computers' displacing people, and that rotten recession in the background. So I played up a "Plan of Action and Programme of Collaboration" for the employees on this theme of the Human Use of Human Beings, a term that had been in our employee manual since 1969.

What I tried to link was the sale of discrete products to such "Human Use." I averred that *Tide* and Folger's didn't need any human intervention. They could be sold by machines. We have since edged closer to that as supermarkets adopt scan-it-yourself check stands. The operational theory is that the labor savings from having no checker offsets the fraudulent scanning by customers. I certainly do think that checking is an inhuman use of human beings. That's one reason Trader Joe's has no permanent checkers, why everyone in the store shares the burden.

Small batches of wines, Brie that was a bit over the hill; explanations of why we were able to sell Armour Dinner Classics for one-half the price of the supermarkets: these required the use of people. And for people to exploit their human potential, that took product knowledge. That product knowledge could be best attained not by "training" but by "engaging the interest" of each employee in what we sold.

Ah, well. How much of that was genuinely meant, and how much of it was Kirby vacuum cleaner talk? Even I don't know. It was well intentioned, anyhow. But what we wound up doing was discouraging our employees from doing any unnecessary selling.

I especially didn't want them "selling" vitamins because of the problems with the FDA, which I've mentioned; and I didn't want them selling wines because that is very time-consuming. The *Fearless Flyer*, as I've explained, was intended to be the primary selling tool.

Yet we wound up with an intensely "human use" of our employees' judgment. Those compensation policies from way back there in 1962 kept paying off. The Macintoshes in the stores were demanding new, "human" skills. The continual hiring, training, and promotion of people for new stores, and of part-timers in existing stores; the new cultural changes of sex and race; all the new government regulations from OSHA: these are human uses. What our full-time employees became more than anything were administrators. Yah, they still put up loads, but here's something about people who like to work in grocery stores: they like a certain amount of physical exertion. It's very satisfying to go home at night and know that you "put up" X hundred cases that day.

And a lot of employees did get their "interest engaged" in the products. We continued to hold wine tastings at the office. But what was really interesting was the five times a year when the buyers went out to the stores to explain the upcoming products in the next *Fearless Flyer*. Boy, did they get an earful!

Still, we badly lacked formal administrative and management training for the store personnel. We had recognized that lack time and again since the late 1960s, but we did very little of such training as opposed to training in the physical tasks and money-handling chores. We simply lacked the internal skills for the job. I hoped that John Shields could help us find the outside help, but I left the company before that materialized.

## Encore, Succes De L'argent

Mostly, FYP '82 extended FYP '77 but with a much better handle on how to do it. Sales in 1988 were 240 percent of 1982's; profit before taxes was 355 percent of 1982's.

## Five Year Plan 1988

This plan was written in December 1987, just after the stock market crash of October, and after I'd hired John Shields, who helped me to prepare it.

The plan foresaw grim times in post–Cold War California until 1994, a pretty good forecast. (I think that the recession would have lasted longer had it not been for the January 1994 Northridge earthquake, which pumped $20 billion into the economy from insurance companies and the governments.) Still, it forecast that we would open twelve stores in demographic-rich Northern California, a plan that worked out exactly, including San Rafael, the highest-volume store in our history.

That's as far as I'll go. I resigned in April 1988, just four months after writing the Plan, and left on December 31, 1988. I cannot judge the success or validity of the Plan since I wasn't there. It did raise the issue of replacing Top Management. How little did I know!

# FIRST I SELL,
# THEN I LEAVE

# 22

# Employee Ownership

No man acquires property without acquiring with it
a little arithmetic also.

–Ralph Waldo Emerson

Thus far in this book I have recounted the story of Trader Joe's without any reference to the fact its ownership changed radically in 1979, two years after the start of Mac the Knife. I saw no need to interrupt the narrative flow, or the exposition of the workings of Trader Joe's, to go into something that was a nonevent in terms of running the company.

We, the employees and I, sold Trader Joe's to the Theodore Albrecht family of Essen, Germany, in 1979; to my surprise, I stayed on for another ten years after that.

## The Goal of Employee Ownership

From the beginning of Pronto Markets, one of my basic principles, one of my basic goals, was employee ownership of the business. Getting there, however, was complicated.

For internal reasons, Rexall had incorporated each Pronto Market separately. So we had seven corporations from Rexall; the 1962 deal with Adohr added an eighth. I didn't, however, want the employees to invest in only one corporation or store. That smelled of franchising; more importantly, we transferred employees among stores—and therefore corporations—all the time.

To unify the eight corporations so the employees could invest in the entire enterprise, the Pronto Market Investment Club was created.

Its creator was my former Stanford roommate, Charles W. Froehlich Jr. Froehlich was the principal attorney for us during my thirty years at Pronto and Trader Joe's. The problem was that he kept going off on other ventures, as a professor of taxation at Boalt Hall at UC Berkeley 1960–64, as a Superior Court judge during 1972–82, and then as an Appellate Court judge during 1987–96.

But always in the background he was Virgil leading this Dante through the Inferno of taxation.

Froehlich was teaching taxation at Boalt Hall when I bought Pronto from Rexall. He created the Pronto Market Investment Club as a vehicle to hold stock in the eight corporations without getting into unnecessary complications with the California Corporations Commissioner. Why didn't we just merge the corporations?

Because there was a tax advantage that was of tremendous help in building the balance sheet of our feeble enterprise. Under the tax code of that era, each corporation, whether General Motors or Pronto Market No. 1, Inc., paid both regular corporate income tax and a surtax on income over $25,000.

Avoiding the surtax on the first $25,000 meant a savings of $12,500. This meant nothing to General Motors but it meant, potentially, a total tax saving of $100,000 per year if we could get all eight corporations sufficiently profitable. To put this in perspective, our net worth was less than $500,000 at the end of 1965. In those days we came nowhere near to making enough before-tax profit in each corporation to save the full $100,000, but the savings were still significant. *But . . .*

To keep the surtax exemptions, we had to keep the ownership of the eight corporations sufficiently diluted so that the eight corporations were not "controlled."

Under the rules of "attributed ownership," the stock owned by the Pronto Market Investment Club was "attributed" to each member of the club in proportion to their individual ownership of units in the club. As long as the five biggest stockholders, including me, didn't own more than 80 percent, the corporations were not "controlled" and could enjoy the surtax-avoidance savings.

Year after year, the multiple-surtax savings piled up, and please adjust for inflation since the 1962–1977 era. It was a hell of a lot more money then than it is now. Froehlich's device probably ensured the financial success of what we called, justifiably, the Pronto Market Complex. When we developed Trader Joe's in 1967, we simply opened the new stores under the old Pronto Market corporations.

Employees were eager to have the chance to invest in the business, a touching faith that was not always justified. As I pointed out in an earlier chapter, however, all transactions were at book value. There was no blue sky, no premium over book. If an employee left, we had the right to buy back any units of ownership in the Pronto Market Investment Club that employee owned. We kept the name even when there were no more Pronto Markets. There was no problem in finding existing or new employees to take the units; more importantly, there was no problem in maintaining the dilution of ownership that we needed to keep the potential $100,000 per year of tax savings.

## Houses Si, Club Units No!

The system worked well until 1975, when a sea change occurred in the economic background. After everything hit bottom in 1974, as described in the opening of the "Uncorked!" chapter, the economy roared back—above all, the price of houses in Southern California. From 1974 to 1977, the price of houses at least doubled!

In the background was a court ruling, one of the most important women's-right rulings in history. The court ruled that (a) a single woman could not be denied a mortgage, and the lender had to rely on that woman's income in determining the size of the mortgage; and (b) for a married working couple, the wife's income had to be included in judging the amount they could afford to pay.

I don't think enough attention has been paid to this profound institutional change. It tremendously increased the ability of women and working couples to afford houses. Women went to work so they could afford the houses they wanted. Suddenly the wives of our employees saw housing prices soaring out of sight. In 1975, a family had to choose between buying a house (or a bigger house) and investing in the Pronto Market Investment Club. The club lost.

The situation was complicated by the death of a couple of employees who were in their sixties. I have always made a point of hiring people over fifty-five. They have a wonderful way with customers, and if they're the right kind of people, they have a lot of product knowledge. Well, a couple of my old guys conked out and their widows wanted their Pronto Market Investment Club units cashed out. I couldn't find enough employees to take their units.

The biggest owners of units—the True Believers like Leroy, Gene Pemberton, Paul Reid, John Epp—were always chomping at the bit to get more units. But I couldn't let them buy more, because of the dilution issue.

First I tried to finesse the issue by paying all the Captains' bonuses in units. That was not real popular. They wanted to buy houses. I also tried paying dividends from the corporations to the stockholders, the Investment Club, and me. That was fine for the club, and gave it some cash for the redemption of units, but for me it was a tax disaster. I was in a 73 percent marginal tax bracket. (It's hard to remember how high tax rates were in those pre-Reagan years.)

Then I began buying units into the eight corporations. Because I was the controlling stockholder, however, part of those units were attributed to me, intensifying the dilution issue.

Please understand there was no shortage of cash in the corporations. In 1975, in fact, we paid off the last of the bank loans from Bank of America: Trader Joe's has never had any fixed debt since 1975. I would have happily bought all the units that were for sale, except that we would lose the $100,000 of after-tax money each year.

## The Employee Stock Option Plan

Clearly a crisis would arrive within a couple of years. So Ed Weissman, our attorney since Froehlich was on the Superior Court, and I began an exhaustive study of Employee Stock Option Plans (ESOPs), a rather new concept in 1975.

The idea: we would establish an additional retirement plan for the employees, with Trader Joe's contributions equal to about 10 percent of each employee's income per year. These contributions, of course, were tax deductible. The accumulated cash at some point would be used to reduce my ownership of the enterprise, in stages, over a long period of years, down to 25 percent, while I maintained voting control.

This Employee Stock Ownership Plan required our giving up the $100,000 per year tax saving, and merging the corporations, but the tax savings on the Trader Joe's contributions would more than offset this, as far as total cash within the business was concerned.

At the end of the years-long process, my wife and I would own 25 percent; the employees, 75 percent of Trader Joe's.

## Bye Bye Fair Trade, and the ESOP

It took us a year to work out all the details. Then, in the autumn of 1976, we started the final process, an outside appraisal of the value of the stock. We hired the leading corporate appraiser in Los Angeles. And then, on the eve of getting their appraisal, the startling announcements about Fair Trader and milk pricing came from the state government.

Given these new, radical uncertainties, the appraisers could not issue an appraisal. And even if they had, the employees would have lacked confidence in it, because many of them thought that Trader Joe's would now go bankrupt. And thus the stage was set for the abandonment of my twenty-year-old goal of employee ownership, and for the sale of Trader Joe's to the Albrechts.

# 23

## The Sale of Trader Joe's

"Risk management," you say?
Risk management is asking,
"What am I risking if I say yes;
and what am I risking if I say no."

—Bernard McDonell, Vice President of Provigo Inc., Montreal
and one of the most astute people I ever worked with,
quoting his former boss and mentor, Saul Steinberg

### A Not-So-Small Town in Germany

In 1919, the parents of Karl and Theodore Albrecht, who were infants at the time, bought three tiny grocery stores in Essen, Germany, and they bought them on credit. It was just after World War I and just before the Weimar inflation. When that inflation hit a few years later, it wiped out the value of the fixed debt they had incurred to buy the stores. It's an ill wind . . .

During World War II, the brothers, now in their early twenties, served as enlisted men in the Wehrmacht. When they returned to Essen, they took over their parents' tiny stores. They found Germany torn apart. Essen, the home of the Krupp ironworks, had been blasted by the bombing raids. They heard that the big American grocery chains were ready to move in. Backs against the wall, in 1949 they did something that has profoundly influenced the economic history of Germany ever since: they designed the "box" store.

Their concept of the box store has about six thousand square feet and carries six hundred SKUs. These SKUs are the most basic groceries, bought at the cheapest costs possible, and sold at a gross profit as low as Costco's today. The box stores, called Aldi (an acronym for Albrecht Discount), were one of the major factors in the postwar German "miracle," growth without inflation. If the DMark had been one of the world's premier "hard" currencies since 1949, it wasn't just because of the famous finance minister Ludwig Erhard. It was the Albrecht brothers, relentlessly keeping grocery prices low in Germany. And along the way they introduced many innovations, including beer in cans, which had been unheard of in Germany.

Sometime around 1970, although still living fifteen minutes apart in Essen, the brothers split their empire, I was told. Karl, the eldest, took Germany south of Essen, Austria, Spain, and the United Kingdom. Theodore (or Theo, pronounced TAY-o, as I came to know him), took northern Germany and West Berlin—where, to stick it up the Communists' nose, he opened eighty stores in a city of two million—the Lowlands, and France.

In 1975, Karl came to the United States and bought a moribund supermarket chain in Iowa, the *Benner Tea Co.* Using this as a logistical base, he began more or less replicating Aldi in the Midwest. He had to make a lot of changes. But the operating principles were the same: you put out the formula for generic products like mayonnaise, oil, paper towels and get manufacturers to bid to these specifications. The lowest bidder takes the contract; Aldi sells it at a gross profit percentage about one-third of the typical supermarket. There are few fresh products. Only in recent years have there been refrigerated and frozen products.

The "box store" concept looked easy. Lots of chains, including the giant *Jewel Tea*, tried it and failed. Today, Karl's Aldi Benner chain is the sole survivor and has more than two thousand stores spread across thirty-six states.

## Sale of Trader Joe's

Perhaps with a little sibling rivalry going on, Theo hired the investment bankers *Dominick & Dominick* to search for an American chain to buy, and to launch his own Aldi's here. Because Trader Joe's operated about the same size stores, they contacted us. I told them to forget it, but they persisted and the upshot was that, on a wine-buying trip to Europe in March 1977, I flew to Essen.

There I met one of the finest, smartest men I have ever known, Dieter Brandes. Dieter, thirty-five (he was born during the Hamburg firestorm in 1942 so it was easy to track his age), was a spare, scholarly man with a PhD in economics. He'd been hired by Theo only a couple of years earlier, and had rapidly risen to be crown prince in Theo's empire. He held the special responsibility for non-German operations: the low countries, and now America. He spoke excellent English: financial, legal, and conversational.

He showed me some of their stores and explained their modus operandi. I was very impressed. Three months later, Dieter and his wife, Karen, who also spoke perfect English, came to Los Angeles and spent a few days with us. He kept urging me to sell, and with additional pressure from Dominick & Dominick, I finally agreed to go to Germany in October and negotiate to sell Trader Joe's.

In Essen, Alice and I met Theo, his charming and intelligent wife, Cilly, and their two sons, Theo Jr. and Bertholdt, who were then in their twenties. Theo, then about fifty-eight, was an impressive, handsome, quiet, intelligent man. He had the demeanor of an architect, which is what he had wanted to be had economic circumstances permitted. Aldi can be described as an architectural operation in the spare, austere Bauhaus mode. I was really impressed. I wound up working for him for ten years.

But not then. After getting a second look at Aldi, I hit the wall. Another look at Aldi's operations gave me what can only be described as an allergic reaction. It violated every management concept that I held dear. It was great for the German economy and for German kultur, but I couldn't take it. I pulled out: Alice and I escaped to Paris, where Young Joe was working. Dieter was crestfallen.

I felt that no way could Trader Joe's be used as a launching pad for Cal-Aldi. I didn't think it would work (I have no idea of Karl's Aldi Benner financial results). It violated Whole Earth Harry; it violated my employee policies.

Furthermore, I felt that the Germans didn't understand the threat posed by the end of Fair Trade on alcohol, which was still in the courts. After all, some of my own employees thought we were going to go bust if Fair Trade ended. So they were trying to bail out of the Pronto Market Investment Club.

On the other hand, perhaps Dieter figured that if we did fail to survive deregulation, so much the better. They could proceed with Trader Joe's as the launching pad for Cal-Aldi. In any event, the deal was washed up, as far as I was concerned.

In 1978, Fair Trade ended and Dominick was immediately on the phone. I told them that we were not in distress, that by God we were going to solve this problem. In short, I told them the same thing I told my employees: freedom from government regulation is always good. And over the next months we did solve deregulation, with Mac the Knife. This just made Essen more eager, and they kept raising the price.

Finally, in October 1978, Dominick called me with a radically revised offer:

1. They were sold on Trader Joe's post-deregulation future.

2. No changes would be made in the way Trader Joe's was run.

3. I would not have to sign a management contract.

4. The price was about three times what had been offered a year earlier. On the other hand, we were already making a lot more money under Mac the Knife.

I responded that the sales contract could be no more than one page long. No holdbacks, givebacks, or whatever. Theo wired word that he'd take the one-page contract, if I would guarantee that I had conducted the business for the past five years as a prudent man would. He knew damn well that I had. So now we had to have the one-page contract.

Back in 1977, at my instigation, the Germans had hired a prominent law firm to represent them in those negotiations. When they got word that the 1979 contract was to be a one-pager, they threw up their hands and refused to write it. So my attorney wrote the contract. Physically, it was more than one page long but spiritually it was a one-pager.

Curiously, my insistence on that simple agreement led to my being retained as a consultant for Thrifty Corporation ten years later, in 1989. Jim Ukropina had become CEO of *Pacific Enterprises* (*Southern California Gas Co.*), which had bought Thrifty, and he remembered "one-page Joe."

## How It Worked Out

As soon as the deal closed in 1979, we at Trader Joe's went back to work, almost as if nothing had ever happened. I'd like to make a few things clear:

1. We did not "sell to a German company." The stock was put in a family trust or *stiftung* for the two sons, Theo Jr. and Bertholdt. This is a matter of public record with the Department of Alcoholic Beverage Control.

2. The Albrechts never invested a pfennig directly in Trader Joe's. There were no debt guarantees, no nothing. Nor did they take

dividends. Trader Joe's has continued to expand with no financial support whatsoever from the Albrechts or Aldi. Nor were there any buying links or ties between Trader Joe's and Aldi.

3. The Albrechts and Dieter Brandes never took an active part in the management of Trader Joe's. For one thing, they had their hands full in Europe. For another, well, that was the deal. I wrote them a report once a month and visited them once a year in Essen, as part of a wine-buying trip in Europe. Dieter usually showed up here once a year; Theo about every three years. In the first years they did lean on me to open more stores, but I resisted while we worked out the knotty logistical problems that you've read about in previous chapters.

4. I never took any part in their European operations. The year after they bought us, however, Dieter, who was charged to find more American investments for them, caused them to buy a 10 percent interest in *Albertson's*. Albertson's management blew up when the filing was made public with the Securities and Exchange Commission. All of top management threatened to quit over what they saw as a German invasion. It didn't help that Sol Price had sold *FedMart* the previous year to another German capitalist, a sale that ended in an explosive exit by Sol, and the subsequent collapse of FedMart. So I was pressed into service to persuade the Albertson's people that the Albrechts were good guys. Then Dieter, Theo, and I flew to Boise and met with top management for three days. The people in Idaho were astonished that Theo and Dieter didn't act or talk like Otto Preminger, Erich von Stroheim, or any of those actors who were the heavies in the World War II movies. They were promised the same hands-off deal that I had, and the meeting was successful. As far as I know, the relationship has been warm ever since; the Albrechts even bought more stock.

5. Two years after the sale of Trader Joe's, the IRS audited our 1978 results and came after us for $100,000 of additional taxes because the corporations' ownership hadn't been diluted enough to enjoy the eight surtax exemptions. The Albrechts never said a word of complaint about the "one-pager" having no holdbacks. When we sold the *Insider's Report* name a few years later for $100,000, I felt we had at least partly made up for this.

> There are three kinds of money: "Getting by" money, "doing nicely" money and "up yours" money.
> —Frederick Forsyth, *Los Angeles Times*, 1983

## Why Did I Sell? Sophrosyne!*

Frequently, people who see the enormous success of Trader Joe's ask me why I sold. Let's put it this way: I ran Bernie McDonell's risk calculus: What do I risk if I sell? What do I risk if I don't?

That calculus of *what do I risk if I don't* included inter-spousal death taxes: not until several years later did Ronald Reagan end the hateful tax that my widow would have had to pay if I died, a tax that could bankrupt a now-leaderless company. That calculus included President

---

* Sophrosyne is an ancient Greek concept of an ideal of excellence of character and soundness of mind, which when combined in one well-balanced individual leads to other qualities, such as temperance, moderation, prudence, purity, decorum, and self-control.

Jimmy Carter's threat to end capital-gains tax preferences in 1980: a threat that would have increased capital gains taxes for me from 33 percent to 73 percent. That calculus included the certain loss of $100,000 of surtax exemption benefits in Trader Joe's. (In fact it had already happened for 1978.) That calculus included my concern that the Kondratieff Wave depression would occur at its scheduled arrival about 1985. (And when 1982 hit, that forecast didn't look so bad.) That calculus included the fact that our after-tax proceeds from the sale would be large enough to permit us to be free of economic worry for the rest of our lives, assuming I didn't do something stupid with the money.

The calculus of *what do I risk if I sell* included the fact that Trader Joe's was my Zen window on the world. I experienced the world mostly through Trader Joe's. That's an advantage of being self-employed. That window can never be as open while you're an employee, even a Frederick-Forsyth rich one, even one given great discretion by absentee owners. The calculus of risk also included the fact that I knew I'd be selling my shadow. (Appropriately, Peter Schlemihl is a German folk tale.) That insight proved all too true. Sometimes the gods offer one a premonition. I was blind to it.

But, Joe, didn't you think about the risk of not making an even greater fortune if you said "Yes"? No. At Stanford in 1947, I had studied and, apparently, retained Aristotle's concept of the Golden Mean, the "Hellenistic ideal of sophrosyne," nothing too much. The amount that the Albrechts offered was enough by the "nothing too much" standard.

In short, I ran Bernie McDonell's risk calculus, and sold. We have led a very comfortable life ever since. It's just that my shadow, the persona "Trader Joe," is owned by the Albrechts. Perhaps I should have taken Alice's suggestion, back in 1967, and called it "Trader Mom's."

# How About Our Children?

How about our children? Weren't they going to go into the business? This is another question I'm frequently asked. The answer: no way.

In France I'd seen all those family wine businesses where, generation after generation, the father and son sit facing each other at a desk specially designed for that very purpose! The son, if competent, was miserable and felt the weight of ages hanging on his shoulders. I have always felt sorry for people who inherit the family business. No matter how successful they prove to be, they always have the nagging doubt about whether they could have done it on their own.

No one, of course, really does it strictly on their own. Both Alice and I were lucky to come from families of strong character, if limited financial resources. And with eleven years of Stanford education between us, we could never be poor, just temporarily impecunious at times.

Young Joe and Charlotte worked in the business from the time they were old enough to count. They counted Raleigh cigarette coupons, and they more than earned the 10¢ per hour I paid them. Later they helped us address the *Fearless Flyer* when we had individual subscribers. Madeleine came along too late for that, but all three kids accompanied me on my endless driving to find locations; and we took them to Europe on my buying trips every chance we had. So one of the really nice things about my career is that I was never an absentee dad. Workaholic, yes, but not absentee. What price glory? When is enough, enough?

Any of my kids would have been competent to run the business, but I would not have permitted it. Young Joe did play an important role in computerization as I discussed, but it was never in the context of a career. Joe went on to work in IBM's think tank in Raleigh; presently he's in Microsoft's think tank in Seattle. Charlotte is a high executive at the Getty, which she helped construct; Madeleine runs a profitable internet business out of her home. These are first-rate people.

One aspect of the sale: back in 1976 when the consensus was that Trader Joe's stock was almost worthless, I gave some to each kid. It didn't help the dilution of ownership, because the shares were still attributed to me. But two years later, when we sold, it meant that each child was fully funded, not rich, but with enough money to have a shield against slings and arrows. By the way, I was audited on the gifts and the IRS agreed that, given the situation in late 1976, the stock was worth as little as I claimed.

## No Exit?

"Well, Joe," the first-year graduate business school student might ask, "what was your 'exit strategy' if it wasn't to sell or let your kids take over the business?"

I detest the term "exit strategy" when I hear young entrepreneurs bragging about theirs, as if a business is something one builds and casts off.

My financial "exit strategy" had been the Employee Stock Ownership Plan. I had never planned to exit by way of sale to outsiders.

In fact, in the year just prior to deregulation, I had turned down offers from two major supermarket chains. I said I would never sell to a big American corporation. They would make me write all kinds of reports; worse, they would strip Trader Joe's of its cash reserve, putting it, my employees' jobs, and my name at risk.

That was something I liked about the Albrechts. They were as financially conservative as I was: do things for cash except for real estate. And I was confident they would never "flip" it. Europeans tend to buy and hold.

My personal "exit strategy," pre-sale, was to work in the business as long as I was able. And this didn't change with the sale, because I thought I'd spend the rest of my career reporting to Dieter Brandes, who was ten years younger, and with whom I had such remarkable rapport.

So I sold. Do I regret it? I'll answer that in the next chapter.

The sale was transparent to the customers and vendors; it was almost transparent to the employees except that some of them suddenly had huge capital gains taxes as a result of having invested in Trader Joe's at book value, some of them having started in the early 1960s.

My deal with the Albrechts called for no changes in the way we ran Trader Joe's. The only overt change was that we merged all eight corporations into one, something we would have been forced to do anyway because the ownership no longer was diluted enough to save the eight surtax exemptions.

# 24

## Goodbye to All That

Like great works,
deep feelings always mean more
than they are conscious of saying.

—Albert Camus, *The Myth of Sisyphus*

**S**ix years after selling Trader Joe's, in 1985, we had an excellent year for Mac the Knife, but there were a couple of bumps in the road.

Frank Kono dropped dead of a heart attack. He was only fifty, but a heavy smoker. This gentle, intelligent Japanese American had been with us since 1960; by 1967, he was our buyer; by 1980, he was supervising half the stores. So much of the "culture" of Trader Joe's stemmed from Frank's personality. People loved to work for him; he was a great trainer; and Frank, whose family had run a produce stand, was into product knowledge before any of us. He was largely responsible for the early experiments in wines. We missed him very much.

Then, at Christmastime, I got shocking news: Dieter Brandes had quit Aldi. This isn't supposed to happen in Europe. My forecast of spending the rest of my career working with him blew up. Dieter was the only member of top management in Essen who spoke fluent or even semi-fluent English. (Theo and I conversed mostly in hotel-level French.) Thereafter a translator was used, but let's just say that the "user interface" no longer met Frederick Brooks's criterion of "ease of use."

Commencing in 1986, a series of small frictions arose that had not existed before. Only one was major: a change in top management, which I wanted to make and which Theo blocked. It was argued somewhat dispassionately, but with growing heat from August 1987 until April 1988 when I faxed my resignation to Essen, effective January 1, 1989. I felt that the change was imperative for the future of the business. Furthermore, I sensed that my prerogative of complete control, the prerogative of an entrepreneur posing as an employee, was being progressively eroded as the user interface eroded.

Theo and his staff were upset; they flew here and most graciously asked me to stay. But I felt the inevitable time had come for these reasons:

1. The time for leaving a company is when it is running well and is well staffed. I felt that John Shields, who would have been with the company seventeen months by the time I left, would be quite capable of running it, and this proved to be a good forecast. When I announced my resignation to the troops in July 1988, I told them that the real measure of my ability as a manager would come about two years after I left. By that yardstick, I was super competent. And there were few changes in the Skunks in the Office for at least five years after my departure, except John hired a former colleague from Mervyn's, Mike Parker, who, until he left in 1997, handled some of my former functions like real estate and budgeting.

2. After thirty years at the same job, I felt I had better leave if I ever was going to leave. I was fifty-eight, and time was running out for me to serve as a CEO elsewhere or start another business.

3. I could see still other disagreements in the future. The remarkable thing was that we got along so well for so many years despite incredible differences in culture.

I learned a lot from the Albrechts and I will never regret my years of working with them.

I consulted with Trader Joe's on secondary issues of leases and accounting during 1989 and then the amputation was complete. That's the way it should be: the old guy shouldn't hang around. In my case, however, my shadow remained behind.

## Second Thoughts?

The same people who can't understand why I sold can't understand why I quit. After all, I was on my way to becoming one of the most famous retailers in the country; they thought I spent all my time tasting wine, or going to France or broadcasting on KFAC.

Do I regret having quit? No. The succeeding ten years were so full of fascinating experiences that I am glad I exited. Furthermore, I simply do not make a good employee. In 1989, I went back to my own entrepreneurial character, and have been self-employed ever since, even when technically employed by Thrifty Corp. and others.

But do I regret having sold? Yes. I admit it. To mine own self I was not true when I sold. I regret not having had the guts to ride out the loss of the surtax exemptions, the employee ownership problem, the threat of death taxes, Carter's threat to eliminate capital gains preference, and all the other fears, real or phantom, of late 1978.

> There exists an obvious fact that seems utterly moral:
> namely, that a man is always a prey to his truths.
> Once he has admitted them, he cannot free himself from
> them. One has to pay something.
>
> –Albert Camus, *The Myth of Sisyphus*

I have to admit the truth, that I regret having sold Trader Joe's. And I have had to pay something for this, beyond the loss of my shadow. Thanks for listening, Joe Coulombe.

# POST DE-PARTUM

# Addendum

## *Post De-Partum*

There's no way that St. Augustine, who died six hundred years before there was much of a French language, could have said that in French. It must have been in Latin. But the warning is just as valid. Never have I said, *ça suffit*; I agree completely with the Bishop of Hippo who lived (354–430) a few (increasingly few, if that's not an oxymoron) years longer than I have. I hope that I never say, *ça suffit*.

When I left Trader Joe's, I had no idea what I was going to do except that Alice and I were going to circumnavigate Sicily by train, an idea that made our Sicilian friends blanch. It turned out wonderfully well, even when we innocently walked through the public market in Palermo and dropped in for lunch at a trattoria occupied by men in very black suits mumbling to each other something that sounded like "omertà."

We didn't linger at the table. In Catania, the newspaper headline read, "The Mafia exists; does the State?"

Sicily has the most complex cuisine in the world, as well reported by Richard Condon in his *Prizzi* novels; the Pinot Nero from the slopes of Mt. Etna is, I suspect, Pinot Noir brought there by the Normans who owned the island from 1100 to 1400; the red sandstone ruins at Agrigento (imagine the Parthenon twice as big and in red sandstone) is one of the wonders of the world; and the pink-nippled domes of Palerman churches are enough to make one convert to Robert Graves's matriarchal cult.

When we got back, I rented a hole-in-the-wall office in Old Town Pasadena. It was so much like Raymond Chandler's 1930s office that my friend brought me a Maltese falcon but not, regrettably, Mary Astor.

I began to explore other businesses; also I had a couple of leads to run other companies. Eventually that did happen, and I did wind up in charge of eleven companies during 1992–95 after wandering into and through consulting work during 1989–91.

## Nobody Knows the Troubles I've Seen— And I'm Not Going to Tell Them

I commenced this book with Umberto Eco's admonition,

> Perhaps the mission of those who love mankind is to make people laugh at the truth, to make the truth laugh, because the only truth lies in learning to free ourselves from insane passion for the truth.

Well, we're going to have a few laughs here as I try to reframe the truth to protect the guilty, my clients and employers of the past ten years. An insane passion for stating the truth of the last ten years would be most unwelcome in some quarters. (Did I hear the whisper, omertà?)

My post de-partum life can be broken into three categories: running companies in terrible trouble; consulting for companies in terrible trouble; and serving on boards of directors, some troubled, some not, which is my current occupation.

## Running Companies in Terrible Trouble

### Thrifty Corp.

In 1986, Pacific Enterprises, the holding company whose principal asset was Southern California Gas Co., sought to diversify away from the heavily regulated utility business. Anyone who has dealt with government regulators can certainly understand this. They chose Thrifty Corp. as their escape from regulation.

Thrifty had six divisions with sales of $3.4 billion. The biggest, Thrifty Drug, with 650 stores, did $1.8 billion. Then there was Pay 'n Save Drug, with 100 stores, the market leader in Washington State, with branches in Hawaii and Alaska; and *Bi-Rite*, a thirty-unit strange but profitable company in Oregon. It operated hardware stores with pharmacies attached.

There were three sporting goods companies: Big 5, *Gart Bros* in Denver, and *Michigan Sporting Goods* in the Rust Belt. The latter two chains were taking gas in the post–Cold War recession.

For three years, 1989 through 1991, I consulted on the six divisions for Jim Ukropina, the former O'Melveny attorney, who was now CEO of Pacific Enterprises, on Thrifty Corp.

By December 1991, five of the six divisions of Thrifty Corp. were in acceptable to downright good condition. Pay 'n Save Drugstores had turned the corner. Bi-Rite in Oregon was fine; Marty Smith, its president, was probably the most competent executive in all of Thrifty. The crown jewel, Big 5 Sporting Goods, had been okay all along, running autonomously under its founders, Bob Miller and his son, Steve. Michigan Sporting Goods, under new management, had stopped hemorrhaging cash. Gart Bros. in Denver was still in trouble, but Denver was beginning to recover from the recession. So, by the end of 1991, light could be seen at the end of the tunnel for Thrifty Corp. except for . . .

## Thrifty Drug

Look, Thrifty Drug was all broke. Every part, every component of it, as you may have inferred by my references to it in previous chapters. The only thing that worked was the wonderful ice cream it made. (Each year we sold three gallons of ice cream for every man, woman, and child in California.)

An accumulation of sins of omission and commission caused Thrifty Drug to have the lowest sales per store of any major drug chain in America, and by far the lowest prescription sales. Its problems at the time of Pacific Enterprises' purchase, however, had been masked by the Cold War defense boom of the 1980s, and an attempt by its chief competitor, Sav-on, to commit suicide.

*American Stores* had bought Sav-on a few years earlier and, since they owned *Osco Drug* in the Midwest, they made the typical big company decision to homogenize. They changed the name to Osco, pulled out the ice cream stands that had helped Sav-on's destruction of Owl Drug (please see the "God of Fair Beginnings" chapter), and sales collapsed. By 1989, however, they had recognized their mistake and went back to the Sav-on logo. That was bad news for Thrifty Drug. As 1989 unfolded, Thrifty Drug began sinking; then the post–Cold War recession hit California real hard.

Thrifty Corp.'s management refused to own up to the changed circumstances of recession and Sav-on redux. At this point Jim Ukropina forced change. He sent his troubleshooter, Dan Seigel, into Thrifty

Corp. in Autumn 1990. Not until months after Dan arrived did Thrifty Drug begin to have even the most basic financial reports needed to operate a $1.8 billion business. Actually, I'm not certain the pre-Seigel management even knew what was going on.

Various other management changes were made in Thrifty Corp. and Thrifty Drug in 1991 (that's omertà speak), but the red ink kept rising. Jim resigned as CEO of Pacific Enterprises in December 1991 and was succeeded by Bill Wood, a plainspoken Oklahoma oilman, who was head of the Gas Company. I'd met him only once before, but he asked me to come to work as Executive Vice President of Pacific Enterprises in charge of Thrifty Corp.

After five days of meeting with lawyers, CPAs, and investment bankers, we decided to liquidate Thrifty Corp. Morgan Stanley was selected; their work made me appreciate just what investment bankers can achieve in this kind of environment, and at fees that were not astronomical.

In May 1992, we made a deal with Leonard Green, a prominent Los Angeles venture capitalist. But right up until the last day, September 24, 1992, it was touch-and-go whether all the necessary approvals could be obtained from the thirty banks and insurance companies involved. A Japanese bank was the last holdout, because all the decisions had to be made in Tokyo.

And that was it. According to some estimates, Pacific Enterprises, whose stock had fallen from $57 to $17, had lost $1.6 billion in six years of retailing. But once we unloaded Thrifty, its stock did recover to $25. Not a bad gain for eight months' work. Working with the top executives at Pacific Enterprises, Bill Wood, the CFO Lloyd Levitin, the general administrative officer Chuck Weiss, and so many others was a pleasure because there was never any bullshit. We had a miserable job to do, and we did it.

My luxurious office at Pacific Enterprises was on the fifty-fifth floor of the Library Tower, the newest, tallest, and most prestigious building in downtown Los Angeles. It was downright unnerving for a guy whose previous hangout had been a toolshed converted to an office with not quite all the building permits required, but with a very profitable company. I'd rather have the latter. Eight months of deep carpeting and gold-plated private bathroom facilities were a bit much, but there was one bonus.

On Mother's Day, 1992, I took my parents to the Library Tower. They had never been fifty-five stories high before. My mother was in a wheelchair (it was her last Mother's Day), so we could roll her around what was then one of the greatest collections of modern art in the United States. She saw the special security windows of the boardroom so there could be no electronic eavesdropping, the enormous board table that had been lifted into place by helicopter, the furniture bolted into place in case there was an earthquake, and on and on. I think it was one of the brightest days of her life.

Leonard Green separated the three sporting goods chains from Thrifty Corp. Then he merged the remainder, Thrifty Drug, into *Payless Drug* in March 1994 in a deal with *Kmart*, which owned Payless. In 1996, he merged Thrifty-Payless into *Rite Aid* and replaced all of the Thrifty signs with Rite Aid signs.

## A Reason Why?

A final word about management. Thrifty had been a very effective, powerful retailer in the 1950s, 1960s, and 1970s. I kept asking the old-timers what went wrong in the early 1980s. I kept getting this answer: it was when they moved the offices from the old warehouse at Rodeo and La Brea to the former IBM building on Wilshire Blvd. At the old offices, everybody could see everyone else, everybody knew what was going on, and you could always go into the warehouse to see what was really being received and shipped.

The IBM building was an administrative nightmare. There were twelve stories, none of them very spacious, so management was physically fragmented. There were about a thousand people in the building. To maintain security, each floor had to have its own receptionist, another expense. Leonard Green gave it to the Archdiocese of Los Angeles as soon as those terrible computers in the basement had been outsourced.

I firmly believe in a factory atmosphere for headquarters with no private offices, pretty much what I've read about the headquarters of the Mars Candy Co. The next terrible company that I ran, in Northern California, had offices as bad as Thrifty's. Is there a message here?

## Northern California

At about the same time as Pacific Enterprises' mistaken purchase of Thrifty, a giant Canadian supermarket chain made a similar bad move. It bought a moribund wholesale grocery company in Northern California called *Market Wholesale*. And then to pump up its volume, the Canadians bought three terrible supermarket chains, the gourmet-level *Petrini's*, a bottomless black hole named *Cost Less*, and a bagged-out chain in Modesto called *New Deal* whose sales were imploding at the rate of 20 percent per year. For that matter, so were Petrini's sales when I was hired in February 1994. The sales of this complex were $500 million per year, about half of it wholesale.

The parent company in Montreal itself had been in trouble in 1993, leading to the ouster of its jet-set management, who were replaced by some really sharp guys who had created *Price Club*-Canada, which had the highest volume Price Clubs in the world. Pierre Mignault, the new CEO, after a downer visit to California, called his old boss, Sol Price, who put him in touch with me.

With the forbearance and support of Alice, I took an apartment in Marin County near the horribly misplaced, abysmally inappropriate headquarters building. I was not quite sixty-four, and I figured I could take the physical pounding, complicated by commuting home, one more time. Running a company is a twelve-hour-a-day job, week in and week out. And this one was spread from Bakersfield to Sacramento.

Pierre Mignault and Bernie McDonell are probably the two best retail executives I've ever worked with. Intelligent, experienced, tough yet visionary, they had a real mess to clean up in Canada. They gave me three years to clean up California. To help, I brought in Bob Johnson, one of the Senior Project Directors at Trader Joe's who had quit in 1990 to join Canned Foods Grocery Outlets, as head of buying.

## New Deal Markets

Its management refused to accept the fact that Modesto had gone 60 percent Hispanic. I replaced them and we went Hispanic. The key to Hispanic merchandising at that time was to sell money orders, because billions of dollars are sent to Mexico every year. We installed money orders in all stores, put up signs in Spanish, and promoted pork instead of turkeys at Thanksgiving.

We brought in about four hundred SKUs of Hispanic groceries including the bootleg *Ariel* detergent, something made by Procter & Gamble in Mexico that isn't supposed to be sold here, only every Hispanic market carries it. Under the leadership of Don Way, who had been head of Human Resources for *Provigo Corp.*, we turned New Deal around in ninety days. New Deal is a great example of demographic coherence. Almost all of its stores' locations had become Hispanic. All they needed was merchandising to match the demographics.

## Market Wholesale

We got this one turned around, too. It was based on three elements. I take credit only for the first. The rest were handled expertly by . . . well, the experts.

1. Putting Market Wholesale back in the Hispanic food business. Incredibly, the previous management had sold off their Hispanic line only two years before! To stock New Deal, we put those four

hundred SKUs into Market Wholesale. It was just what so many of Market Wholesale's small grocery store clients needed.

2. The head of Market Wholesale had been nursing a pet project: making us a specialty frozen food distributor of frozen baked products for supermarket bakeries. Almost nothing is made "from scratch" at supermarket level; most of it is thawed, or thawed and heated. In the course of 1994, Bill got the contract to supply the in-store bakeries in sixty *Lucky Stores*, and was on his way to getting *Raley's Supermarkets* as well (another sixty stores), when we got rid of the company.

3. The big grocery wholesaler *Fleming* decided it would not serve any accounts that bought less than $10,000 per week. In late 1994 we were picking up lots of small accounts from this windfall.

## Cost Less Markets

This eight-store chain, of which I closed two as soon as I could, consisted of giant, warehouse-sized stores that sold everything below cost, as near as I could tell. The only reason to keep it was that it put volume through Market Wholesale's Modesto warehouse—a poor reason. But, as I revealed in the "Too, Too Solid Stores" chapter, it had "continuous operation" clauses in the remaining six stores.

## Petrini's

When I arrived at Provigo Corp., I found a jewel, Igor Cherkas, a Ukrainian immigrant. Igor is the highest-energy man I've ever known, and the energy is potentiated by a razor-sharp mind. He had been Controller of Petrini's. We made some radical moves, some of them unwise, but we did shift Cost Less's sales into ethnic foods, like fish heads, with some success. Closing those stores was the answer and that would have involved breaking the leases.

Taking advantage of Igor's energy and deep knowledge of the chain, I also gave him Petrini's. It had been the premier meat chain of the Bay Area under a great old man, Frank Petrini. As Frank aged, however, Petrini's began sinking. When the Canadians bought it in 1988, it was already failing. Successive Canadian managements, one of whom insisted on installing anti-snow barriers in the stores, tried every retailing formula known to idiots. By 1994, the clientele was totally confused about what it was. I immediately closed two of the eighteen stores, but again, the really horrible stores had continuous operation clauses.

Let's go back to earlier chapters where I talked about supermarkets running on branded products, whose manufacturers pay them slotting and co-op ad allowances. Four weeks after I got there, the grocery buyer, a competent veteran named Bob Saisi, came to me and said he could not "fund" the ads for the next month. Petrini's had milked those cows dry. The manufacturers had realized Petrini's didn't have sell-through. That's when I compounded the problem by moving too fast with too many changes: I felt a sense of urgency, but I should not have yielded to it.

Still, we were beginning to turn it around by December. Among other things, the wine buyer trebled wine sales and the meat buyer scored some triumphs in Dungeness crab and other seafoods. One of Petrini's many afflictions was a shift in demand from meat to fish.

After it was all over, Pierre Mignault was gracious enough to say that he was confident we would have succeeded if he had been able to give us the three years that had been promised. But he was not able to do so because of new pressures in Montreal to get out of California right away.

## Sale to the Kohlbergs

We had a hard time finding anyone who would buy the California operations. Fortunately I had gotten to know Jim and Jerry Kohlberg back in 1992 when I was finishing Thrifty. I did some consulting for them in 1992–93.

After months of tough negotiations in which Bernie McDonell proved his mettle (and taught me about "risk management"), we sold to the Kohlbergs in early January 1995. We were able to close only through sterling work by our head of real estate, whose personal relationships with Petrini's landlords made possible the change of ownership. The ability to assign a lease is one of the key clauses in leasing. Petrini's, typically, had failed to get a broad enough assignment clause in its leases, so it took personal salesmanship to pull us through.

As I've already discussed in "Too, Too Solid Stores," the Kohlbergs simply closed Cost Less; they sold Market Wholesale to another wholesaler; and they closed or sold the Petrini's to various parties. The only thing they kept was the Hispanified New Deal, something that rather pleased me.

As for the parent company in Montreal, as soon as we closed California, its stock went from $5 to $8, a 62 percent increase. Voila!

## Sport Chalet

I was totally burned out when I went home to Pasadena in January 1995. Ten months of playing Laocoön to the snakes of Northern California, however enriching, had me ready for some R&R in France. Ten days after I got home, however, I got thrown into the breach again.

*Sport Chalet* was a chain of forty-seven big, upscale stores in Southern California. Their personnel are known for their expertise, whether in skiing, mountaineering, or fishing, and it was the biggest SCUBA retailer in the U.S. (mostly by default, as most SCUBA is sold by individual retailers). I had served on its board in 1993 a little while after it was taken public. The founder sold 25 percent of his interest to the public at about $9 in October 1992. I had quit the board in 1994 when I took the Northern California job.

Just as I returned home to Pasadena, the board parted company with its CEO and asked me to fill in and recruit a new CEO. The stock was down to $3 and there was some sense of urgency. I guess! My first meeting was with their banker who told me that as soon as Sport Chalet's line of credit expired fifteen months hence, they would not renew. That does focus the mind wonderfully.

The company had suffered from a year with no snow, 1994–95, yes, but its real problems were structural—of which the most glaring was an almost total lack of controls in buying merchandise. I forget how many hundreds of thousands of dollars of merchandise we liquidated in the next few weeks, but it was a lot. Briefly, because I was there only nine weeks, but nine weeks in which I think I did some of my best managerial work, and we cleaned it up.

I hired Kim Robbins as General Merchandise Manager. She had been a major executive at the *Carter Hawley Hale* department store complex. Kim, who stayed her one-year contract, did a great job of rationalizing inventory and buying procedures. Dennis Trausch, the veteran director of stores, came up with innovative compensation plans for the stores, which took hold quite quickly. And Bob Haueter, the head of advertising, and I hit it right off.

We stopped virtually all newspaper advertising, thereby taking a great strain off the buying department—assembling hundreds or thousands of SKUs for a print ad is a nightmare—and went exclusively to radio. That really worked. As Bob told me afterward, Sport Chalet "own[ed]" radio in the sporting goods field.

This is one of the most important things I can impart: in any troubled company the people at lower levels know what ought to be done in terms of day-to-day operations. If you just ask them, you can find answers. In the case of Thrifty Drug, those poor, beat-up store managers gave me an earful. A deeply troubled company is always the fault of the CEO, the board of directors, and the controlling stockholders who appoint those worthies. It is never the fault of frontline troops.

As to why I quit: given the environment, I was unwilling to lure a competent person into the CEO position. Enough said. Tom Petruno did a very good job of covering the story in the *Los Angeles Times*.

Enough progress was made after I left so another bank stepped up to the plate in 1996 and renewed the line of credit. And then it began to snow, so Sport Chalet remained among the living, unlike Thrifty and those Northern California businesses.

In the latter two, my tenures were successful in that the stock of the parent companies jumped sharply after we liquidated their problem subsidiaries. They were financial successes. But Sport Chalet, curiously, was the most satisfying because it was an operational success.

It was a good way to end a career as a CEO that had begun in 1958.

## Consultant Coulombe

Ever since I left Trader Joe's, companies have called and asked me to "consult." I have always had an allergic reaction to consultants. At

Hughes Aircraft in the 1950s, I had observed that consultants were brought in to tell management what the latter already knew but didn't have the political clout to say.

The would-be clients who called me out of the blue, however, didn't want consultation, they wanted a magic wand. These clients were in such desperate shape that, figuring they had nothing else to lose, they brought me in as a consultant for $200 per hour. Some of them thought that the "miracle" (in their ignorant eyes) of Trader Joe's could be re-created on no matter what rotten foundations of financing; employee relations; screwing around with the female employees; terrible real estate leases; and a general absence of planning, organization, or control.

Not too surprisingly, therefore, most of my "clients" who showed up were already in such extremes that they are no longer with us. Among them are a liquor store chain with a debt to equity ratio of 1,600:1 (you think I'm kidding!); a convenience market chain that I hastily dropped as soon as I learned that the owner had canceled his workers' compensation insurance because it was too expensive because the stores had been held up so often; and a chain that sold spandex garments to teenyboppers. There, the visual compensation exceeded the monetary.

That was a pretty good business, but it was mall-traffic dependent. In the pit of the post–Cold War depression, almost every department store in California was in Chapter 11, which killed traffic in the malls that they anchored.

Spandex-bop, we'll call it, had a rather unique personnel problem: the store managers were all women who had been promoted because as teenaged sales clerks they were profitably empathetic with the teeny-bopper clientele from whose common chrysalis they had so recently emerged.

As they aged, however, to let's say, over twenty-five, their ability to serve as role models for squeezing teenyboppers into spandex seemed to, uh, sag. Their vocabulary no longer was, like, au courant. They were killing the business. They were like thirty-eight-year-old quarterbacks but without beer distributorships to retire to. Sure, here and there we found a Lou "The Toe" Groza, still kicking field goals at age fifty, but most of them, taking a snap from center, kept it right at the waistline.

They had to be replaced: I could envision a class action age discrimination lawsuit filed by twenty-five-year-old ex-boppers. Too late did I think to reread the last, sad encounter between Humbert Humbert and a now-matronly Lolita, just in case Nabokov had encoded some advice for us. Fortunately, I guess, the guy financing the enterprise correctly foresaw four more years of California depression and empty malls, and pulled the financial life-support system. So everybody, super-annuated or not, got laid off.

Speaking of spandex, more than once I got involved with clients where the CEO had a very special assistant who ran customer relations or advertising or merchandising. One of those men being very specially assisted into oblivion was an heir in his fifties trying to prove, successfully, that it does not require three generations to go from short sleeves to shirtsleeves, just two. What I remember most vividly was the well-stocked mirrored bar behind his desk in which my disapproving frown was captured at each of our consultations.

Partly, however, that disapproving frown was directed at myself, as in "What in the hell am I doing this for? You know this jerk won't close the bad stores; or he should start paying decent wages; or . . ."

Now, I consult for troubled clients only on a pro-bono basis. It is psychologically more profitable. And I get a lot of Umberto Eco laughter from the crazy schemes that get presented to me.

## Serving on Boards

Since 1989, I have served on the boards of directors of some really interesting companies. The four years with Canned Foods Grocery

Outlets were quite rewarding. How else would I have seen Blackfoot, Idaho? The company is tremendously successful and, better yet, it really helps poor people have access to cheap food.

The two years on the board of a California bank during the depths of the real estate depression in 1992–94 were really, how shall we say it, tense? The Federal Deposit Insurance Corporation regards itself as a secondary insurer of your bank deposits: the net worths of the directors are primary. On the other hand, I did have a degree in monetary policy from Stanford and it was sort of fulfilling to sit at the same table with controllers from the Federal Reserve while the status of the Bank hovered between CAMEL 3 and CAMEL 4. If you don't know the meaning of that acronym, you're lucky.

I quit the board at the time I took the Provigo job because you cannot afford to be an absentee bank director. I attended not only the monthly board meetings but loan committee meetings and audit committee meetings. There's no way I could do that from Northern California. The bank's condition, however, did improve. Its stock rose 50 percent during my tenure. So, when I left and cashed in my stock options, I made a $185,000, profit which we gave to the Los Angeles Opera Co. to underwrite a production of my favorite opera, *The Marriage of Figaro* starring the great baritone and nice man Tom Allen.

Presently I'm on the boards of several companies, and since they're very much among the living, I'll say no more except that I find board work satisfying, challenging, and appropriate to my age.

## Au Revoir. . .

What can be said of board work can be said about writing this book. It was satisfying, challenging, and appropriate to my age. Joseph Conrad said in *The Mirror of the Sea,*

To deal with men is as fine an art as to deal with ships. Both men and ships live in an unstable element, and are subject to subtle and powerful influences, and want to have their merits understood rather than their faults found out.

I hope you have understood my merits more than you have found out my faults.

# List of Companies

Here is a partial list of companies with which Joe Coulombe has been associated, whether as an owner, chief executive officer, member of the board of directors, employee, or consultant:

Owl Rexall Drug Co.
Drug King Drugstores
Thrifty Drug Stores
Pay 'n Save Drugstores
Bi-Mart
Pronto Markets
Loblaw Markets (Canada)
Provigo Markets (Canada)
Petrini's Markets
Cost Less Markets
New Deal Markets
Bristol Farms
Passport Foods
Canned Foods
Grocery Outlets

Market Wholesale Grocery
Gales's Coffee Shops
Denny's Restaurants
Winchell's Donuts
El Pollo Loco
Big 5 Sporting Goods
MC Sporting Goods
Gart Bros. Sporting Goods
Sport Chalet
Standard Shoe Stores
Cost Plus World Markets
Vroman's Bookstores
Imperial Bank
PIA Merchandising
Trader Joe's Markets

As for the others, *omertà!*

# Index

accounting function, 156–57, 198
Adamson, Merritt, Jr., 3–6, 19, 24, 25
Adamson, Merritt, Sr., 4–5
Adobe® PageMaker, 70
Adohr Milk Farms, 4–6, 22, 24, 25, 44, 212
advertising, 29–33, 178
    informative, 69–70
    radio, 72–75
    traditional, 100–101
    word-of-mouth, 78–79
Aggazotti, Dr., 54
The Akron, 134
albacore tuna, xviii, 128
Albertson's, 222
Albrecht, Bertholdt, 219, 221
Albrecht, Cilly, 219
Albrecht, Karl, 196–97, 216, 217–22
Albrecht, Theodore, Jr., 219, 221
Albrecht, Theodore, Sr., 196–97, 211,
    216–19, 221–24, 226–27, 229, 230
alcohol sales, 20–21, 36, 43–44, 47, 183. *see
    also* wine
Aldi, 201, 218–20, 222, 228
Alhambra, Calif., 148
Allen, Tom, 250
almond butter, xxii–xxiii
almonds, 63
Alta Dena milk, 62, 114, 115, 117, 137
altruism, selfish, 16–17
"always in stock," 170
Alzheimer's Disease, 128
Amazon, 173
American Stores, 238
Amman, Robert, 159, 160
*Amos 'n' Andy*, 29, 133, 178
AM-PM chain, 25
Anacin, 32, 101
Ancient Mariner Retailers, 143
Annenberg School of Communications, 118

A&P, 32, 112
Appert, Nicolas, 28
apple cider vinegar, 128
Apple II computer, 118, 119
Apple Macintosh, 70, 77, 118, 121, 150, 157,
    188, 207
architecture, 180
ARCO, 25
Ariel detergent, 242
Aristotle, 224
Armour, 135, 207
assortment, 163–71
"attributed ownership" rules, 213
average sale, 111

back room areas, 142, 192
bags and bagging, 29, 77–79, 106, 169, 171
Baker's Chocolate, 28
bakery products, 108, 111, 117–19, 135,
    172, 191
baking powder, 127
baking products, 131
Bane, Dan, 157
Bane, Sandra, 157
bankers, 195
banking crisis of 1990, 10
Bank of America, 12, 24, 38, 196
Barmash, Isidore, 104
Barney's, 161
BATF, 107
Beaujolais, 56
bees, 55–56
Benner Tea Co., 218
Bennion, Dave, 55–56
Beringer, 50
Berning, Bob, 51, 52, 54, 55, 57, 58, 94, 99,
    103, 114–15, 123, 151, 153, 154
berry pies, 128
Bershon, Nate, 25

Best Foods Mayonnaise, 33, 94
Beverly Hills, Calif., 3, 161
"biggest variety in town," 163–66
Big 5 Sporting Goods, 237, 238
biosphere, 60–61
Bi-Rite, 237
blackmail, 5
Blake, William, 159, 160
Blueberry syrup, 130
Blue Chip, 187
boards, serving on, 249–50
Boeing 747, 26
bologna, 136
bonuses, 39, 149, 154, 214
Bordeaux wines, 49–51, 59, 137
Borden, Gail, 28
bourbon, 55, 79, 98
box stores, 218–19
bran, xxii, 63
Brandes, Dieter, 219–20, 222, 226, 228–29
Brandes, Karen, 219
brands, 28–34, 100–101
Bran the Blessed, xxii
Braudel, Fernand, xiv
bread, 117–19, 172
Bretton Woods Agreement, 46, 50
Breyer's, 135
Brie, xxi–xxii, 64, 103
Brooks, Frederick P., Jr., 204–6, 229
Brooks Brothers, 79, 131, 137–39
Brookstone, 179
Budget Gourmet, 135
Budweiser, 27, 94, 101, 164, 190
"Built to Last" (study), xiv
Bullock's, 88, 180
burglaries, 201
Burke, Julian, 5
butter, xviii–xix
Button, Jack, 44
buyer orientation, 96
buyers, 102
buying function, 154, 198
"buying power," 109

Cabernet Sauvignon, 59, 85, 125
cable TV, 33–34
Caesar, Julius, 37
Caillouette, James C. "Jim," xxii, 62–63, 175
Cal-Aldi, 220
California, xix, 4, 6, 20, 21, 47–51, 62, 63,
    83, 87, 93–94, 181, 183–84, 195. see also
    Fair Trade laws; specific cities
California Bureau of Milk Control, 117

California Department of Alcoholic Beverage
    Control, 57
California Institute of Technology, 62
California wines, 43–44, 47, 52, 54–57, 59,
    85–86, 94, 114
Camel Caravan, 30
Campbell, Mike, 117
Camus, Albert, 228, 231
Canada, xviii
Canned Foods Grocery Outlets, 123, 135,
    139, 176, 242, 249–50
canning, invention of, 28
cans, solder-free, 127
capital gains taxes, 224, 230
Captains, 41, 42, 44, 149, 151–52, 154, 155,
    169, 214
Carnation, 136
carp, 73
carpeting, 180
Carson, Rachel, 60–61
Carter, Jimmy, 223–24, 230
Carter Hawley Hale department stores, 246
cartoons, 68–69
case pack, 108
cashews, 63
cash reserves, 196, 226
cat food, 130
catsup, xxiii–xxiv
Cavanaugh, Richard E., xiv
Central Management, 153–57, 175
Central Valley (California), 84–85
Certified Grocers, 116, 157, 191, 192, 193
Chain Store Age, 186
champagne, 58, 77, 184
Chardonnay, 40, 59, 85
charities, 76–77
Chase & Sanborn coffee, 30
Chavez, Cesar, 84
checkers, 206–7
cheese, xviii–xix, xxi–xxii, 63–64, 94, 95,
    103–5, 107, 111, 114–17, 128, 137, 147,
    151, 156, 167–69, 190
Cheez Whiz, 101
Cherkas, Igor, 243–44
Child, Julia, 75
cholesterol, xxii
Christie's, 50–51, 57
Christmas, 219
"chunking," 41–42
cigarettes, 192–93, 201
Civil War, 28
Claremont College, 121, 122
Cliff, Bernice, 21, 186

Clifford, Donald K., xiv
closeouts, 109, 134–38, 171, 176
Club of Rome, 61
Coca-Cola, 27, 29, 62, 101, 108, 132–33, 190, 191, 193
coconut milk, 168
coffee, 105–7, 110, 115, 126, 128–31, 167
Colbert, Jean-Baptiste, xii
Cold War, 204, 208, 238
Colgate, 101, 171
Collier's, 29
Columbus, Christopher, 159
"common area" charges, 19
company culture, 185
company parties, 155–56
compensation. see wages and compensation
computerization, 101, 118–22, 145, 206, 225
conceptual integrity, 205, 206
Concord, Calif., 146
Condon, Richard, 236
Confessions of an Advertising Man (Ogilvy), 68
Conrad, Joseph, 250–51
"constitutional contempt," 186
consulting, 247–49
Consumer Reports, 68
Continental, 117
"continuous operation" clauses, 147
continuous products, 132–33, 137
"contract pricing," 190
convenience, 172–75
convenience stores, 6, 19, 25–26, 27. see also 7-Eleven Markets
"core" customers, 145
Cornish game hens, 135
Corona computers, 120, 121, 157
Costco, 96, 98, 144, 170, 171, 173, 175, 179, 180, 201, 218
Cost Less Markets, 147, 148, 241, 243–44, 245
Cost of Goods Sold, 197
Cost Plus World Markets, 123
"co-tenancy" clauses, 194
cottonseed butter, xxiii
Coulombe, Alice, 6, 12, 42, 56, 62, 70, 72, 75, 77, 87, 171, 215, 219, 220, 224, 225
Coulombe, Charlotte, 131, 225
Coulombe, Joseph Steere, xxiv, 118, 124, 225
Coulombe, Madeleine, 131, 225
coupons, 101, 172
"coyote" truckers, 184
CPM, 120
Crate 'n Barrel, 179

credit cards, 53–54, 176, 186
creditorship, 182–83
crime, 198–201
Crosby, Bing, 30
Cucamonga, Calif., 54
Culinary Historians Society, xvii
Culver City, Calif., 13, 44, 141
customers, consumers vs., 69
Cybernetics (Wiener), 206

Dairy Fresh, 116
dairy products, 108. see also cheese
Dart, Justin, 9–10, 12
Day, Tony, 58
Dayton Hudson, 123
Deane, Tom, 12, 25
Delano, Calif., 84–85
Delors, 50–51
demand side retailing, 163–81
    and accepted modes of payment, 176
    and assortment, 163–71
    and convenience, 172–75
    and pricing, 171–72
    and showmanship, 177–81
demographics, 24, 27, 44, 74, 75, 141, 143–45, 148, 174, 208
Denny's Restaurants, 119
dental insurance, 150
deodorants, 127–28
Department of Labor, 183
department stores, 80, 111, 172, 176
DeSilva, Joe, 16, 20
Dessin, Ron, 43
detergents, 128, 129
Deukmejian, George, 58
diesel cars, 65
Diet for a Small Planet (Lappé), 61
differentiation, 23, 26, 27, 38, 69–70, 127–29, 137, 173, 175, 206
Dillard's, 80
direct store deliveries (DSDs), 96, 113
direct store vendors, 190–91
discontinuities, 22, 97, 126, 132–34
discounts, full-case, 96
Disneyland, 40
DMark, 218
dog food, xxiii
"dogs," 143
dollar sales, 66, 141, 168
Dominick & Dominick, 219–21
"double coupons," 101
double entry accounting, 159–60

double entry retailing, 160–62. *see also* demand side retailing; supply side retailing
Dow Jones Industrial Average, 40, 46
dried fruits, 63, 98, 169
Drucker, Peter, 24, 27, 102, 104, 121, 157–58, 185
Dumas, Blanche Greenwood, xx
Dun & Bradstreet, 9
dyslexia, 8

earthquakes, 116, 208
Eco, Umberto, 236, 249
economic downturn of early 1970s, 45–46, 49
*Economist*, 15
*Edgar Bergen and Charlie McCarthy*, 30
edibles, focus on, 97
efficacy, 177
eggs, 21–22
Ehrlich, Paul, 61
Eisenhower, Dwight D., 7–8
El Paso Natural Gas, 10
Emerson, Ralph Waldo, 211
employees
    empowering, 41–42
    knowledge of lower-level, 247
    nonexempt, 82
    ownership by, 26, 211–16
    and showmanship, 177–78
    and supply side retailing, 197–98
employees, paying, 15–18
Employee Stock Option Plans (ESOPs), 215, 226
energy conservation, 65
enthusiasm, 197
Epp, John, 155, 214
Erhard, Ludwig, 218
Ervin, Sam, 5, 64
Essen, Germany, 217–18
"exclusively at our stores," 166
"exit strategies," 226
express lanes, 174
extra large eggs, 21–22, 133

Fair Labor Standards Act, 17, 82, 83, 183
Fair Trade laws, 21, 29, 36, 46–53, 64, 66, 93–94, 97, 98, 107, 114, 115, 166, 173, 216, 220
family businesses, 225
fascism, 4
*Faust* (Goethe), 64
*Fearless Flyer*, xxi, 46, 67–79, 81, 106, 121, 127, 131, 136, 146, 169, 188, 189, 207, 225
Feast for One, 136

Federal Deposit Insurance Corporation, 250
Federal Reserve Bank, 250
FedEx, 140
FedMart, 222
Felker, Clay, 68
*Fibber McGee & Molly*, 30
field supervisors, 155
"first in town," 166–68
First Union National Bank, 195
Fisher, Wayne H. "Bud," Jr., 8–11, 22, 25, 38, 198
Fitzgerald, Roger, xiii
Five Year Plan '82, 204–8
"Five Year Plan '77" (white paper), 94, 97–99, 101, 113, 116, 191, 203–4, 208
fixturization, 179, 194
Fleming, 243
"float," 195
flooring, 180
floor safes, 201
flour, 129
Folgers Coffee, 33, 62, 94, 97, 101, 206
food, groceries vs., 97, 132
Food and Drug Administration (FDA), 71, 107, 207
food stamps, 176
foreign currency risk, 107–8
Forrester, Jay, 61
Forsyth, Frederick, 223, 224
fossil fuels, 144
France, 46, 52, 59, 103, 151, 225
franchises, 20
Francis, Jim, 39
"Frederick the Great" merchandising, 101, 102, 110
French wines, 48, 56–58
fresh juices, 114, 115, 117
freshness, 168–69
fresh-squeezed orange juice, 168–69
Friedman, Milton, 201
Froehlich, Charles W., Jr., 212, 213, 215
frozen foods, 110, 116–17, 127, 129, 135, 137, 156, 167, 173, 192, 200, 218
Frusen Gladje, 135
Fry's Electronics, 79
full-case discounts, 96
Fuller, Buckminster, 65, 204
Fullerton, Calif., 44, 145
Fyleman, Rose, 125

Gallo, Ernest, 85
*The Galloping Gourmet*, 75
Gallo wines, 132, 134

Gart Bros., 237, 238
General Dynamics, 12
General Electric, 33
Genest, Mary, 124, 154, 156–57
geodesic domes, 65
geographical convenience, 172–73
Germany, 151, 220
Getty Museum, 225
GI Bill of Rights, 26
Gillette, 30
gin, 98, 125
gingko biloba, 168
glass containers, 107
"God Bless America," 32
Goethe, Johann, 64
Golden Mean, 224
gold prices, 46
Good-Bank Bad-Bank, 10
"Good Time Charley," 35–44, 46, 62, 67–68,
    133, 151, 160, 163–66, 180
Gould, Stephen Jay, 35
government regulation, 183–85
grape juice, 127, 128
Graves, Robert, 69
Great Depression, 4, 9, 21, 29, 83
Green, Leonard, 239, 240, 241
Green Movement, 66
greeting cards, 173
grievances, listening to employee, 18
groceries, food vs., 97, 132
grocery stores (grocery business), 4, 5, 9, 33,
    53, 84, 89, 93–94, 102, 111, 128, 133,
    160, 171, 173, 175, 176, 180, 183, 186,
    191, 193, 197, 203, 206, 207, 217–18. see
    also supermarkets
gross profit percentage, 111
Group of Seven, 58
Guentert, Robin, 75, 121, 123, 155
Guibert, Jacques, Comte de, 100, 112
The Guns of August (Tuchman), 14–15

Hadley's, 62
"hairballs," 80–89
Halloween stores, 194
Hamlet (Shakespeare), 140, 179
handedness, 8, 10
handshake, value of a, 25
Hanson, Bob, 61
Hardin, Carmelita, xx
hard liquor, 20–21
Haro, Steve, 155
Harvard University, 8
Hatch, Orrin, 71

Haueter, Bob, 246
Hawaii, 199
Hawaiian music, 41
Hawaiian shirts, 178
Hawken, Paul, 69
Hayakawa, S. I., 75
health foods, 61–63, 71, 95, 118, 126–27, 136
health insurance, 150, 188, 199
heavy products, 184, 187
Heisenberg, Werner, 130
Heitz, Joe, 125
Hemingway, Ernest, 50
Hershey, 63
Hetzel, Dave, 155
high fiber diet, xxii
Hill, George Washington, 29
Hispanic merchandising, 242
Hoffritz, 189
holidays, 175
home delivery, 173
homogenization, 27
Hope, Bob, 30
housing prices, 214
Hughes Aircraft, 9, 26, 248
human use of human beings, 206–8
The Huntington hospital, 42, 144
Huntington Library, 77
Hutchinson, G. Evelyn, 60

IBM building (Los Angeles), 240–41
IBM computers, 118–20, 204
ice cream, 135
iconotropy, 69
immigration, 34
Income Continuation Insurance, 150
income taxes, 212
inflation, 46
informative advertising, 69–70
inner cities, 173
In 'n Out Burger, 79
In Search of Excellence (Peters), 41–42
Insider's Food Report, 68
Insider's Report, 44, 67
Insider's Wine Report, 67–68
institutions of learning, 144
in-store convenience, 174
insurance, 187–89
    health and dental, 150, 188, 199
    product liability, 188–90
    workers' compensation, 187–88
Intensive Buying, 100–113
Internal Revenue Service (IRS), 5, 196,
    223, 226

internal theft, 198–200
internet, 22, 34, 105, 140, 142, 173, 189, 225
Interstate Bakeries, 117–18
Interstate Commerce clause, 173
interviews, employee, 18
investment bankers, 195, 239
Italian products, 64, 131

*Jack Benny Show,* 30
Japanese products, 130
Jarlsberg, 137
Jarlsberg cheese, 190
Jello, 30
Jergens, 32
Jewel Tea, 219
Johnson, Bob, xxii, 110, 117, 123, 135, 154, 242
Johnson, Lyndon, 39
Johnson, Samuel, 67, 72
Johnson's Wax, 30
Johnston Frozen Pies, 135
juices, 107, 114, 115, 117
Jurgensen's, 43, 53

Kansas, 47
keg beer, 187
Kennedy, John, 11
Kennedy, Robert F., 39
Kent State Massacre, 46
Kepler, Johannes, 35
Ketchy, xxiii–xxiv
KFAC, 72–74, 78
Khayyam, Omar, 132
Kibble, xxiii, 130
kid shows, 30
Kilmartin, Jack, 123
Kipling, Rudyard, 7
Kirby, Patrick James, 42
Kirby vacuum cleaners, 37
Kmart, 240
Kohlberg, Jerry, 147, 245
Kohlberg, Jim, 147, 245
Kohlberg Kravitz Roberts, 94
Kondratieff Wave, 224
Kono, Frank, 41, 43, 62, 94, 99, 129, 155, 228
Korbel, 86
Kornell, Hans, 88
Kraft brown paper bag, 29
Kraft Cheese, 30
Krupp ironworks, 218

labeling, 107
*Lancet,* 63

landlords, 193–95
Lane Drug, 10
Langendorf, 117
Lappé, Francis Moore, 61
"layering," 102
layoffs, 143
leases and leasing, 12, 19, 42, 140–48, 156, 181, 193–95, 198, 230
Leave Bank, 150, 186
L'Eggs, 191
Leroy (employee). *see* Watson, Leroy
Lever Bros., 30
Levin, Bernard, 201
Levitin, Lloyd, 239
Liberty Mutual, 188
Lido Isle Market, 180
life insurance, 150
Liggett Drug, 10
lighting, 180
Lindt, 29
liquor, 20–21, 36, 44, 66, 98, 125. *see also* wine
Liquor Barn, 58, 94
loading docks, 145
Loblaw's, 67, 104
Lockheed, 153
logistics, 123
Logo, Trader Joe's, 40
Long Beach State, 144
Long Beach Veterans' hospital, 144
Los Angeles, Calif., 3, 5, 8, 25, 34, 41, 45–46, 54, 72, 75, 77, 117, 118, 122, 124, 239–41
*Los Angeles Times,* 40, 45, 52, 58, 247
Louis XIV, xii
Luckman, Charles, 29, 178
Lucky Stores, 22, 94, 243
*Lucky Strike Hit Parade,* 30
Lucky Supermarkets, 11
Lundberg, Guy, 119, 121–22, 124
*Lux Radio Theater,* 30
Lydia Pinkham (patent medicine), 28

MacFrugals, 135
"Mac the Knife," 35, 89, 93–99, 111, 113, 115, 116, 134–35, 142–47, 154, 162–64, 220, 221
Macy's, 123
mailings, 70
mainframe computers, 119, 120
Malibu, Calif., 5–6, 24
Manhattan Beach, Calif., 144
manufacturers, visiting, 103

maple syrup, xx–xxi, 56
Marie Callender, 40
market testing, 171
Market Wholesale, 241, 242–43, 245
Marks & Spencer, 103–5
Marqués de Olivar (wine), 48
Mars Candy Co., 149, 241
Master Charge, 53, 176
Master Wine Grower's license, 54–55, 78
Maui pineapples, 127
Mazda, Ahura, 202
McCoul, George, 43, 44
McDonald's, 180
McDonell, Bernard "Bernie," 217, 223, 224, 242
McKellen, Ian, 80
M&C Trucking, 117
Medical Tribune, 128
Medici Bank, 159
merchandising, 178–79
Mervyn's Department Stores, 123, 229
Mexican products, 130
Michigan Sporting Goods, 237, 238
Microsoft, 225
middlemen, 109
Mignault, Pierre, 241–42, 244
milk and milk business, 4–5, 21, 25, 27, 28, 66, 84, 93–94, 97, 117, 142, 168, 169, 183, 184
Miller, Arthur, 84
Miller, Bob, 238
Miller, Steve, 238
Milton, John, 202
Minute Maid Orange Juice, 33
Modesto, Calif., 241, 243
molasses, 127
Mondavi, Robert, 59
money orders, 242
monopolism, 109
monosodium glutamate (MSG), 127, 136
Monsieur Henri, 48, 50
Monterey Park, Calif., 65, 148
Monteux, Pierre, 185
Montgomery Ward, 80
Moore, Rosella, 155
Morgan Stanley, 11, 239
Morris, Merv, 123
mortgages, 144
Mozart, Wolfgang Amadeus, 200–202
Mrs. Paul's, 110, 135
Munger, Charlie, 172
Mussolini, Benito, 4
The Mythical Man Month (Brooks), 204–5

Nader, Ralph, 68
name, origin of Trader Joe's, 40
names, product, 130–31
Napa Valley Eight wineries, 84–88
Napoleon, 28
National Recovery Administration, 4
National Tea, 32
negatives, positive, 170
Nestlé, 50
network TV, 32–33
New Deal (supermarket chain), 241–43, 245
New England-associated products, 131
"newest in town," 166–68
Newport Beach, Calif., 180
new product development, 105–7
Newsweek, xvii
New York magazine, 68
Nichol, Dave, 67, 104
99¢ Stores, 135
Nixon, Richard, 45, 46
"no label" products, 98
nonexempt employees, 82
non-merchandise vendors, 187
non-profits, 76–78
Nordstrom's, 42, 80, 177
Northern California, 115, 117, 120, 146, 155, 186, 208, 241–42
Northridge earthquake, 208
Northwestern University, 10
nuts, 63, 98, 169

Oakville Winery, 55
"occupancy expense," 181, 195
occupational and safety regulations, 184
Odd Lots, 135
Odette (JC's granddaughter), xxiii
office organization, 153–58
"offset" goods, 108
Ogilvy, David, 68
operating decisions, 158
orange juice, 168–69
Oregon, xix, 237
organic gardening, 61, 66
organizational theory, 102
Orsten, Leo, 148
Ortega y Gasset, Jose, 37–38
Osco Drug, 238
Otrona computer, 119–20
Ovaltine, 30
overtime, paying, 17
Owl Rexall Drug Co., 8–11, 21, 22, 124, 198, 238
ownership, employee, 211–16

Pacific Enterprises, 221, 237, 238, 239, 241
Pacific Palisades, Calif., 200
Pacific Union Club, 10
Pacioli, Fra Luca, 159
Pampers, 101
paper bags, 29, 106
paper towels, 128
Pareto, Vilfredo, 35
Parker, Mike, 229
parking lots, 30–31, 181
parties, company, 155–56, 200
part-time employees, 150
Pasadena, Calif., 40–44, 116, 144, 180, 236
Pasadena Planned Parenthood, 61
*Patton*, 83
Patton, George, 38
Pauling, Linus, 62
Paul Masson, 13, 21
Payless Drug, 240
payment, methods of, 176, 186
Pay 'n Save Drug, 199, 237
PBS, 75
Peacock, 116
peanut butter dog bones, xxiii
peanut oil, 128
Pear's Soap, 28
Peat Marwick, 157
Pemberton, Gene, 94, 154, 155, 214
Penfold, Russ, 155
Pennsylvania, 47
*Pentagon Papers*, 46
Pepperdine University, 24
Pepsi Cola, 48
Pepsodent, 29, 133, 178
Perdue, 135
personal appearances, promoting via, 78
Peters, Tom, 41–42, 153, 185
Petrini, Frank, 244
Petrini's Markets, 78, 79, 241, 243–44
Petruno, Tom, 247
physical condition, of products, 168–69
Pic 'N' Save, 135
Pilchard, xvii–xviii
Pilgrim Joe's, xxi
Pillsbury, 135
pineapples, 127
Pirsig, Robert, 163
pistachios, 63
pizza, 79, 129
Placentia, Calif., 145
*Playboy*, 44
policies, 158
Pomona College, 8

positive negatives, 170
potato chips, 130
President's Choice, 67
Price, Sol, 222, 241
Price Club–Canada, 241
Price-Costco, 98
Pricewaterhouse, 11
pricing, 49, 64, 71–72, 95, 111–12, 160,
    171–72, 189–90, 216
Princi, Carl, 72
printing, outsourcing of, 121–22
private label products, 125–31
Procter & Gamble, 104, 171, 242
product development, 105–7
productivity, 18–20
product liability insurance, 188–90
product managers, 135
product names, 130–31
Programmes of Collaboration, 187, 188,
    195, 206
Prohibition, 47
Project Directors, 153–55
Pronto Market Complex, 213
Pronto Market Investment Club, 212, 214, 220
Pronto Markets, xiii, 3–6, 9–12, 14, 15, 18,
    21–27, 36–39, 42–44, 54, 80, 84, 95, 141,
    145–46, 155, 170, 200, 201, 211, 213
Provigo Corp., 242, 243, 250
prunes, 127
PSA (airline), 49
public television, 33, 34, 75

Rabelais, 45
radio and radio advertising, 31–32, 72–75
Raley's Supermarkets, 243
Ralphs Supermarkets, 88
Randolph, Eddie, 48
Rauch, Doug, xxii–xxiii, 8, 99, 103, 106,
    110, 115, 116, 123, 127, 135, 154
Read, Carveth, 14
Read, Steven, 139
Reagan, Ronald, 9, 33, 204, 223
Recession of 1962, 14
Recession of 1974, 66
Red Flannel hash, xx
refrigeration, 116–17, 167–68, 173, 194,
    201, 218
Regional Project Directors, 155
Reid, Paul, 214
Renoir, Jean, 113
Retail Clerks Union, 16–17
retailers, fundamental job of, 95
retailer screening, 169

retail square footage per capita, 142
retirees, 144, 174
*The Revolt of the Masses* (Ortega y Gasset), 37–38
Rexall Drug Co., xiii, 3, 5, 6, 9–12, 15, 19, 21, 26, 32, 38, 84, 142, 147–48, 175, 193–94, 212
Reynolds, Gloria, 124
rice, wild, xxi
rice milk, 168
Richard, Dick, 180
Richfield, 30
Riesling, 85
Rindge, Rhoda, 5
Riordan, Dick, 25
Rite Aid, 240
robberies, 200
Robbins, Kim, 246
Robert Mondavi (brand), 54, 86
Roosevelt, Franklin D., 4
Royal Baking Powder, 28

S. S. Pierce, 79
safes, floor, 201
Safeway, 94
St. Augustine, 235
St. John, Pat, 70, 77
Saisi, Bob, 244
salaries (salaried employees), 39, 82, 149, 154. *see also* wages and compensation
"sales area," 142
sales function, 154–56
sales per square foot, 142
sales per store, 142
sales taxes, 173
Sandburg, Carl, 130
San Diego, Calif., 22, 117
sandwiches, 169, 187
San Francisco, Calif., 27, 62, 77, 78, 107, 123, 124
San Francisco State University, 75
San Francisco Symphony, 185
San Marino, Calif., 87–89
San Rafael, Calif., 208
Santa Ana, Calif., 61, 62, 199
Santa Ana winds, 180
Santa Barbara, Calif., 142
Sara Lee, 135
satellite TV, 33–34
*Saturday Evening Post*, 29
Sav-on drugstores, 8, 32, 194, 238
saw palmetto, 168
scanning, 174

Schama, Simon, 100
Schick, 136
Schlossberg, Herbert, 81
Schrage, Michael, 93
Schroeder, Fred, 40
Schumpeter, Joseph, 93
*Scientific American*, 26, 60–61, 119
scotch, 98
Scott, George C., 83
screening, retailer, 169
SCUBA, 245–46
*Seafood Leader*, xxiv
seafoods, 110, 127, 135, 244
Sears Roebuck, 39, 80, 104
Second Energy Crisis (1979), 65
secrecy, 39
Securities & Exchange Commission, 11, 222
selfish altruism, 16–17
selling power, 109
"Sell the Mail Room," 157–58
senior discounts, 172
Senior Project Directors, 153–54
7-Eleven Markets, 6, 9, 14, 19, 20, 23, 24, 26, 27
*Seven Kinds of Inflation* (Skinner), 182
sexual harassment, 140
Shakespeare, William, 140, 179
Shields, John, 122–24, 154, 208, 229
shoplifting, 200
shopping bags, 77–78
shopping centers, 32
showmanship, 177–81
Sicily, 235–36
Siegel, Dan, 238–39
signage, 40–41, 179, 180
*Silent Spring* (Carson), 60–61
Skinner, Richard Dana, 182
Skunkworks, 153
slip-and-fall claims, 189
Smirnoff, 101
Smith, Kate, 32
Smith, Marty, 237–38
*Smithsonian* magazine, 203
SNAP program, 176
soap operas, 30
solder-free cans, 127
Sony, 33–34
sophrosyne, 223–24
Southern California Gas Co., 221, 237, 239
Southland Corporation, 6, 24–26, 62
South Pasadena, Calif., 55, 57
soy milk, 168
Sport Chalet, 197–98, 245–47

"standards of identity," xxiii
Stanford Business School, xiv, 8, 9, 18, 19, 122–23, 158, 160, 224
Stanford University, 7, 8, 26, 61, 212
the State, 37–38
Steere, Bill, 26
Steinberg, Saul, 217
Stew Leonard's, 142, 170, 179
stockholders, 196–97
stock keeping units (SKUs), 96, 98, 111, 118, 122, 124, 137, 146, 163–64, 167, 170, 174, 218
stock market crash of 1987, 138
Stolichnaya vodka, 48
store location criteria, 143–47
sugar, 128, 129, 184
sulfites, 127
*Sunset* magazine, xxiv
supermarkets, 4, 22, 31–34, 69, 71, 74, 82–83, 93–95, 97, 106, 110, 117–18, 126, 129, 133, 142, 170–75, 190, 191, 206, 207, 218. *see also specific supermarket chains*
supply side retailing, 182–202
    and bankers, 195
    and cash flow, 196
    and company culture, 185
    and crime, 198–201
    and direct store vendors, 190–91
    and employees, 197–98
    and government regulation, 183–85
    and insurance, 187–89
    and landlords, 193–95
    and non-merchandise vendors, 187
    and number of vendors, 192–93
    and stockholders, 196–97
    and systems, 185–86
    and theft by deliverypeople, 191–92
    and underpricing of highly branded products, 189–90
Supreme Court, 4, 17, 82, 83, 140
Swanson TV Dinners, 33
swap meets, 198–99
"sweetheart" sales, 199
Switzerland, 50, 151
systems, 185–86

Tail O' the Cock (bar), 3, 4
tamales, 128
Tannenbaum Latta, Lori, 118, 124
Teamsters, 86
technology, 33–34
television, 31–34
temperature-controlled displays, 168

tenacity, 15
Tennis, Diane, 124, 156–57
Texaco, 30
Texas, 20
"thanks for listening" tagline, 74–75
Thanksgiving, 175
theft, 191–92, 198–200
Theodore Payne Foundation, 87–88
Thompson Seedless grapes, 84–85
Thornton, Tex, 14
Thrifty Corp., 120, 157, 190, 199, 221, 230, 237–41, 245
Thrifty Drug Stores, 10, 11, 124, 142, 143, 147, 148, 176, 237–40, 247
Tide, 206
"tied house" laws, 47
Tillamook, xviii–xix
time convenience, 175
time off, 150
toilet paper, 129
Trader Charlotte, 131
Trader Darwin, 128, 130, 136
Trader information, losing access to, 193
Trader Joe's Biosphere, 65
Trader Joe's Vintage Dated Canned Corn, 126
Trader Madeleine, 131
Trausch, Dennis, 246
travel, 26–27
truckers, 184, 199
True Believers, 78–79, 214
*True Grit*, 33
TRW, 144
Tuchman, Barbara, 13–15
tuna, xvii–xviii, 128
Tupperware, 9–10
turnover, 18

Ukropina, Jim, 221, 237, 238, 239
unbranded products, 110
underpricing, of highly branded products, 189–90
Underwood's deviled ham, 28
unfiltered wines, 128
uniforms, 178
unions, 17
Union Theological Seminary, 86, 87
United Farm Workers (UFW), 84–88
United Parcel Service, 140
United Way, 76
University of California at Berkeley, 212
University of California at Davis, xxiii
University of California at Los Angeles (UCLA), 144

University of California at San Diego, 118, 144
University of California at Santa Cruz, 62
University of Southern California, 18, 118
University of Toronto Medical School, 104
U.S. Department of Agriculture (USDA), 107
U.S. Department of Labor, 81–84
U.S. dollar, 46, 57–59, 107–8, 204, 242
U.S. Growers, 117

"vacuum-packed" coffee, 105–6
value, delivering, 96
value per cubic inch, 36
vanilla extract, 127
VCR, 33–34
vendors, 101–5, 113, 187, 188, 190–93
Ventura, Calif., 142
Ventura County, Calif., 5
Veuve Clicquot, 29
Vietnam War, 26, 39, 45, 46, 192
vinegar, 128, 130
virtual retailers, 173
Visa, 53, 176, 186
vitamins, 62–63, 71, 98, 107, 114, 115, 124,
    128, 130, 136, 144, 168, 207
vodka, 125
Von's, 94

W. T. Grant, 142
wages and compensation, 15–20, 23, 36, 39,
    81, 82, 102, 140, 148–50, 187, 197, 207
Wall Street Journal, 11, 26, 157–58
Walmart, 144, 170
Walton, Sam, 18, 190
Wang, 122
warehouses, 115–16
warfare, rules of, 100
War on Drugs, 201
Washington (inventory service), 187
Washington State, 47, 173, 237
Watergate, 46
Watergate hearings, 5
Watson, Leroy, xxi, 22, 41, 62, 63, 94, 99,
    107, 110, 115, 116, 119, 121–24, 136,
    151, 154, 155, 199, 214
Way, Don, 242
Wayne, John, 33
Webb, Ezra, 49, 51, 52, 57

Weber's Bread, 30, 97
Weiss, Chuck, 239
Weissman, Ed, 215
Westinghouse, 33
West Los Angeles, Calif., 44, 144, 145
wheat bran, xxii
Wheaties, 30
whey butter, xviii–xix
White, Betty, 33
The White Goddess (Graves), 69
The Whole Earth Catalog, 61
"Whole Earth Harry," 35, 44, 47, 56, 60–67,
    87–88, 113–14, 116, 125–27, 151, 197
Whole Earth Review, 69
whole lines, avoiding carrying, 98
Wiener, Norbert, 206
wild rice, xxi
Wilshire, Calif., 180
Winchell, Walter, 32
wine, 42–44, 46–59, 62–64, 67–68, 72–74,
    76–78, 84–86, 88, 94–96, 98, 106–8, 114,
    115, 124–29, 132–34, 165–68, 170, 175,
    207. see also specific types of wine, e.g.:
    Cabernet sauvignon
Wine Bank, 52–53
wineglasses, 97
Wine Spectator, 68
The Winning Performance (Clifford and
    Cavanaugh), xiv, 185–86
Wisconsin cheese lobby, 63–64
Wodehouse, Barbara, 75
Wolfgang Puck's frozen pizza, 129
Wood, Bill, 239, 243
word of mouth, 78–79
workers' compensation insurance, 187–88
work rules, union, 17
World War I, 14–15, 29
World War II, 4, 9, 31–32, 148, 217
Wright, Frank Lloyd, 179
Wynn, Ed, 30

yeast, 56–57
Yoda, Dave, 7, 22, 119, 150, 156, 186
Yugoslavia, 108

ZIP codes, 70, 144